Climber's Choice

THE BEST CLIMBING WRITERS
PRESENT THEIR WORK

Edited by Pat Ament

Ragged Mountain Press ▪ **McGraw-Hill**

Camden, Maine ▪ New York ▪ Chicago ▪ San Francisco ▪ Lisbon
London ▪ Madrid ▪ Mexico City ▪ Milan ▪ New Delhi
San Juan ▪ Seoul ▪ Singapore ▪ Sydney ▪ Toronto

Ragged Mountain Press

A Division of The McGraw·Hill Companies

1 3 5 7 9 10 8 6 4 2

Prologue, compilation, and contributor introductions
copyright © 2002 Pat Ament

LIBRARY OF CONGRESS CATALOGING-IN-PUBLICATION DATA

Climber's choice : the best climbing writers present their work /
edited by Pat Ament.
p.   cm.
ISBN 0-07-137723-9
1. Mountaineering. I. Ament, Pat.
GV200 .C585 2002
796.52′2—dc21   2001007478

Printed on 55 lb. Sebago by R. R. Donnelley & Sons, Crawfordsville, IN
Design by Irving Perkins Book Design
Production by Faith Hague and Dan Kirchoff
Title page photography of Mount Kilimanjaro, Tanzania, by SuperStock

DEDICATED TO THE MEMORY
OF CHUCK PRATT,
GREAT SPIRIT, GENIUS OF
YOSEMITE CRACKS . . .

Pratt at his cabin, Grand Tetons,
August 1999.

Contents

Acknowledgments

I am grateful to all the writers who contributed to this book and who went to the trouble of drafting introductions, supplying photos, giving deep consideration to their work, and finding, sometimes with difficulty, a piece toward which they were partial. I am also grateful to the photographers whose images appear in this work.

I am indebted to Luisa Iovane for her help translating Walter Bonatti's comments and for all her efforts in communicating with Walter Bonatti and Kurt Diemberger, two men who are never easy to track down. Susanne Skyrm also helped with the translation of Bonatti's piece.

I express my appreciation to Chris Bonington, Royal Robbins, Stephen Venables, Duane Raleigh, Bob Koch, Bill Briggs, Ed Webster, Michael Chessler, and the late Chuck Pratt, who readily assisted me in ways that helped bring this book to fruition.

I am indebted to the various publishers who let me use articles from books, magazines, and journals. Duane Raleigh especially found time to help us, and so ungrudgingly, even though he is the tooth, so to speak, the busy man who must daily take hold of the big world of *Climbing* magazine.

Thanks must be given to Mandi Gardner, Kristie Sheriff, and Dudley Chelton, for their computer genius in improving a number of old photos, and to Laura Snyder for her assistance with technical aspects of manuscript preparation.

My wife, Robin, and our children helped at every turn, a little array of beautiful spirits who make all my efforts worthwhile.

With regard to origins of the writings:

My "Reflections on Being the Best Climber in the World" is from my book of the same title (Two Lights, 1999). Reprinted by permission of the author.

Walter Bonatti's "Concepts of Adventure" is excerpted from a climbing lecture he gave in 1999. It is translated from the Italian by Susanne Skyrm, Luisa Iovane, and Pat Ament. Reprinted by permission of the author.

Chris Bonington's "Drangnag Ri" was originally published in England's *Alpine Journal* (1996). Reprinted by permission of the author.

"On Broad Peak," copyright © 1993 by Greg Child. Text from the book *Mixed Emotions* by Greg Child included with permission of the publisher, Mountaineers, Seattle, WA.

Kurt Diemberger's writing is excerpted from the Raid on Broad Peak chapter of his book, *The Endless Knot*. Copyright © 1991 by Kurt Diemberger. Text from *The Endless Knot, The Kurt Diemberger Omnibus* by Kurt Diemberger included with permission of the publishers, Mountaineers, Seattle, WA, and Baton Wicks Publications.

John Gill's "Get the Hell Off That Rock" and "LifeSavers" were originally published in *Master of Rock*, by Pat Ament (Stackpole Books, 1998). Reprinted by permission of John Gill.

Tom Higgins' "Soarks" first appeared in *Climbing* magazine (March–April 1980). Reprinted courtesy of *Climbing* magazine.

Amy Irvine's "The Path of Destruction" originally appeared in the 2000 Patagonia catalog. Reprinted by permission of the author and Patagonia.

John Long's "The Bird's Boys" first appeared in his anthology *Rock Junction* (Chockstone, 1992), and then in *Long on Adventure*, published in 2000 by Falcon Publishing. Reprinted by permission of the author.

Ian McNaught-Davis' "The Mustagh Tower, Climbed 6th July 1956" is a recent rewrite of an article McNaught-Davis claims may or may not have been published somewhere in the past but long forgotten by everyone, including himself. Reprinted by permission of the author.

Alison Osius' "The Squalor and the Glory" originally appeared in *Climbing* magazine (April–May 1993). Reprinted courtesy of *Climbing* magazine.

Jim Perrin's "Visions and Virians" was written for and broadcast on Radio Wales in 1995. Reprinted by permission of the author. Will Perrin scribbled his little ending in December 2000 while visiting the United States and climbing around Bishop, California.

Chuck Pratt's "The South Face of Mount Watkins" originally appeared in the *American Alpine Journal* (1965). Reprinted by permission of the author.

"Rubble Merchants, Slateheads, and Others" copyright © 1997 by Paul Pritchard. Text from the book, *Deep Play* by Paul Pritchard included with permission of the publishers, Mountaineers, Seattle, WA, and Baton Wicks Publications.

Royal Robbins' "Jack of Diamonds" first appeared in *Climb!*, by Bob Godfrey and Dudley Chelton (Alpine House, 1977). Reprinted by permission of Royal Robbins.

Doug Robinson's "Mountaineering Just Means Glad to Be Here: Eight Alpine Poems" is a collection of poetic tidbits, a few published, many not, and assembled to form a new piece. The title is from a chapter in the author's *A Night on the Ground, A Day in the Open* (Mountain n' Air Books, 1996). Reprinted by permission of the author.

"Up and Out, the Myth of Emergence" is from *Reaching Keet Seel* by Reg Saner (Salt Lake City: University of Utah Press, 1998). Reprinted courtesy University of Utah Press.

Susan Fox Rogers' "Loose Woman" is appearing for the first time in print. Printed by permission of the author.

John Sherman's "Boulevard of the Behemoths" originally appeared in Sherman's column, Verm's World, in the August 1995 issue of *Climbing* magazine, Carbondale, Colorado. Reprinted courtesy of *Climbing* magazine.

"Guilty as Charged" copyright © 1996 by Joe Simpson. Text from the book, *Storms of Silence*, included with permission of the publishers, Mountaineers, Seattle, WA, and Jonathan Cape/Random House Group Limited.

Mark Synnott's "The Maestri Enigma" first appeared in *Climbing* magazine (May 1999). Reprinted courtesy of *Climbing* magazine.

Stephen Venables' "Tierra del Fuego" was rewritten in 2000 from an earlier published version (*Summit Magazine,* mid-1990s). Reprinted by permission of the author.

Ed Webster's "The Fight" is a chapter from his book *Snow in the Kingdom: My Storm Years on Everest* (Mountain Imagery, 2000). Reprinted by permission of the author.

Prologue: The Climber as Writer
PAT AMENT

There is theater in climbing, and we like front-row seats. In lieu of actual climbing, the written word is a magical place to apply our audience. In some cases, the writer crafts with word an experience almost as excellent or beautiful as the original. He or she has had time to look back and reflect on an adventure, to sift through the specifics of it, to ponder relationships, and remember scenes with care.

We are able to do many climbs, with the good climbers who also are good writers.

Climbing writing and "actual" literature once were thought to be separate forms of expression: one legitimate and the other, well, uncertain. That's no longer the case, as more and more writers, in what has come to be known as the "literary mountaineering genre," have stepped into the wider arena of adventure nonfiction publishing. They have demonstrated that climbing writing can be a powerfully focused lens. It is clear there are genuine artists able to sculpt from words the action-oriented experiences of the mountains.

Some climbing or mountaineering compositions are by undisputed poets, such as Reg Saner. Continually in his award-winning writings, Saner's love for the mountains and the outdoors expresses itself.

As to the intent of climbing writing, it seems concerned most with human beings, what they discover and share, how they interpret experience, and the goals they mysteriously set for themselves. Often a piece of writing is not a copy of an outdoor, "motor" activity so much as it is a replica of some feeling about what was shared or experienced. The good writers are true in one or another way to sensory awareness, sound, color, touch, feel, smell, and taste. There is something poetic, if not mystical, in the way such things combine to create for us the stamp of perception. In some cases, the words indeed are a kind of poetry, with sharp images only a more poetic mind is able to cast.

A number of writers in the climbing world have academic credentials, such as Jim Perrin. Yet his doctoral degree in English does not cause his writing to become artificially formal or stilted, and often he appears surprisingly relaxed—his brilliance virtually as unaffected as a young climber first putting pen to page. Perrin observed once that his writing, or much of it, is, in essence, little more than conversation. Still, we know he works at it. But he has understood the motif.

In climbing, and in mountaineering, the best goals belong to a person's own singular world. In a few of the writings in this book, it feels as though the author has only a passing interest in a union between his or her mind and the minds of readers. The suggestion, rather, is that there is something going on more individual, or personal, a being taking note of him or herself, and coming to conclusions, or not coming to them, in some extraordinary, soulful experience. Sometimes the dialogue is between the author and the author, a type of self-talk that serves to explore and test the dimensions of experience. Certain writers seem often to be completely self-contained and able to speak to or with themselves, or to the situation that faces them. Reg Saner might be a little like this, and certainly John Gill is a shrewd self-observer in an isolated setting.

Not often do we find plot in climbing writing. The climbing story tends to dwell in a slightly more nebulous space and, in general, moves forward by virtue of the strength of its author's observations or the quality of his or her discoveries. Almost always, it is more situation, or more intuition, than triumph, more fingers that grasp and minds that savor than a place where everything done is decisive. There are game and destiny. There is a backdrop: a mountain, a rock, a forest, a group of friends. . . . And these backdrops, these settings, have voices themselves, in and around the author's.

In this book, articles brought together from several generations introduce to us the inner minds of men and women. Climbing, a vast detour up and away from humanity's main world, becomes another cosmos with rituals, ceremonies, play, and a language all its own. In the dance, art, risk, and ideologies, a reader senses the serious meanings as these writers weave their golden threads of past and present, their adventures, and write of their glimmering paths upward and inward.

In the classic sense of Wordsworth, a poet muses on a hillside. Climbers take that notion to a greater height and consider the view from often striking or exhilarating realms of snow and rock. It is an intermingling of the world of reality and the world of fantasy or reflection, sometimes a picture that flows from the irreverence of youth. Or it is nostalgia, to look back a bit on life. A few of the pieces are uncomfortable. The story sometimes is a struggle between flesh and spirit, worlds cold yet among friends, or warm yet lonely, but where some sense of a supreme and quiet beauty is almost predictably one of the eventual rare truths.

Climbers do go out into the mountains, or up among the rocks, almost in the spirit of young adventurers who run away from home and go to meet new experience. In certain ways, they are fragile creatures with psyches as delicate as air. In other cases they seem tougher, harder, such as Chris Bonington, an army man who drove tanks and who feels at ease on big expeditions to assault mountains of the Himalaya.

Some write in first-person present tense, a style that seems to allow memories to remain immediate. Others write in third-person past, more typically a reflective style. The writing, like climbing itself, in large part mirrors the culture to which it belongs, yet the language and acts of climbing, upon closer consideration, are also universal. In the finest tradition of the humanities, climbing writing has risen right along with the rise of climbing, and some of the best thinkers in academia will acknowledge the strength and quality of much of what has been achieved—"with rope and with pen."

Thoughtfully perused, there is much brilliant writing on the subject of rock climbing and mountains, and there are many astute portraits of and by the people involved. There is plenty of unworthy literature as well, and it takes a keen eye to sort out the masterpieces.

By nature, it seems, the climber is a creative person. The act of climbing a mountain or a rock, or tromping through the aesthetic realms of any mountain terrain, is itself a theme unfolding always. The mountains, the holds of a rock face, require imagination and an eye for things. Such an individual is a lively and alert creator of experience, as well as an observer of it. Climbing is an attempt to realize, or at least recognize, intelligent relationships in nature. To look at the resplendent outside world and at the very least sense a fullness of meaning is virtually the act of an artist, and thus it seems quite logical for the artful climber to move to the written art and express that fullness.

Some of the individuals in this book have climbed so extensively and with such insight and depth that they naturally build into their writing remarkable shades and nuances. It seems like relative ease, yet the task is not easy. It took Ed Webster twelve years to complete his book, *Snow in the Kingdom: My Storm Years on Everest.* In other instances, a writer churns something out on a whim or a sudden inspiration, and it is nearly perfect immediately—Royal Robbins' "Jack of Diamonds," for example. Yet to write about an experience can be a bit like asking someone to read music on a page rather than hear it. The reader may need a lot of imagination to get as much of the meaning as is there or that may occupy the heart and mind of the composer. The work of art will evoke an impression, at least, a little of the sentience, deep mysteries, and beauty of life. That must be a criteria of the best writing, even if the writing has as its subject "dossing" on a couch in England and ascending slate quarry slabs in rain to fight the despair of no job or money, as described by Paul Pritchard.

A good writer never reveals all. The artist of the rock, who is also an artist of the written word, suggests. He or she is able to give a few images and clues and is clever enough to find the means to shape, through words, a little of the pitch and drop and wisdom and intensity of life, some of the terrain of the perceptions, and a few gendarmes of experience. The writer assists readers, one might say, so that they might fulfill the author's experience, or some of its possibilities, in their own souls.

Like poets, climbing writers notice the position of the stars or the direction of the wind. They hear a waterfall. They hear the sound of a piece of equipment in the eerie acoustical silence of a deserted canyon. They recognize the temperature of air high up in the sweeping expanse of one of Yosemite's granite walls. They bring mythical significance out of what might seem to be normal spheres of language.

Ernst Bocklen, an obscure European writer, many years ago in a study of the creation and development of speech, tried to prove from language that all myth originates in the moon. Likewise, the climber is able to imagine the secret beauty and mystery in precipitous nature. A rock, or a mountain, is known for its various weaknesses, and its strengths, and is a formidable, supernatural presence. Only a climber can know so well how to infuse into writing similar cracks and fracture lines, the logical weakness of language perhaps, and make something that is still and spectral and to which readers are drawn.

Through spatial and color ideas, the mention of time, and the descriptions of people, climbing becomes, in a sense, one vast metaphorical comprehension of the world. It is a relatively new framework for the creative impulses of man and, truly, originates less for practical reasons than in the satisfaction of spiritual, supersensible, and ideological needs. The language seems somewhat to reject the theory that it arises in order that a person make him or herself better understood. It was Yeats who said something to the effect that if you can explain a work of writing it is not poetry. Climbing writing has some of that element. We wonder what we are being told. We are left to feel rather than fully understand. It is required that we imagine, as we enter into the detail of the various angles of approach offered by individuals who have unique personalities and viewpoints.

In *Art and Artist: Creative Urge and Personality Development*, Otto Rank asserts, "There is not a single word of which we know the original meaning." Through such a possibility, we realize we have arrived simply at one more point in time. And this too will pass. We sense the evolving nature of language. Climbing writing, one might think, is so new, relatively, yet already the newer writings look different than those only a few decades earlier. Climbing writing borrows freely from the whole past, is absorbed into the future, and merges comfortably and quickly into the glottis of that voice which might be called time immemorial. It seems to have been given instant intergalactic license to be as illuminative and filled with light, or storm, or gloom, as any of the other valid creative acts of expression throughout the world, academic or otherwise. The climber, however, will concede that his or her writing is not necessarily conclusive and that his or her "studies" are . . . preliminary to . . . deeper investigation.

There will be more climbs and more words about them, new ideas, new feelings, and more creative urges to say what has been felt. We shall continue to make sounds that hint at the unearthly, heavenly, imagined, or abstract. A climber is never independent of such things. What he or she climbs seems almost secondary. The rock always is a symbol of something deeper, and the mountains are vehicles for the soul to rise. The air carries the movements of tongue and lips and mind, and things yet to be worked out, the sound waves, call them, of hidden, more inner realms, the inner places of a person . . . like the colors of steep rock.

Styles of writing grow out of basic personal philosophies, out of the way the authors think, and from the kinds of beings the writers are. Knowing most of the individuals in this book, I can speak well of them as people. They have lived in the pictures they write, and thus some of the words are as delicate as a silhouette. Sea striking against the rock, or a genius effort to fight one's way through a storm. . . . The writing might be defined as imagination stimulated, and it shines on these pages. Climbing is acute sensory action and requires one to hold his or her attention to the rock, sky, mountain, and tasks at hand. There are dangers which require fierce attention, and there are more poetic elements, the strong movements of clouds across a great blue overhead, the sounds of feet as they scrape against rock, or even the sounds of breath or heartbeat. There are colors of many varieties, each one of which can be made into an association or meaning itself. The tastes of climbing, as well, are important and peculiar.

Walt Whitman said in *Leaves of Grass*, "I seek less to state or display any theme or thought, and more to bring you, reader, into the *atmosphere* of the theme or thought."

Climbers perceive the atmospheres of rock and mountain with their bodies as much as with their eyes or minds. Perception occurs inwardly as much as through the senses, and that perhaps is a subtle message, a story, that exists between the lines of good climbing writing. Robbins speaks about the anguish of being forced to hang on the side of a rock wall in cold wind to belay. He speaks of tired legs and how he must force them to take each step forward to keep up with Layton Kor along a seemingly endless trail down the mountain after their strenuous climb. In such images, we feel much more of the man, much more of his world, than if he simply were to describe the wall of rock or tell us the goal was reached.

One thing all the writers in this book have in common is an honesty about themselves and integrity in the experience which they write. We find Perrin, who lovingly moves from hold to hold with his son, and Venables, with mature insights. We find irreverent memories by Long and the slightly boorish comedy of Sherman. Saner notices every layer of sand, and there is the environmentally aware Irvine, who writes movingly of the exhilarating, honest, and *rare* experience that climbing affords us. There is the playful benediction of a fading yours truly, or Higgins, who likens himself and his companions to the Flintstones. Susan Fox Rogers conjures the heady lure of that first climb.

It was difficult for quite a few of these individuals to choose a favorite or a piece that could be called a best work. A humility was encountered with Tom Higgins who said, "Most of my stuff is junk, really." Far from it. Tom's lighthearted scribblings always have reflected his keen, creative mind.

I came up with or was given many names of people who might qualify in terms of their capabilities as writers, and it immediately became apparent that I would not be able to include them all. As for one of the newer writers, I chose Mark Synnott. His piece on the famous climber Cesare Maestri was the first article in a long time, from a climbing magazine, that held my interest from start to finish—almost without allowing me to take a breath.

Ian McNaught-Davis entertains us with the most "unsentimental" writing imaginable. He is a master of understatement.

In just a few words, Alison Osius sketches a revealing picture of the world of competitive climbing.

Chuck Pratt's piece well represents the 1960s and the early days of American climbing writing. In his writing, he speaks so clearly of comradeship and other aspects of pure, childlike fun.

In his account of soloing a scary granite wall in the Tetons, John Gill speaks of the aspect of childlike play: "I pause for a few moments, thinking that at the age of fifty-four my climbing career has come full circle. I have returned to the origins of spirit, found in the simplicity of my earliest and most naive ascents." Jim Perrin, describing his son, writes, "he falls into the subversive void where the rest of us, knowing the folly of taking climbing seriously, have long been content to play." John Long says, "Doesn't shameless youth appeal because it's raw and without guile, and doesn't it endure, however briefly, because it accepts no order but its own? In the heart of the 'just and devout' is a bumbling charlatan, and it is this charlatan that holds out the chance for joy."

Perhaps only Joe Simpson's "Guilty as Charged," a treatise on Tibet, would exempt itself successfully and almost altogether from the compass points of raw childish happiness, pleasure, and direct creative involvement with life. He does not express the feeling of Doug Robinson's title, "Mountaineering Just Means Glad to Be Here."

Indeed climbing is not always happy. Sometimes friends are lost to avalanches or storms, terribly deep experiences, as told by Greg Child and Kurt Diemberger. There is even a certain underlying pain in Walter Bonatti's description of his style.

In the end, the good writing tells us many interesting things but does not necessarily utter the secret. That will be the reader's own revolution, within limitations, to belong to that subtle conquest that sees and also feels. The artist, by virtue of what he is, in his own nature, reacts in a special way to experience. And thus climbing writing leaves the mystery of genius exactly where it has been, is, and always may remain, high up among the radiant, resplendent, elusive, and transcendent revelations of all art: the soul, the imagination, the high landscapes of heart and mind.

Sentinel Rock, in clouds, Yosemite.

Climber's Choice

JIM PERRIN

Jim Perrin, Wales, 1984.

As a young man during the 1960s and 1970s, Jim Perrin was one of England's outstanding climbers. His columns, articles, and books are some of the best writing to come from the British climbing-naturalist world. A sensitive writer, Perrin is clearly a romantic. The range, quality, and human breadth of his writing, together with his outspoken and controversial nature, have made him an important literary figure. Yet he does not try to be "intellectual"—he speaks with a warm and human voice. Here he reflects on aging and parenting as they tie to wet rock in the great climbing destination of Wales, above the Irish Sea. The love he expresses for his son and his understanding of climbing are welcome additions to a literature that tends to be dominated by more ardent voices.

A doctor in English biography, Perrin won the Boardman Tasker Award for Mountain Literature for his 1985 poetic biography of John Menlove Edwards.

Visions and Virians

Climbing with my son William, though I was decades past my own prime, offered some of the most magical experiences of rock ever for me. It insisted on the harshness and danger as well as the singular beauty. Between my ribs I felt the dagger of responsibility for my example set to him. It felt like a blessing too, in a passing along of something that had come to my life as a gift, and that would enhance his. As indeed it has: he is a supremely talented climber now and a funny, lovely, endearing young man whose soundness of approach to the sport educates me as surely as the sport itself has educated him.

JIM PERRIN

The present condition of my son gives cause for concern. He's just turned fifteen, and until last summer he was quite a pleasant, interesting kid as adolescents go, into mountain bikes and computers and den building. All that's changed. He started hanging around the local climbing wall—I suspect initially because a girl at mention of whose name William goes bright crimson and professes to hate was always down there. Then he caught the rock-climbing bug. Talk with him now is a delirious babble of crimps and slaps, dynos and French grades—all the patois of the modern rock ape. He hangs off any excrescence around the house like a great sullen lemur, mopes on wet days, and is off into the quarries at every permitted opportunity, clipping, working, and top-roping God knows what. When I tuck him in bed every night he's propped up reading the Slate guide.[1] He wants a climbing wall for his birthday.

Needless to say, all the members of the Llanberis climbing ghetto—the Crook and Radio Walton, Big G, the Creature, the Fugitive, and the Lone Intoxicant—whenever they call in or he sees them around, regard this as excellent sport, tease his incessant questioning into ever more ludicrously indefinable realms, so that his fingers there on the bullshit edge he and his mates so eagerly grasp loosen their grip and he falls into the subversive void where the rest of us, knowing the folly of taking climbing seriously, have long been content to play. Alas, poor William, we know the state too well.

Me, I get parentally worried, remembering that inability to concentrate on anything as your mind runs over and over the moves of a climb. So what do I do? I insist he finish his homework first. I don't let him go out too often on weekday evenings in case it affects his schooling (and sneakingly, I know that not making it too easy for him, and giving him something to fret against, sustains the allure). I can't share his enthusiasm for the quarries where he climbs mostly—the burden of their industrial history hangs too heavy for me to feel easy among them. But he—without that knowledge to trammel his enjoyment, rejecting empathy with those who worked here—takes them on the uncomplicated plane of egocentric recreation. In which guise I can appreciate their appeal, envy him the simplicity of that response, and envy him also at times—mornings especially—his growing strength and ease of body, as my own creaks and aches its way into decrepitude.

Also I try to bring in the other dimensions, to fill in the gaps our mockery tears in his value systems. So on Sunday, though rain was forecast, the wind blustering around and thick gray cloud scudding in across Anglesey, we set off to climb on the sea cliffs near Holyhead. Our objective goes by the romantic name of *A Dream of White Horses*. It's a rising traverse of four hundred feet across a steep gray slab of rock that forms one side of the deep inlet known as Wen Zawn, near the North Stack lighthouse. There is a famous photograph taken of its first ascent in 1967—embattled, tiny figures and the flung spray of a leaping wave—that William has seen. So there is an element of apprehension in his mind to which I add by telling him about hanging belays above the surging water, rock little better than dried mud, and stances that collapse beneath you into the depths with a sulfurous roar,[2] all of which exaggeration is the currency of those who climbed on these cliffs in the first phase of their exploration.

There is no one in Wen Zawn when we arrive. We creep down the descent route that crosses above its fearful void. I play mother hen, clucking over him, warning him about rock boots on wet grass, roping him to me where the path touches the cliff edge by a three-hundred-foot drop to the waves, explaining to him at the notch on the far edge of the slab where the route begins that from now on we're incommunicado and tugs on the rope are our language. On the slab the wind is less. I concentrate on placing protection that won't pull out when tension comes on the ropes' long parabola. The moves are not difficult by today's standards—even the smallest holds will take most of your fingertips, and the hardest thing is to identify footholds from the dappled cast of rock. I take the hanging stance in the crack of Wen, backing up the belays on each rope, checking his figure-eight and clove hitches when he's across with me, ensuring the ropes will run free.

So it goes on. William relaxes. He's enjoying it, engaging with the differing demands of rope work, circumspect use of the rock, registering situation, relishing the huge drop beneath him from the security of big holds and an angle which puts little strain on his arms. For me it is both pleasure and painful responsibility to see him habituating to this environment of deadly beauty in which so many of my friends have died. When we finish, the sky has cleared. The hills of Wicklow are acid etched on the horizon.

Back where we left our rucksacks, ropes coiled, he asks to go down and look across at what he's done, where he's been. I look with him, see as if for the first time the slab's light dusty gray, like new concrete, seamed and globuled as though some almighty artisan had applied a hasty scratch coat of rough render against the tide roar; I see the patches of ocher and umber in the rock, the delicate pink tints that in summer pick up on the color of tenuous clumps of thrift, I see the rough-cast, quartz-splashed back wall where the grand design is broken into pieces, fragments, where the rock is splintered, hard and veiny as old timber, with the wave surge among black boulders below. The sea's running diagonals merge into opalescent sky, and the choughs[3] tumble with a call like rusty springs as we turn to head out on the white track, amongst sepulchral stones, in the last light.

[Will Perrin, now grown and an excellent climber, adds his own reminiscence.—Ed.]

"Wow! this is a pretty scary place," I thought as I left the vaguely solid ground I'd been belaying from and stepped around onto the huge white slab. I looked down at the void between my frozen feet and saw a piece of driftwood being tossed around in the frothy swell that crashed between boulders and the sides of the Zawn. My body warmed a little, and the climbing became interesting and enjoyable.

As I hung at the next belay, my dad involved in the intricacies of the climb, my mind wandered. I gazed around at the amazing jagged rock scenery all around and at the ferry rocking its way across to Ireland. There must have been some very sick people on that boat. They seemed pretty insignificant out there in the huge sea, and so did we up there surrounded by huge expanses of choss.[4] I shivered as the wind picked up, and I thought of the climbing wall [in the back room of the local pub]. I thought of the increasingly drunk climbers telling tales of adventures and mishaps on these crags. I was not finding it all that bad. It was quite peaceful really, listening to the wind whistle through the huge arch, watching the birds, with nature slowly taking its course. We were soon at the top, wrapped up warm, and I scrambled down to the end of the promontory to see where we'd been. It was beautiful. A patch of sun broke through the blanket of gray and lit up the speckled walls.

My dad came down to look with me. I felt close to him at that moment. Those special moments with special people in special places are what it's all about. Isn't it?

NOTES

1. A guidebook to the climbs on the slate quarries of Wales.
2. Suggesting the fires of hell.
3. Small black seabirds.
4. Loose crumbly rock.

JOHN SHERMAN

*John Sherman at
Moorman's Boulders in
the mid-1990s.*

A boulderer specializes in very difficult climbs on very small rocks, usually no higher than thirty feet. The goal is pure difficulty, without the restrictions of a partner and equipment. John Sherman has established himself as one of the best—for example, with a pure unroped and unpreviewed solo of John Gill's Thimble route in the Needles of South Dakota.

Sherman has bouldered Yosemite's Midnight Lightning and written a wonderful book, *Stone Crusade*, about bouldering areas across the country. Probably no one has visited so many of America's legendary bouldering areas or so many of its good but obscure bouldering locations. In the following piece, he writes about such relatively unknown but well-used places as Carderock, in Maryland, and Moorman's Boulders, near Charlottesville, Virginia.

Besides being a tenacious boulderer, Sherman demonstrates a flair for writing. He has found his element in his humorous column Verm's World in *Climbing* magazine. He lives in Estes Park, Colorado. In the following hilarious piece, he tells about the rugs and little carpet squares some climbers place at the bottoms of boulder problems so they can wipe their shoes clean of dust or dirt or sand grains that might act like little ball bearings and make them slip from the small holds of a boulder. If the ground is wet or muddy, the climber can step on the rug to start instead of having to kick the gunk off partway up the rock. Unfortunately, in certain bouldering areas across the nation, these little eyesores become fixed in place. Sherman's love for the beauty of nature, and perhaps his desire to keep bouldering areas as unlittered as possible, inspired him (at least for a time) to collect these rugs. It evolved almost into a game, tantamount to pure mischief, one might say.

Boulevard of the Behemoths

I think this is my most successful piece. It combined a strong ethical stance with a hearty dose of satire and succeeded on both counts. After it ran, I got several calls from climbers who told me they laughed out loud reading it. The same callers said that the next time they went bouldering they couldn't leave without picking up the fixed rugs. I did get one angry letter from a Moorman's local who felt my article would endanger access if the landowner read it and found out that climbers were trashing his land.

JOHN SHERMAN

Busch ain't bad on a humid June day in Virginia. I know, I just slammed a quart for lunch. It seemed the right thing to do after spending the morning on a successful trophy hunt. No, not turkeys or whitetail. We were after elusive quarry, the *scotchgard immobilius*, better known as the shag-topped sole-scrubber or, to the layperson, the fixed rug.

For years fixed rugs were an endangered species, just clinging on in a few areas best suited to their needs—urban boulder fields rife with spray paint, broken glass, and soft, lazy climbers. But in the 1990s the population has exploded, creating a heyday for the modern hunter.

I'd been to the famous holes in the West: Indian Rock near Berkeley, with its thin but feisty towels; Ilium Boulders near Telluride, a hidden gem where the soft, drippy rugs stand out in front of a background of harsh and inhospitable mountains; and of course Morrison [Colorado], where the Black Hole has set records for trophy hauls for years. I've even pulled a few lunkers out from Hueco Tanks [Texas], though the dry climate and slabby landings don't generally favor these otherwise hardy species. As far as the East goes, I hadn't been there for a couple of years. I surely wasn't prepared for what I'd find there in the 1995 season.

I was traveling with D. Changeling, a cagey newcomer skilled in ferreting out fixies in the overhunted canyons of Stoney Point [near Los Angeles]. We had two months to scour the Midwest and East. I suspected this was where the truly big brutes resided, the granddaddies that took hours to haul in. I first got a notion of how big rugs grew east of the Rockies when I visited Chandler Park in Tulsa, Oklahoma. There my local guide took me to a little-known pocket where I reeled in the heftiest single specimen in my career, a plump deep-shag buck with a mature growth of moss and microorganisms. I struggled with it throughout the descent, its slime-infested haunches and fifty-pound heft proving a true test for my oaken arms. But like Tracy hugging Hepburn, Fields gripping a gimlet, Butkus clenching a quarterback, I hung on. At long last, stumbling through the poison ivy, tripping over the thorny vines, and slipping through the mire, I broke its will. By the time I reached the road we were both exhausted, but I proved stronger. The final quarter mile back to the van was as much victory parade as work.

D. and I cruised the Midwest north of Oklahoma with only limited success. It appeared that Chandler was an anomaly, one of those rare days when you pull in the legend that the old-timers call the General. I was beginning to get depressed and suspected that all the litterbugs had moved into the gyms. Fortunately, I was wrong: New England proved more fertile. Only at the most obscure areas were we skunked. Nevertheless, I suspect we could have done just as well out West. A month had gone by and we'd only pulled in nine keepers.

Finally our luck changed on the banks of the Potomac, just a bent page and a scandal west of D.C. There the rocks were formed ideally for rapid growth of carpets. Planes of schist slice into the mud at a sixty-degree angle, forcing sheets of water from the frequent rains to form long bogs at the base. The carpets residing in this muck quickly become fat. These were tricky sons of guns and hard to track down—sometimes you'd only see a palm-sized patch of pile breaking the surface. We found the best way to sneak up on these was to imitate climbers. The rugs seem to have no fear of being picked up by them. First we'd crank up the boom box really loud, then with chalk on hands and sneer on lips we'd nonchalantly flick a tape wad or cigarette butt onto the ground. When the rug least expected it, we'd grab a corner and heave mightily.

We tugged sixteen chartbusters out of the muck, but at the same time some real beauts got away. The rapid growth rate of Carderock rugs is offset by a short life cycle. Some folks blame it on the acid rain. Whatever the cause, in just a few seasons even the proudest nineteen-dollar-per-square-yard tight-loop bull rug will lose its weave and become just another twirly, spineless pile of slop. More than once we were fooled by these cagey codgers. Spilling a ten-dollar pitcher doesn't compare to the disappointment that comes from stalking a twenty-square-footer, clutching it by the short curlies, jerking like a Titan, and only coming up with a handful of rug ramen.

With a few weeks of vacation left, we bid Carderock adieu and headed south into Virginia. Virginia isn't known for its rug hunting, but for years I'd heard of a small area called Moorman's Boulders, five leagues northwest of Charlottesville. I was warned that there wasn't a whole lot there, just a pair of dinky yet delightful bouldering walls hiding in the hardwoods next to the tranquil Moorman River. Usually you don't see much climber trash in such an idyllic setting, but this place was a gold mine. The first wall, a scant fifteen yards from the car, yielded four fair-sized specimens right off the bat. The real treasure, however, lay a hundred yards farther downstream. Imagine my glee when I emerged from the tunnel through the bushes to see a fifty-foot-wide wall, overhanging, thick with chalk, and the entire base covered in carpets. We're talking everything from small carpet store samples to thirty-square-foot remnants. Thirty square feet! Layer upon layer they were stacked: level loops, plushes, sculptures, even a berber or two and in all the fashion shades—red and brown, yellow and brown, orange and brown, brown and brown. Not only that, there was indoor-outdoor too. The not-quite-natural Astroturf green brought tears to my eyes, I tell you. This was it—Home of the Hogs, the Honey Hole, Boulevard of the Behemoths.

D. and I had already hauled three loads out when a local arrived. I'm sure he thought nobody knew of this place, because you should have seen his jaw drop when he saw our remaining catch. It's a good thing there are no limits on rugs, otherwise the warden would have us in for a good decade. I couldn't help showing off one rug to the kid. Only three by three, but eighteen pounds if it was an ounce—astonishing for a low-pile plush. The mud clung thick to both sides (Lucky Pierre from a three stack), and earthworms slithered in and out of the mesh. There was even a cute little centipede all yellow and squinting in the newfound daylight. The kid was speechless. Jealousy can do that. Fearful that we'd be back again, he told us, "It wasn't this way two days ago. This is really rare." Typical local talk; they'll say anything to keep you away. I've got news, pal— your secret's out. You had your chance to clean up and you blew it. Nevertheless, I felt charitable and offered the kid a chance to get in on the action. I have to applaud his nobility as he declined, knowing the catch was not his doing, and let us have all the fun. He did offer that "there's a dumpster a mile down the road." There wasn't. Oh, those crazy locals.

Before we could get the haul loaded in the van we had to take hero shots. Before we could get the squabs lined up, another local arrived. Younger than the first, he was a slight boy just coming into some peach fuzz. He was heartbroken to see the pros had come in and scored huge. This was worse than the time his school's homecoming queen was caught running deep patterns with the rival school's halfback. He pleaded with me, "Can't you leave just a few back there for us?" His droopy basset hound eyes touched me. I felt cruel, like I'd yanked a pacifier away from a six-year-old, but I held firm. The kid had to grow up sometime.

I did what I could to console the boy. I talked about game management. How we had to take out the trophy specimens so that the young rugs to come could have a chance to get just as plump and juicy. I explained to him how climbing hard and an environmental ethic couldn't mesh. How there is no shortage of insecure, self-centered climbers desperate to ascertain their dominance over the rocks, to piss on the fire hydrant of nature. How these climbers would quickly reseed the areas. How climbers were dumb as dog chow; they still hadn't clued in to carrying their own compact, lightweight strip of carpet with them to *and* from the crags. How carpets carried home after each bouldering session stay clean and dry and always clean shoes better than dirt-choked fixed rugs. How cleaner shoes equate to highest-level performance on the rock.

It was no use. The boy was crestfallen. He looked longingly at our booty. Thirty-two rugs in all. Over two hundred glorious pounds of fiber and filth. He shuffled away with his head hung low. The young fellow was obviously in a tizzy, desperately clutching to the shreds of his rent-apart worldview and wondering if there was anything he could do about such injustice. The urge to catch up to him, clap him on the shoulder, and say "fret not" was great, but I checked myself. I knew this wouldn't be the last such haul from Moorman's Boulders.

STEPHEN VENABLES

Stephen Venables

Stephen Venables, one of Britain's best-known mountain writers and one of its great souls, was born in 1954. He has skied and walked in the hills since childhood and started climbing while studying at Oxford University. His first love remains the European Alps, where he has done many of the classic routes, such as the north face of the Eiger. But he has also made many first ascents farther afield, particularly in the Himalaya. His most demanding Himalayan climb was a new route on the East Face of Everest with a four-man Anglo-Canadian-American team, achieved without oxygen. An account of this ascent is given by Ed Webster later in this collection.

Venables' first book, *Painted Mountains*, won the Boardman Tasker Award, and *Himalaya Alpine-Style* won the Banff Mountain Literature Festival Grand Prize.

Tierra del Fuego

One of the few consolations of middle age is that as your climbing deteriorates your writing gets better. When I was asked to contribute to this book, my first reaction was to dig out articles I wrote fifteen or more years ago, chronicling my proudest moments on hard Alpine and Himalayan faces. Although there was some good stuff there, it all seemed a touch shallow. It didn't really do justice to my memory of the huge, joyful, overwhelming experiences I had been through. So I looked instead at some more recent literary efforts and thought, "Yes—I have actually gotten better at this writing game." That is a gratifying discovery, and I hope my writing will continue to improve. In the meantime, I'm settling for this account of an expedition to Tierra del Fuego.

The article was written originally for Summit Magazine, *but because of some muddle during a change of editors a different version eventually appeared. So this particular account is published here for the first time. It does not describe an earth-shattering first ascent, nor does it recount a desperate escape from the jaws of death. As expeditions go, this one, despite two unlucky accidents, was comparatively low key. That's not the point. Monte Sarmiento—the mountain we went to climb—was really just an excuse, albeit a compellingly beautiful excuse, to visit a fascinating part of the world. There is much more to mountaineering than just climbing mountains.*

When I set off for Monte Sarmiento in 1995 I was ambivalent about the project. This was to be my first serious climb since a near-fatal Himalayan accident three years earlier. I was understandably nervous, particularly since I was now the father of two young boys. Despite the anxiety, however, I was also excited at the prospect of seeing Tierra del Fuego. I had always been fascinated by the land of forests, fjords, and mountains at the far southern tip of South America, ever since I had read Eric Shipton's accounts of his explorations there in the sixties. I was also thrilled to be joining a very special team. Tim Macartney-Snape's ascent of Everest's Great Couloir in 1984 was a landmark in Everest climbing history and had inspired my own ascent of the East Face of Everest in 1988.

Charlie Porter was one of those legendary figures I had read about in magazines, one of the great stars in that mecca of climbing centers, Yosemite. I had also known for years about Jim Wickwire, pioneer of many Alaskan climbs and the first American to climb K2. As for John Roskelley, he was simply one of the world's greatest Himalayan climbers.

This, then, was the talented group I joined in 1995 to attempt an obscure but beautiful mountain, rising elusively above the Straits of Magellan. I hope this account gives some idea of why we do these things.

STEPHEN VENABLES

Tierra del Fuego was a crazy idea. I love climbing, but these days I rarely have the chance to get away. For my first expedition in three years I should have chosen somewhere warm, dry, and accessible—a place to maximize the climbing potential of each precious day. Instead I chose perversely to visit a remote, sodden, wind-battered island at the southern tip of Patagonia, knowing that in one month I would be lucky to get two or three days of actual climbing. Why on earth did I do it?

The answer, of course, is that there is more to climbing expeditions than the individual pitches of rock and ice. A mountain is often just an excuse to visit an interesting place, and after years of Alpine and Himalayan ventures, I find myself drawn increasingly to the Southern Hemisphere, in particular the wild mountains on the fringes of Antarctica. In 1990 I spent three months on the island of South Georgia, relishing the combination of mountain, sea, and teeming wildlife, and learning to live with the almost incessant wind. Tierra del Fuego would be similar but with the added attraction of trees, for although it is glaciated country on the same latitude as South Georgia, the toe of South America is dipped in slightly warmer water. Those few extra degrees of warmth—and the infinite humidity of the Pacific weather system—nurture a glorious profusion of temperate rainforest that cloaks the intricate shoreline of the world's most extensive system of coastal channels.

So I was drawn by the landscape. More important, I was attracted to the team, which originated serendipitously, many thousands of miles away, on Everest. In 1988 I spent three of the happiest months of my life there, climbing a new route on the Kangshung Face with an American team. Five years later two of my companions were back on Everest, this time on the north side, camped alongside John Roskelley and Jim Wickwire, telling them all the old yarns about their days on the Kangshung with an oddball Brit called Venables. Soon after that a letter from Wickwire arrived in England, asking if I would be interested in joining him and Roskelley on a trip to Monte Sarmiento, in Tierra del Fuego.

Given our introverted national psyche, it is a truism for Britons to talk about American openness and friendliness, but on my first American expedition there really had been a refreshing warmth and generosity of spirit, which I remembered fondly. Wickwire's letter promised more of the same, and when I eventually met him in England I knew that a trip with him would be fun. I wasn't quite so sure about Roskelley, the self-confessed redneck from Spokane, whom I hadn't yet met but who carried a reputation for seeing life in absolutes. This was a man who had frequently upset the American climbing establishment with his outspoken criticisms, a man who seemed, by all accounts, intolerant of fools and weaklings. How would he take to an oversensitive, unfit Englishman, only just recovering from a bad knee injury sustained in a Himalayan accident? How would I match up to one of the world's toughest and most successful mountaineers?

I was curious, intrigued, and a little apprehensive when I left home at the beginning of April, forsaking the English spring for fall in Patagonia. When I arrived in Punta Arenas two days later, my apprehension evaporated. Roskelley was open, friendly, uncomplicated, and funnily observant, with a quiet, dry Clint Eastwood voice. His eyes twinkled flirtatiously at Chilean waitresses, but it was the harmless joking of a man who is actually fiercely loyal to his wife and who spends the greater part of his life at home on the farm, looking after his two children. There was a lot of talk of home, both from him and from Wickwire, who for thirty years has sustained a brilliant juggling act, balancing the demands of a large family in Seattle, an ambitious climbing career, and a successful law practice representing Indian and Eskimo land rights in Alaska.

The fourth climber arriving in Punta Arenas was Tim Macartney-Snape, who led the first Australian ascent of Everest in 1984. He is a backwoods natural—tall, lean, self-contained, with huge lungs and an unerring competence lurking beneath an apparently diffident manner. An outstanding mountaineer, he is also experienced with boats, and when we arrived at Ushuaia on the Beagle Channel he quickly endeared himself to the fifth team member, Charlie Porter, whose yacht, *Gondwana*, Wickwire had chartered for the expedition.

Twenty-five years ago Charlie Porter was a big name—a very big name—in Yosemite, where he spent countless days, often alone, hammering, hooking, drilling, and jiggery-pokering his way up what were then some of the hardest artificial big wall climbs on El Capitan. Two of his routes in particular, the Shield and Zodiac, have become famous classics. His 1977 swan song was a phenomenal solo effort on Mount Asgard, on Baffin Island. Then he vanished from the climbing world and headed south to Chile, where he embarked on a nine-month solo kayak trip of two thousand miles through the Patagonian channels. He has been in Chile ever since, kayaking, sailing, botanizing, geologizing, occasionally climbing, and generally immersing himself in one of the world's most beautiful wildernesses. In these days of increasingly off-the-shelf adventure, he remains a true original—eccentric, opinionated, and infectiously enthusiastic about the land he has made his home.

Charlie was our guide and skipper for the oceanic tour up the Beagle Channel—that improbable creek linking Atlantic and Pacific, winding between Tierra del Fuego's main Isla Grande and a maze of smaller islands to the south and west. For five days we motored into the wind, occasionally hoisting the jib when the direction changed. In memory the days blur into a slow-moving picture of black water, blue ice, and reddening leaves of *Nothofagus pumilio*—one of the southern beeches—intermingled with dark *Nothofagus betuloides*. Each evening we would anchor in a cove, landlubbers fumbling with ropes as Charlie shouted orders. Only Tim was really trusted; Roskelley, Wickwire, and I dared not so much as touch a rope and slouched around like disgraced schoolboys, calling ourselves the Three Stooges—Larry, Mo, and Curly.

On the fourth day we battered through the gray lumpy water of the Bahía Desolada, named by Captain Cook during his epic eighteenth-century circumnavigation of Antarctica. Then on the final day we rounded the Brecknock Peninsula and emerged briefly on the Pacific coast of Chile, to feel the oceanic surge of waves that come all the way from Australia, before slinking back east into the shelter of the Cockburn Channel for the final run into Sarmiento.

The main group of peaks on Tierra del Fuego is named after the naturalist who came here in the *Beagle* in 1832, at the start of a voyage that would eventually result in a book challenging the whole basis of Western civilization. Just west of the Cordillera Darwin, isolated on its own little peninsula, rises another peak, Monte Sarmiento, that is perhaps the most spectacular in Tierra del Fuego. It is certainly the most prominent and was described in Darwin's *Voyage of the Beagle* as the "most conspicuous and the most splendid object in these regions. Rising abruptly from the sea to a height of about 7,000 feet it terminates in two sharp peaks, which seem absolutely in the sky, so lofty does the mountain appear when you are close to its base."

Those twin peaks of Sarmiento have eluded many expeditions over the past 126 years, since Domingo Lovisato first explored the southwest approaches in 1869. The first climbing attempt was led by Martin Conway in 1898, but he never really came to grips with—or even saw—the upper slopes of the mountain.

Conway was followed by a man whose name is synonymous with Patagonia—Alberto de Agostini. Agostini spent the best part of his life away from his native Italy, serving in Patagonia as a Salesian missionary. An assiduous photographer, he posed stilted groupings of the native Indians, scrubbed clean and decked out in unnaturally fine furs; but his mountain photographs make no attempt to tame the grandeur of the wild landscape. For over forty years he explored the length and breadth of Patagonia, mapping, photographing, and climbing. Of all his first ascents, the most important was probably the magnificent peak of San Lorenzo, between the two Patagonian ice caps. Down in Tierra del Fuego he led expeditions to several peaks including Sarmiento. His first Sarmiento attempt was in 1913 and his second in 1956, when he was seventy-three. On that second attempt Clemente Maffei and Carlo Mauri attained the South Ridge and finally succeeded on a very steep, direct line up spectacular rime mushrooms to the higher East Peak (2,235 meters). The West Peak eluded three further Italian expeditions, but a fourth, in 1986, was successful; Daniele Bosisio, Marco Della Santa, Mario Panzeri, and Paolo Vitali reached the summit by its Northwest Ridge. A British attempt on the East Peak in 1993, led by Caradoc Jones, was unsuccessful.

That was the state of play when we arrived in April 1995. Each night in the cabin of *Gondwana*, Charlie had squinted through his stereoscope at aerial photos, convincing us that the original southwestern approach up the Lovisato valley was our best bet; so we anchored in the cove nearest to the mouth of the Lovisato River, Stooges looking on while Charlie trussed

up his precious *Gondwana* in a spiderweb of shore lines, tied off
to every tree in sight. Finally he chuckled happily, "If she moves
now, she'll take the whole forest with her. What d'ya think,
Tim, huh?"

Macartney-Snape nodded his approval, and we all went
ashore, leaving the boat in charge of Minos, the French-Cre-
tan cook. So far we had seen no sign of our mountain, or indeed any high mountains. Dank gray drizzle was to remain
the pattern for most of our trip, and when the mountain finally
did appear it was only in brief, flirtatious glimpses. From a
climber's point of view it was frustrating; the only way to cope
was to immerse yourself (literally) in the experience and learn
to love the soft light, the dripping trees, the oozing emerald and
orange bog, the glistening of jade green lichen festooned luxu-
riantly in the forest where we made our home, a few yards from
the beach. Charlie introduced us to the peppery taste of canella
leaves ("full of vitamin C, the Indians ate lots of 'em") and the
bittersweet calafate berries. Macartney-Snape wielded the ax,
building our kitchen and the "bridge over the river Lovisato"—
two wildly flexing *Nothofagus* trunks lashed a few inches above
the vicious glacial torrent.

Roskelley, mindful of the French mountaineer Poincenot,
drowned near Fitzroy, wasn't too sure about the bridge at first.
"I don't want anyone taking risks: it's not worth dying just to
have a mountain named after yourself." Eventually he agreed
that we should use the bridge, provided no one ever crossed it
alone. All the while Wickwire, expedition leader, kept a low
profile. One night, sitting around the fire at base camp with wet
cagoules and gumboots steaming on the line, I asked him why
he didn't get a grip and tell us all what to do. He looked up
from his book of poetry and said, "I wouldn't dream of telling
you lot what to do." And he was right, because in a small group
of equals consensus worked. On the whole, Macartney-Snape
and I tended to be more pushy, backed by Charlie's insistence
that in Patagonia you can't sit around waiting for good

weather—if any good weather does come it probably only lasts a day, and you have to be up there on the mountain, ready to go. Roskelley was the check on any impetuousness. A born hunter, full of tales of stalking bears and deer in the forests of Washington, on the mountain he reversed roles, becoming the prey, every sense acutely tuned to potential danger. Now in his midforties, his life seemed to be focused increasingly on home—on family and community, his work as a volunteer fireman, his zealous concern for the local environment, and his soon to be realized political ambitions; he wasn't going to risk all that for any mountain.

We were reminded soon enough that even a comparatively simple mountain like Sarmiento can be dangerous. A day came, after three long trips carrying loads across the bridge and up steep slopes to the rocky platform of camp 1, when there was enough visibility to allow us onto the Southwest Ridge above. It was only a rocky scramble, followed by an easy-angled glacier slope, but for me it was a symbolic moment when we reached the ice and stopped to put on crampons. Those steel spikes symbolized more than anything else my return to the world of high mountain glaciers. The last time I had worn them, three years earlier, they dangled uselessly by their ankle straps, wrenched from my boots as I hurtled 80 meters down the precipitous flank of Panch Chuli V—a remote peak in the Indian Himalaya. By some miracle I survived the fall, but I had broken my left ankle and badly smashed my right knee. It had been a long, slow struggle to get back to the mountains, and now, three years later, bending forward to ease my left boot into the crampon, I noticed the incongruous gleam of sharp new metal amid rusty burrs and remembered that it was a replacement section: during the fall one spike of hard-forged steel had bent ninety degrees as my foot hammered into granite. That graphic reminder should perhaps have filled me with dread, but now there was no fear—just nervousness about how I would perform alongside my companions. Would I enjoy my climb, or would it turn out to be the drab postscript to a finished career?

The slope was not steep, but in places the snow crust had melted away to reveal hard, polished ice. Sudden gusts of wind came blasting unannounced across the ridge, threatening to catch us off balance, and we had to move carefully, ice axes ready to check any slip. My momentary nervousness was lost in concentration, and I began to enjoy the steady rhythm and the reassuring sound of steel biting into ice. Like skiing or playing the piano after a long layoff, it felt right, with old familiar reflexes quickly returning.

After a couple of hours we reached a good site for our top camp—a deep bank of snow tucked into the lee of a rocky outcrop, sheltered from the prevailing westerly wind. The plan was to leave food and spare gear here and return the next day with the largest tent. First we had to excavate a tent platform. Half an hour later, still immersed in practicalities, the five of us were hacking away with ice axes and shovels when someone shouted and we all looked up to see the clouds swirling up and away to reveal, at last, the twin crystalline summits of Sarmiento, luminous in the sky, three thousand feet above us.

This was what I had really come for—this theatrical transformation scene, this transcendental moment of revelation, earned by hard, patient slog. Suddenly we all talked at once, throwing opinions back and forth, arguing different routes, trying to gauge scale and steepness, but all agreeing that this mystery mountain had been worth all the effort of reaching it.

Charlie, Tim, and I lingered to savor this precious luminous scene while the other two started down, and it was only when we returned to camp 1 that we heard about the accident. Wickwire had been descending easy terrain, unroped. Suddenly, without warning, at the precise vulnerable moment when he was lifting one foot, a particularly violent gust of wind had caught him off balance and flung him through the air. He had landed on a sheet of ice, spun out of control, and crashed feet

first into a pile of boulders, badly spraining his right ankle. He
had managed to hobble painfully down to the camp, but now,
as five of us gathered for supper in the communal tent, he ad-
mitted sadly that he would have to abandon the climb.

When we said good-bye to Wickwire the next morning, he
did not expect to see us again for two or three days. But by
evening we were back, this time with a more serious casualty.
Roskelley and Macartney-Snape were already at camp 2 when
this accident happened. I had nearly reached the camp when I
heard Charlie shouting below me. I turned around to see him
crouched motionless on the ice. I couldn't hear any words above
the noise of the wind, so I descended a little and began to catch
the word "arm." Just to make quite sure, I climbed down closer.
He was kneeling on the ice, clutching his right arm, and gri-
macing with pain. "I've dislocated my shoulder. Get the others
and tell them to bring a rope."

By the time we were all back with him, Porter was shivering
and in shock. But he remained as garrulous as ever while we
escorted him down, furious with himself for letting the wind
catch him out, apologizing to us for the nuisance. Halfway
down, safely off the ice, we stopped to inspect the damage.
Roskelley, a trained paramedic, insisted we should try to put
the shoulder back as soon as possible, before it seized up completely. We should ideally have done it then and there, but we
needed somewhere flat and dry, out of the wind, so Porter's
shoulder had to wait until we were back with Wickwire at
camp 1.

It was like being in the labor room, and I wanted nothing
to do with all that pain. I looked the other way, concentrating
on cooking the supper, while Wickwire held Porter down on
the tent floor, only mildly sedated with codeine, and the other
two tried repeatedly to wrench his arm back into position. After about fifteen agonizing attempts, Porter begged for relief.
Everyone rested while I served up supper. After the meal,
Macartney-Snape, who had once in a remote bush hospital

been taught how to put a shoulder back, asked to give Charlie's one more try. This time I had to assist in the torture chamber, adding more weight to immobilize the victim. I held Porter's head and shoulders down. He chewed on a piece of beef jerky and dug his fingernails into the left leg of Wickwire, who sat on his hips. Roskelley and Macartney-Snape stood over him, repeatedly pulling with all their might on the arm, sweating and gasping with the effort, as they tried to rotate the shoulder joint back into its socket.

After a while it grew cold, and Roskelley said, "Wait a minute—I'm just going to get up and close that door." At which we all burst out laughing, envisioning some stranger peering in at the weird spectacle of five grown men grappling with each other in the semidarkness, one of them screaming through his teeth as he chewed frantically on the pink, pulpy remains of dried beef. The laughter gave us strength for more attempts, but eventually, after wrestling for over an hour, Macartney-Snape announced, "I can't do it. You can rest now, Charlie." It was now several hours since the accident, and the muscles around the joint had seized up completely. He needed expert help at the nearest hospital, which was ninety miles to the north in Punta Arenas.

My reaction to the second accident was a selfish one: I was bitterly disappointed that it probably spelled the end of our hopes for the summit. Wickwire was more magnanimous. First, he insisted on carrying down a full load, hobbling painfully on his sprained ankle; second, he was determined that, even if he had lost his chance, someone should climb the mountain, putting the official stamp of success on the expedition he had worked so hard to organize. Back at the boat, while Minos cooked up a hurried meal, Jim persuaded Charlie that he and Minos could crew for the one-armed skipper, crossing the Straits of Magellan that night and reaching the hospital the next day. The old sea dog stomped around the cabin clutching his bundled-up, distorted arm in an old jacket, muttering into his beard about wanting a bigger crew. "I really need Tim," he said. The Stooges said nothing. I said nothing. Tim appeared to do nothing but afterward said, "I gave Charlie a quick hard look."

It obviously did the trick, because the skipper agreed to sail with a crew of two, leaving Macartney-Snape, Roskelley, and me with just enough time for one crack at the summit. Wickwire promised to return, in some boat or other, within five days. Roskelley was not entirely convinced, and as the three of us paddled back ashore to base camp that night, he muttered darkly, "We're marooned, stranded. I sure as hell hate being away from the sound of an internal combustion engine." Less practical and more susceptible to romanticism, I found it deeply moving: *Gondwana* chugging away, navigation lights fading north into the dusk as we slid silently back to shore, staring ahead at Sarmiento, the whole mountain visible for the first time, orange in a violet sky.

Of course it was raining again in the morning, and the wily old fox Roskelley tried to persuade us to be sensible, but we coaxed him back up to camp 1, and the following day, in equally squally weather, we fought our way up to camp 2 to lash our tent to the platform we had prepared four days earlier. We spent a contented, domestic sort of evening in the tent. Macartney-Snape cooked supper while Roskelley argued the basic right of the American citizen to carry firearms. Then we drifted asleep in our cocoons of goose down, trying to ignore the battering of the wind outside.

The wind howled to a climax in the early hours of Wednesday, then died down at dawn. As we left, pink light suffused diaphanous clouds, dispersing rapidly beneath us. I dared to hope we were going to be lucky, and sure enough, as the day brightened to luminous tranquility I realized we had been given a wonderful gift. Only two things marred it. First, Charlie and Jim should have been there; second, we had to abandon hopes for the slightly higher East Summit, untrodden since 1956. To reach Mauri's route from this side would have meant traversing a zone of avalanche debris, and when Roskelley stopped in front of it, with his look of deliberate purposefulness, I knew there was no point in arguing. My feeling—and I think Tim's—was that you have occasionally to hurry past nasty places, but Roskelley was adamant that there should be no unnecessary risk. The man who had climbed K2 with Jim back in 1978—and followed that with a succession of brilliant Himalayan successes—was not going to take any chances on Sarmiento. So we opted for a shorter, safer new route up the southwest face of the West Summit.

It was a pleasure to climb with two superlative mountaineers—both a hundred percent alert, concentrated, and always following the safest line, seeking out islands of solid ice amid suspicious slopes of windblown snow. In the shade, on the south side, there was little freeze-thaw, and the choice lay between deep powder and rime-encrusted ice. Whenever possible we stuck to the ice, relishing the joy of crampons and axes sinking effortlessly into purpose-built Styrofoam.

It was wonderful to be ice climbing again for the first time in three years. As my initial nervousness evaporated, I thought, "Why should they do all the leading?" Overawed by the others' experience, I had let them take turns in front, but now, toward the top of the south face, as our summit came into view, I said, "Do you mind if I lead for a bit?" Above us was a steep ice gully that promised to be the most exciting part of the climb, but to reach it we would have to wade through a long, tedious snowfield. Macartney-Snape, ever the gentleman, suggested, "Why don't I break trail for a bit, then you can lead the interesting bit higher up." For "interesting" read steep, technical, absorbing. But I insisted: "No, thank you, I'll take over here. It's time I did some trail breaking. I can't have you colonials doing all the work." Self-esteem had to be assuaged, and after taking the end of the rope from Roskelley it was good to throw myself into the hard labor of kicking through deep powder, panting hard, and doing a little jump each time I had to lift my still imperfectly bending right knee.

The reward for that hard slog was the final series of ice walls up the gully—real climbing, stepping up almost vertically, poised on just the front points of my crampons, with the whole three thousand feet of the south face now dropping beneath me, and below that the fractured glacier tumbling far down into the red and green tapestry of the forest. Above me the gully emerged onto a gangway beneath the giant overhang of the summit. This gangway was the final question mark, and we hoped desperately that it would coincide with a little notch we had spotted in the summit bulge.

Macartney-Snape led up the gangway. Roskelley followed. Then the rope came tight, and it was my turn. The summit overhang was now leaning right out over me—a two-hundred-foot-high mushroom hanging thirty feet out in space, encrusted with swirling crystalline feathers of rime—but as we had hoped, the gangway led right up underneath it to a notch, where the other two now stood silhouetted against the sky.

From the notch it was an easy walk to the top of the mushroom, which we reached at three o'clock in the afternoon. The sun shone and the air was miraculously still. I was reminded of a fine winter's day near home in Scotland. There was the same intricate, glittering pattern of mountain and sea, but on a grander scale, with huge glaciers and ice caps and the wonderfully surreal rime battlements of Sarmiento to remind me that we were in Tierra del Fuego, suspended between Atlantic and Pacific, at the uttermost ends of the earth.

Forty minutes passed all too quickly, then it was time to descend, hurried down by Roskelley, who was rightly anxious to get down as far as possible before the light faded. His urgency was vindicated soon after dark when the wind returned suddenly, without warning, transforming the benign face of Sarmiento into a hideous maelstrom of spindrift, pouring down relentlessly on our heads, stinging eyeballs raw. It seemed that every one of the billion tiny granules of snow on the mountain was being funneled deliberately, malignantly, onto our heads, down our necks, and into our mittens every time we took them off to fumble with rappel brakes. We were being forced to pay for our summit gift, and if we failed to find our way off the mountain we would have to spend the whole night out in this smothering icy torrent. I was very glad that Roskelley, without my impediment of lousy eyesight, was going first, rope length by rope length, finding the way out of this hellhole.

There were moments, suspended on the rappel ropes in the swirling blackness, when I thought of that other descent in the dark, three years earlier on Panch Chuli, when the pin came out. The terrain here was different, with no jagged rocks. I wondered whether one might even survive a fall to the foot of the face, then remembered all those ice bulges we had climbed that morning and graphically imagined the life being pounded from my body. Each time I set off down the ropes, I couldn't help glancing anxiously at the anchor, just to reassure myself that it was sound. In fact they were bombproof, and my fear, like most fear, was irrational. Most of the time I was far too busy to be frightened. As always on these occasions, there was a grim satisfaction in coping efficiently, concentrating one hundred percent, keeping discomfort to a minimum. It was horrible, but the unpleasantness lasted only two hours. By nine o'-clock we were back in the tent, congratulating ourselves on our fantastic luck as the stove's roar challenged the noise of wind outside.

Packing up the tent on Thursday morning, Macartney-Snape and I told Roskelley to get inside and hold it down while we untied it from its moorings. A moment later Roskelley's hand shot out of the door and grabbed a piton as the wind picked up the tent with him in it, threatening to fling them both over the edge. He looked at us suspiciously and said, "I don't wanna seem like an old fuddy-duddy or anything, but I really think we should rope together down to camp 1." So we roped up for slopes less than thirty degrees, clawing our way horizontally on hands and knees, like a replay of the famous Monty Python sketch of people climbing the pavement. It looked very silly, but we weren't taking any chances. To misquote another British humorist, Oscar Wilde, two accidents had been unlucky; a third would have looked careless.

Two days later Macartney-Snape and I did the final load carry down from camp 1, while Roskelley cleared up base camp. The loads were heavy, and my bad knee twinged uncomfortably on the final slog through the bog, lurching from hummock to hummock, struggling to keep up with Tim's effortless stride. It was another typical damp overcast afternoon, but the bog seemed more luminous than ever—orange, yellow, crimson, and green, with brilliant white lichen encrusted like coral on the skeletal remains of long-dead trees. I had to admit to myself that the beauty of it all was enhanced by success. It had been wonderful to live for three weeks in this enchanted landscape, but as always I needed the simple satisfaction of a job completed, a goal attained. That fulfillment was reinforced when we tramped into base camp to discover that Roskelley had cleared away every trace of our stay and was waiting for us on the beach, listening delightedly to the deep throb of a diesel engine. A hundred yards offshore, a Chilean fishing boat rocked in the swell, and as we were rowed out to meet it we could see from the smile on his face that Jim Wickwire, despite his own bad luck, was equally pleased with our eleventh-hour success on Sarmiento.

JOHN GILL

*John Gill at the
Hagermeister Boulders,
Estes Park, Colorado.*

The great boulderer John Gill began to make his fame as a young man in the Air Force in 1961 when he free-soloed the overhanging side of the Thimble, a thirty-foot spire in the Needles of South Dakota. That was an astonishing and legendary rock climbing achievement. In 1958, on Baxter's Pinnacle in the Tetons, he had led one of the first 5.10 climbs anywhere. With his one-finger pull-ups and one-arm front levers, but also with incredible technique, he has remained a hero to climbers throughout the world.

Because of Gill's tremendous strength, he has suffered a number of injuries—in some cases, it seems, because human ligaments are not designed to contain so much power. For example, he suffered an incapacitating form of tennis elbow and spent a long time recovering and redesigning his approach to bouldering. In October 1987, at age fifty and bouldering hard on a very difficult route, the Micro-Shield, his weight came down suddenly onto his extended right arm. The biceps was torn from the forearm bone. Aside from the pain, there was the gruesome effect of the muscle more or less rolling up to his shoulder under the skin of the arm. The muscle was reattached surgically.

Not only a great climber, Gill also has set a standard as a person, possessing remarkable insight and humility. He has been a distinguished professor of mathematics at the University of Southern Colorado, retiring in 2001.

Throughout the years, Gill has continued to write and produce tale after tale of his climbing adventures, articles that with the passage of time are more and more infused with his wonderful sense of humor, keen wit, and spirit of play.

Two Pieces from *Master of Rock*

My climbing career began—almost fifty years ago—in a traditional fashion, with ropes and hardware, lengthy leads, and inspiration from immortals such as Hermann Buhl. I soon found I lacked the temperament for conventional rock climbing. Yet I have survived a few interesting moments while linked to a supportive companion. Recalled from the perspective of so many years, any exaggeration in the first tale that follows is purely undetectable.

Often I have felt the need to break away from bouldering and get a little air beneath my heels, to achieve a kind of existential balance by going solo above the treetops. The second of these two pieces describes an exposed scramble up Trinity Buttress in the Tetons on a warm and sunny day in August 1991. The climb is typical of what I seek in the autumn of my life: to maximize adventure while minimizing difficulty—ironically the opposite of much of my previous bouldering.

JOHN GILL

"Get the Hell Off That Rock"

[Visiting the Needles in 1975, John was ascending a hundred-foot spire a short distance from the Needle's Eye parking lot on a humid summer afternoon.—Ed.]

I found myself pathetically grappling with slippery quartz crystals, patiently belayed by my wife, Dorothy. As I turned a corner halfway up the spire, two huge beer-drinking motorcyclists, clothed in what appeared to be uniforms of the Romanian Iron Guard, spotted me. As they sat on the hood of the car of a petrified tourist, whose casual acquaintance they had just formed, they yelled to me, "Get the hell off that rock!" With sweat pouring into my eyes and a dismal climbing performance jading my thoughts, I promptly shouted back, "Come get me!" A moment of tense silence gripped the Black Hills. Automobile traffic came to a halt, and touring families exchanged worried looks as they quickly rolled up their windows, locked their doors, and stuffed their small children into the back seats. The two motorcyclists focused their attention on me with a look that was a perfect blend of cruelty and serendipitous pleasure. One of them effortlessly and with quiet arrogance pulled a beer can apart. The pieces tinkled to the ground. Remembering Dorothy on the ground, I quickly began mental calculations of distance and rappelling and running speed.

Suddenly the two cyclists shook their heads, and their expressions changed to (of all things) bland indifference. They slid off the hood onto their Harleys and roared off with only

John Gill on "the Scab," Needles of South Dakota.

GILL COLLECTION

the quickest glance at the daily and predictable casualty that unfailingly warmed the hearts of climbers: the Greyhound tour bus, as usual, had jammed against the rock and become stuck in the Needle's Eye tunnel, shedding its glassy tinsel to the satisfaction of children and climbers alike.

My spirits bolstered by these fortuitous developments, I shouted around the corner of the spire to my belayer, "It's OK, Dorothy, they've gone," only to hear her reply coming from a quarter mile away, "That's good. I'll see you at the campground."

LifeSavers

[In August 1991, in the Tetons of Wyoming, Gill found himself soloing on smooth, water-polished granite, making a few airy steps high up on the third tier of Trinity Buttress.—Ed.]

I move across a boulder field and up a steep grassy slope to a tiny cave hidden in the trees at the base of Trinity Buttress—a tiered cliff. After stowing my blue daypack, I put on my climbing shoes, belt pack, and coiled rappel line and move up around the left corner of the cave onto an exposed but undistinguished ridge. I scan the buttress above. My route will be devious—three large cliffs are separated in a complex fashion by huge ledges covered with trees and brush.

The transition from scrambling to climbing, that moment when you first glance down and see rocks and grass far beneath the contours of your feet, induces a heightened perception and a subtle change in body chemistry. I feel more locked into the evolving matrix of the present and less prone to drift in time and place. I move up the arete, ascending several minor steps in an increasingly airy environment, frictioning over rounded corners. Easy terrain on my right—I could scramble, practically walk, up there if I wished—steep cliffs on my left, long and exposed. That's where previous climbs have been made.

I move into a thirty-foot dihedral with abundant holds and climb quickly upward, passing in astonishment what appears to be a fresh Charlet-Moser piton: is this to be a dreamlike day in the twilight zone of a thirty-year distant past? Whatever the context, this is the first fun pitch of the day—no grass, dirt, or shrubs, just clean, firm rock. Above, I enter a strange, chaotic realm of precipitous rock walls, steep grassy ledges, and towering evergreens, some leaning over the corners of vast overhangs, their roots groping blindly into space. Color is everywhere— in the texture of the rock and the brilliant green of the trees.

I move up through this turbulent landscape, guided more by whimsy than strategy. I imagine myself in an ancient poem—a medieval fairy tale—as I scramble along vertiginous ledges and over short bulges of lichen-covered granite, across precariously steep dirt slopes on the very edge of concave palisades, until finally reaching a broad shelf guarded by stately firs, the sentries of time. Beautiful white and tan slabs of polished granite sweep upward from here, two hundred feet to the top of the second tier of cliffs, capped by an uneven but continuous overhang. I pause for a few moments, thinking that at the age of fifty-four my climbing career has come full circle. I have returned to the origins of spirit, found in the simplicity of my earliest and most naive ascents.

With some apprehension, I scan the long line of the overhang above me until spotting an obvious break where exposed scrambling may carry me through. Tiptoeing now, up and across to the west on lovely, firm, and slightly sculptured rock, an occasional optional move of unnecessary difficulty to add spice to my adventure, and I am suddenly near the crest of the overhang. I sense the tingle of exposure as I move up an easy crack to a foot-wide ledge directly beneath an abrupt, ten-foot step. If I negotiate a couple of elementary moves now, with my hands above on slabby holds, I'll be up and through the barrier.

As I balance on my exposed perch, I hear voices of a climbing party across the couloir on the southwest ridge of Storm

Point—a half mile away. A female climber, assertive to the point of belligerence, is leading two good-natured men up a series of granite slabs. Her instructions ring clearly through the canyon. Instinctively I begin to move in the direction she indicates! I knew long ago that the tough, hard-man, thoroughly masculine image of climbing would eventually vanish. I didn't foresee the peculiar androgynous analogue that would evolve, however.

My attention interrupted by this display, I step over the bulge—exaggerating a simple move in the process. A trivial distraction, yet my technique has been degraded. I move quickly up onto dirt and scree slopes leading to a large boulder sitting a few feet from the vertical immensity of white and yellowish granite that forms the last, most significant part of Trinity Buttress.

It's not good that I lost my concentration for a moment on the pitch below. That's not the way to endure in this solitary and dangerous meditation, this slowly deliberate, vertical stroll on edges of hard granite reality. In soloing, the margins of safety are maximized by shutting out anything other than the immediate technical requirements of climbing.

Time for a few LifeSavers. After some deliberation, I decide to climb on the eastern part of the buttress wall on rock that rises to a prominent shelf two hundred feet up. To the west, the rock is vertical and has few if any comfortable resting places. From my philosophical perspective, it lacks the virtue of available relaxing sections where a middle-aged explorer can recharge. I move upward and to the left, following a diagonal seam toward a small rectangular block perched high on a minor ridge. The face I ascend becomes vertical toward the end of the pitch, capped by a slight overhang, but the holds are large and the climbing easy. I fully expect to find a simple way up the last twenty feet above the block to the shelf seen from below. But when I arrive at the block I am face to face with uniformly steep, smooth yellowish rock of severe appearance and considerable exposure—far too risky for unroped exploration.

To the right of the crest, however, I see a favorable pattern of holds. Amazing how one's perspective changes. A few seconds ago, while beneath this section, I dismissed the possibility of going straight up, due to the exposure and wickedly smooth nature of the rock. Now I see that a couple of elementary but airy moves on newly discovered ledges will take me up the remainder of the face.

Several minutes of increasingly disciplined, tentative steps off the block, onto the rock above, then back onto the block bring me to the point where determination exceeds the sense of jeopardy, and I move up a steep dihedral for several feet. I step around a corner, stretching my right leg to reach a ledge that slopes down away from me and is carved into the wall above a small overhang far above the trees. I would never attempt this elementary but unprotected move without the new technology of sticky rubber soles.

A short scramble leads to the shelf. Without pause for rational planning—deplorable but typical behavior when I get wound up in this frenetic sport—I start up a high-angle crack that appears to terminate thirty feet above at a ten-foot vertical face. The face seems replete, from its rough facade, with abundant edges. It should provide an easy exit into dirt gullies above that are filled with scree and bordered by shrubs and trees. The climbing on the smooth stone quickly becomes a little harder, and I run out of comfortable, horizontal holds. I move continuously, stemming and cross-pressuring my way up an inside corner until I reach the small face. At last some sloping footholds and a good hold for one hand . . . a chance to secure and pause and suppress the niggling anxieties that threaten to disturb the smooth flow of climbing technique.

Slightly out of balance and with considerable space beneath my toes, I can see no more holds above me. Feeling that I am at the end of my hypothetical rope, I search for a way to negotiate a few feet of intimidating rock without calling on bouldering skills that I have largely avoided since my injury.

I still my mind and press tiny sparks of apprehension into the subconscious and calm the viscera, and I am ready to receive instructions. And . . . yes . . . my body drifts a step to the right, above the emptiness, and I am now nearly below a ledge, and I find a handhold and sloping foothold and step up and stand above this thing of which I have become part.

It is over, and I scramble the remaining few feet to the top. I lose the descent path on the bottom tier of cliffs and wander back and forth across the wilderness of overhanging walls and tree-covered shelves. I follow ledges that lead nowhere. I traverse steep, dangerous earthen slopes, rappelling three times, until I am down to the level of the cave and my blue pack. It is 4:30, and I am weary and hungry. This day has been a bit more than I expected. The difficulties were, I am certain, less than they seemed, but the continual probing of the unknown strains the eye and the nerve and leaves the mind unsettled, insecure in the subtle turbulence of an existential ripple.

CHRIS BONINGTON

Chris Bonington, Buxton, England, 1984.

Chris Bonington was born in Hampstead, England, in 1934. In 1956 he was commissioned in the Royal Tank Regiment and commanded a tank troop in northern Germany for three years. He became a mountaineering instructor with the Army Outward Bound School and started climbing in the Alps, participating in the first British ascent of the Southwest Pillar of the Drus in 1958. He made the first ascent of the Central Pillar of Freney, on the south side of Mont Blanc, in 1961, with Don Whillans, Ian Clough, and Jan Dlugosz, a climb considered at the time one of the great classics of the Mont Blanc region. In 1962 Bonington was on the first British ascent of the North Wall of the Eiger. Over the years he has pursued a career as a writer, photographer, and mountaineer, planning and participating in expeditions all around the world and to the world's highest peaks. In 1996 he was knighted as Sir Christian Bonington. A kind of elder statesman of British mountaineering, he has won numerous awards for his books and films. His documentary *The Everest Years* won the highest award at the 1988 New York Film and TV Festival.

40

Drangnag Ri

Drangnag Ri was a very special trip, both because it was to celebrate the tenth anniversary of my ascent of Everest with a Norwegian team and because at age sixty I felt I was going as well as, indeed better than, I had for some years. There was plenty of life in the old dog yet!

It was a lovely mountain, but even more important, I was climbing with a group of individuals with whom I'd formed a lifelong friendship ten years earlier on Everest. That friendship was further strengthened by our experience on Drangnag Ri. We didn't climb the mountain in the purest manner. Indeed, we ran a line of fixed rope to the very top, but that was to enable as many of the team as possible, Sherpas and Europeans, to reach the summit. The shared experience and friendship seemed more important than an ethical stance.

CHRIS BONINGTON

We'd climbed the headwall of the glacier through the night and reached the crest at dawn. As we pulled over the top of the slope, my eyes were drawn to a peak that formed a natural focus immediately in front of us. It was a steep and almost perfect pyramid, black rock defined by ice and snow—forbidding, unattainable, and therefore immensely attractive. The moment was the end of our expedition to Menlungtse in 1988 when I was attempting an unclimbed peak on the southern rim of the valley on the Tibetan–Nepalese border. Checking the map, I discovered that it was called Drangnag Ri, meaning Black Rock Peak, and was 6,801 meters high. It stuck in my mind as something I'd love to climb. Research indicated that no one had ever attempted it, so when Arne Naess, leader of the 1985 Norwegian Everest Expedition, of which I had been the sole British member, decided to have a tenth anniversary expedition, I suggested this as a possible objective.

All but one of the members of the 1985 team joined us in Kathmandu at the end of March 1995, together with six of the Sherpas who had also been with us on Everest. Just getting to Drangnag Ri was an expedition in itself. We flew into Lukla, the airstrip south of Everest, and then had to cross the Tesi Laptsa, a 5,750-meter pass leading into the Rolwaling. On the other side a long glacier snaked its way through the mountains toward our objective. The view at its head was amazing, for the glacier became an airy shelf perched above an immense drop into the deep-cut valley that leads up to the Nangpa La. It was like being in the dress circle of a gigantic open air theater, with a backdrop of some of the highest mountains on earth— Makalu, Lhotse, Everest, Gyachung Kang, and Cho Oyu.

It was 20 April before we turned our attention to the mountain, establishing a camp at its foot at around 6,200 meters, which left 600 meters to go to the summit. Since it looked extremely steep, we had already decided to put out fixed ropes to enable as many team members as possible to reach the top. We had chosen as the most likely route the right-hand skyline, which we could reach at a small col or notch about a third of the way up. After three days' work, we reached a point just below the notch. It was my good fortune to be out in front that day on sixty-degree ice, my first lead on the mountain. Climbing ice at altitude is an exhausting business. You are poised on the points of your crampons, each swing of your ice tool takes several pants, and yet the fatigue is hardly noticed in the tension of the moment. I was nearly at the top, a bulge of snow pushing me off balance. I planted my ax, pushing it in to its head, and heaved up. Suddenly the view opened out. Menlungtse, partly hidden by the ridge, seemed very close. Shishapangma sprawled in the distance. In the immediate foreground the notch offered a perfect campsite with a neat platform of snow for our tents. Glancing above, the ridge soared in a series of ice towers and pinnacles. It was not going to be easy. Stein Aasheim and I ran out a single rope length beyond the notch before the afternoon cloud and snow rolled in. We had made a start.

The following morning it was good to snuggle into my sleeping bag and listen to the others in the tent next door preparing to set off. I emerged at eight to make the first radio call. The reception wasn't good, but I learned that Ralph Høibakk and Bjørn Myrer-Lund were coming back up that day to establish a camp on the notch and keep going until the mountain was climbed. I dropped back down to advance base at this point, but returned two days later to join Høibakk and Myrer-Lund on the notch. It was slow going, and in two days' hard ice climbing they had run out four rope lengths. I suggested they take a rest the next day. I volunteered to push the route out, climbing with the Sherpas.

Next morning I set out with Mingma Gyaltzen and Rinzin. We now had five 50-meter rope lengths run out. It didn't sound much, but it felt a long way as I jumared up it. I was impressed with just how hard the climbing seemed, up and across steep icy runnels walled by spurs of snow and ice. The route even went through an icy arch and up over little rock walls and then, suddenly, I was at the high point, at the end of the fixed rope, a bundle of pitons and carabiners hanging from an ice peg. Getting ready was a long drawn out process. First we had to haul in all the slack of the fixed rope, then sort out the climbing rope, rack the gear I thought I'd need, and at last we were ready. I couldn't help feeling apprehensive.

"Is it all right if Rinzin belays you?" asked Mingma. "He's more used to it than I am."

"Yeah, sure, no problem." There was another little delay while Rinzin caught up on the fixed rope. Time for me to begin to feel nervous. Was I up to it? Would I make the same progress as the others had the previous day?

Rinzin arrived. He was younger than Mingma, with a long, narrow face which nearly always held a broad, wolfish grin. He had a Figure of Eight, but I loaned him my own Black Diamond belay plate and showed him how to use it. It was time for action. I glanced down the ridge to the camp far below, the tents, tiny boxes perched on the only available flat snow ledge on it. Time to start. I swung an ice tool in a curve, flicking the pick as it touched the hard, smooth ice. It penetrated neatly, and I knew it would hold. I banged the other one into the snow on the side of the runnel. It cut through easily but felt firm. Kicking in a cramponed boot and stepping up, my nerves vanished. I was concentrating and felt good, although panting hard now at 6,500 meters. A few more moves and I was 10 meters up, the drop spiraling below for over 300 meters to a snow shelf which concealed the further drop of over 2,000 meters to the valley below. I pulled up around the bordering snow ridge toward some broken rock protruding gray brown from the ice, decided it was time for some protection, and put in an ice screw. I felt an intense elation. This was why I was still climbing at age sixty. I was going better than I had for years, reading the ground, attuned to this environment in which I had worked and ventured for so many years.

Mingma and Rinzin were now out of sight. Alone, barely aware of the rope snaking behind me, I picked my way up past a huge cone of snow that clung to the crest of the ridge. Sometimes on rock, then on snow or ice, I slowly gained height until a shout from below warned me I had nearly run out all the rope. I found a tiny rock ledge, put in a couple of ice screws, and shouted to the two Sherpas to start moving up. A long wait ensued, followed by the complex work of fixing the rope, hauling it through, and tying it off to the intermediate runners. That day I led just one more rope length before the afternoon flurries of snow swept in, the same distance as Bjørn had achieved the previous day.

We slid down the ropes back to the camp, well pleased with what we had done. It was 29 April. Ten years ago this week we had all been taking our turns to top out on Everest. I thought there was probably just one more rope length before the angle started easing and we would be able to make a push for our latest summit. We could go for it the following day.

The camp on the notch had become a small village. Klaus Eric Okstad, the cameraman, and Ola Einang had moved up, pitching a tent on the very brink of the ledge. Everyone wanted to have a go at the summit—this meant that ten of us would be heading for the top the next day. It was Bjørn's turn out in front. On reaching the top of the rope I had fixed the previous day, he disappeared behind an ice bulge and was out of sight for over an hour. In the meantime the rest of the team, all nine of us, caught up to wait, festooned on various ice pitons, as the sun slowly climbed into a cloud-flecked sky. It took Bjørn nearly two hours to run out 50 meters of rope while we waited anxiously below. Ralph Høibakk, who was belaying him, then followed up, and I followed Ralph. I could see why it had taken Bjørn so long, for it was steep and hard and the difficulties were not over. Bjørn had belayed in an open gully of steep snow that soared into a convex bulge. It was no longer technically difficult, but the snow seemed bottomless and we discovered that we only had one snow anchor with us. The rest had been used on our tents in the camp below. The morning had slipped away, it was beginning to cloud over, and ten people on the route were too many. Ralph and I talked it through and decided that some of the team would have to go back down—but who? I certainly wanted to go to the top, and besides Bjørn, I was the only team member who was happy leading on this steep ground. Ralph then suggested that Bjørn, Pema Dorje, our *sirdar*, and I should go for the summit. I knew how much he wanted to go for the top and was impressed by his self-sacrifice.

By this time Bjørn had run out another rope length, so I followed to take a spell out in front. On reaching him I found him wedged in a small crevasse, acting as a human belay. He didn't have the solitary snow anchor, and there was no ice in sight for an ice screw. I floundered up some more snow to reach a rocky outcrop and at last fixed a solid anchor by driving a rock peg into a crack. Half an hour later Pema Dorje arrived, accompanied by Lhakpa Gyalu and Ralph. Pema had wanted

CHRIS BONINGTON

Ola Eineng on ridge above camp 2, Everest in background.

Lhakpa along to carry some more rope, so Ralph had felt justified in coming along as well.

I felt good, out in front and focused on reaching the summit. The angle had now eased, but the snow was deep and prone to avalanche. I moved forward tentatively, sinking up to my knees at each step as I traversed out across the slope toward a serac wall which would give me an ice anchor, but the rope ran out before I could reach it. Nothing for it, I buried my solitary snow stake horizontally in the soft snow. It just about held. I sat on top of it and waited for the others to arrive. The two Sherpas came first. Pema had another rope with him, and on easy angled ground the Sherpas were stronger and faster than I was.

I waved him through and he broke trail up to the serac wall, where we got in an ice anchor. By this time the cloud had swirled in around us and we were limited to a gray white world, the serac wall stretching as far as we could see on either side. Pema was happy to yield the lead—the Sherpas have little experience of climbing steep ice. After wallowing in deep, insecure snow and nearly falling into a bergschrund, I decided to tackle the ice wall direct. It was just off vertical, but the ice was quite soft. It was easier than I had anticipated. Above, the angle eased. I slowly plodded on until once again the rope ran out. I'd recovered our one snow stake, put that in, and waited for the others to catch up. The cloud shifted above, and I glimpsed another serac wall ahead. Surely we should be somewhere near the summit, and yet in the mist the glimpses of ice seemed far above. The angle being easy, I now abandoned the rope and plodded on up the slope until Lhakpa Gyalu caught me up and surged ahead toward the next ice wall. This proved to be another bergschrund, but he produced yet a further rope from his sack. I belayed him across. He reached the ice and put in an ice screw, and once again I took over for the next steep section.

We were now on the crest of the ridge, and as I pulled over it, the slope dropped away giddily on the other side. I hardly noticed the altitude, my concentration on the summit was so great. It was as if forty years had dropped away from me. I had all the drive and single-minded focus of my youth to take me up the steep ice of that soaring ridge. I ran out of rope just short of the crest. Nothing for it. I hammered in my ax, tied the rope to it, planted my ice hammer over the top and heaved up onto a little platform, glanced up, and suddenly realized that I had nearly run out of mountain. I could see the ridge tapering just above me into a gentle knife-edged curve. We'd made it. We were very nearly on the summit of Drangnag Ri. I let out a whoop and waited for the others. Lhakpa Gyalu was first up, so I waved him past. It seemed only right that he should be first to stand on this unclimbed summit in his own country. He had been with me in 1972 and 1975 on the Southwest Face of Everest and then again in 1985 on our Norwegian Expedition, but he had never been to the summit of Everest.

He demurred, but I pushed him past me and followed up. He was standing balanced precariously on the knife-edged ridge, the slope dropping away on every side into the mist, when suddenly I felt an electric shock course through me. The air around me seemed alive with an all-pervasive hissing. I yelled at Lhakpa Gyalu to get off the summit and fled back to the platform a short way below. Bjørn and Ralph had just arrived. I shouted we should get the hell out of it, but Ralph was prepared to take the risk and had started for the final little summit ridge when the atmosphere sizzled again. We turned tail and one at a time slid back down the top-rope. I was the last, feeling very vulnerable as I waited my turn. I abandoned my ax, which was acting as anchor, and rappelled carefully down the summit crest.

The descent seemed endless, but at last the tents came into sight. The others were awaiting me as I stumbled down, embraced them, and couldn't stop myself crying from relief, exhaustion, and an immense feeling of affection for my Norwegian and Sherpa comrades who had shared the experience with me.

CHUCK PRATT

Chuck Pratt in the 1960s.

In the 1960s Chuck Pratt was probably the best off-width crack climber in the world. One of the magic lights of Yosemite climbing in that golden era, he also was perhaps the best writer in American climbing. He wrote very little, however. Readers savored every word, and he certainly left people wanting more. His calm, his humility, his insight, his humor drip from the two main articles he wrote, "The South Face of Mount Watkins" (*American Alpine Journal*, 1965) and "View from Deadhorse Point" (*Ascent*, 1970).

Chuck was a shy fellow and never for sale to the media. Many people asked him to write something, yet he didn't. He often declined interviews or other media opportunities. Even to get him to comment on his past climbs was no easy task, although he was warm to friends he trusted. His brief introduction to the following piece reflects his simple approach. He was a man of few words, and that introduction might just as well have been excluded except for how well it reflects the precise, succinct, and laconic Pratt. He was a true legend and one of the great spirits of the climbing world. He passed away, only in his midsixties, in December 2000.

The South Face of Mount Watkins

My choice would be "The South Face of Mount Watkins," because it was published only once. People will not be as familiar with it as with "View from Deadhorse Point," which has appeared in several places.

CHUCK PRATT

The historic first ascent of Yosemite Valley's El Capitan in 1958 opened a new era in Yosemite climbing. In subsequent years, three additional routes, each over 2,500 feet in height, were established on the great monolith. El Capitan's height, the sustained nature of the climbing, and the resulting logistical problems required that the first ascent of these routes be accomplished in stages, with the use of fixed ropes to facilitate a retreat to the valley floor. Since the initial ascent of El Capitan, eight ascents of the various routes have been made, and climbers involved in this latter-day pioneering have gained confidence and experience in sustained, multiday climbing. By the summer of 1964, with new improvements in hauling methods and equipment, the time seemed ripe for someone to attempt a first ascent of such a climb in a single, continuous effort.

One of the few walls that remained unclimbed by the summer of 1964 and which afforded a challenge comparable to El Capitan was the south face of Mount Watkins. Rising 2,800 feet above Tenaya Creek at the east end of Yosemite, Mount Watkins rivals in grandeur even nearby Half Dome. Despite the obvious and significant challenge presented by the face, the mention of Watkins seemed to produce only a certain apathy in the resident climbers of Camp 4. Though many of them, including me, speculated on who would climb it, few of us were moved into action. Then one pleasant July evening at Warren Harding's High Sierra camp on the shore of Lake Tenaya, when the wine and good fellowship were flowing in greater quantity than usual, Warren showed me a flattering photograph of the south face and invited me to join him. In a moment of spontaneous rashness I heartily agreed, and we enthusiastically shook hands, confident that the fate of Mount Watkins had been sealed.

Several days later we were strolling through Camp 4, two rash climbers looking for a third, having agreed that on this climb a three-man party was a fair compromise between mobility and safety. However, our recruiting was unrewarded. The experienced were not interested; those interested lacked the necessary experience. By evening we had resigned ourselves to a two-man party when Yvon Chouinard walked out of the darkness. He had ten days to spare and wondered if there were any interesting climbs planned.

Within the week, after a reconnaissance trip to study the face and plan a route, we were assembling food, climbing equipment, and bivouac gear for a four-day attempt on the face. The three-mile approach to Mount Watkins began at Mirror Lake. As we unloaded packs at the parking lot, two young ladies approached us to ask if we were some of *the* Yosemite climbers. Yvon modestly pleaded guilty and pointed out our destination. They asked if it was true that Yosemite climbers chafe their hands on the granite to enable them to friction up vertical walls. We assured them that the preposterous myth was true. Then, with perfect timing, Harding yanked a bottle of wine and a six-pack out of the car, explaining that these were our rations for four days. We left the incredulous young ladies wondering about the sanity and good judgment of Yosemite climbers. And so the legends grow.

After following the Sierra Loop Trail for two miles, we eventually began contouring the slopes above Tenaya Creek until we reached the base of Mount Watkins, where we sought out a suitable camping spot for the night. In the darkness we noted with apprehension that the granite bulk of Mount Watkins completely obliterated the northern quadrant of the sky. The following morning, we awoke grim and significantly silent. With lowered eyes we approached the base of the wall.

Unlike most major Yosemite climbs, Mount Watkins has very little climbing history. Warren had been 700 feet up some years before, and climbers had studied the face from the southern rim of the valley, but ours would be the first and only all-out push for the summit. On his brief reconnaissance, Warren had been stopped by an 80-foot headwall above a large, tree-covered ledge. After studying the face three days before, we had elected to follow his route, as it involved only third- and fourth-class climbing and would allow us to gain a great deal of altitude on the first day. By climbing a prominent corner at the left end of the tree-covered ledge, we could gain enough height to execute a series of pendulums in order to reach a comfortable-looking ledge at the top of the headwall, thus eliminating the necessity of bolting 80 feet. This ledge would then give us access to an 800-foot dihedral system on the right of the face. The dihedral eventually connected with a thin, curving arch leading westward across the face. We hoped this arch would take us to the great buttress in the center of the face and that the buttress would in turn take us the remaining 500 feet to the summit. These speculations, however, would be resolved only after several days of sustained, technical climbing. The personal challenge, the unsuspected hardships, the uncertainty—in short, the unknown—that separates an adventure from the commonplace was the most appealing and stimulating aspect of the course of action to which we had committed ourselves.

Our immediate concern was transporting 100 pounds of food, water, and equipment up to Warren's previous high point. Loading everything into two large packs, Warren and I struggled up the hand lines left by Yvon as he led ahead of us up an intricate series of ledges and ramps. By noon we reached the tree-covered ledge and the base of the headwall where Warren had turned back before. Having volunteered to haul the first day, I began repacking our loads into three duffel bags while Warren and Yvon worked their way up the shallow corner at the

left end of the ledge. Two free-climbing pitches brought them
to a ledge where they investigated the problems of the long pendulums necessary to reach our goal for the first day—the comfortable-looking ledge 80 feet above me at the top of the headwall. By midafternoon Yvon had descended 75 feet, climbed
across a delicate face, and after trying for half an hour to place
a piton, resigned himself to a bolt. Descending once more,
Yvon began a series of spectacular swings trying to reach the
ledge above the headwall. After numerous failures he finally
succeeded by lunging for the ledge after a 60-foot swing across
the face. Warren rappelled to Yvon. After dropping me a fixed
rope, Warren joined Yvon in an effort to reach the great dihedral which we hoped to follow for 400 feet.

Prusiking up the fixed rope, I could watch Yvon leading an
overhanging jam-crack in the dihedral. From the ledge I began
hauling all three bags together. I was using a hauling method
developed by Royal Robbins for the El Capitan routes. It consisted of a hauling line which passed through a pulley at the
hauler's anchor. By attaching a prusik knot or a mechanical
prusik handle to the free end of the line, it was possible for me
to haul the loads by pushing down with my foot in a sling instead of hauling with my arms. The method was highly effi-
cient and far less tiring than hauling hand over hand.

Yvon and Warren returned to the ledge after leaving 200
feet of fixed rope, and we settled down for the first bivouac of
the climb. After only one day on the wall, it was evident to all
of us that our greatest difficulty would be neither the climbing
nor the logistics but the weather. It was the middle of July, and
temperatures in the valley were consistently in the high
nineties. We had allowed ourselves one and one-half quarts of
water per day per person—the standard quantity for a sustained
Yosemite climb. Still, we were not prepared for the intense,
enervating heat in which we had found ourselves sweltering
for an entire day. Those mountaineers who scorn Yosemite and
its lack of Alpine climbing would find an interesting educa-

tion by spending a few days on a long valley climb in midsummer. Cold temperatures and icy winds are not the only kinds of adverse weather.

The following morning Warren and I ascended the fixed ropes and continued climbing the great dihedral, hoping to reach its top by the end of the day. The climbing was both strenuous and difficult as we resorted more and more to thin horizontal pitons and knife-blades driven into shallow, rotten cracks. However, our biggest problem continued to be the heat. We were relieved only occasionally from the unbearable temperatures by a slight breeze. Although we tried to refrain from drinking water during the day, so as to have at least a full quart each to sip at night, we were all constantly digging into the climbing packs for water bottles. Every few minutes we found it necessary to moisten our throats, since even a few breaths of the dry, hot air aggravated our relentless thirst. Even the hauling, which should have been a simple task, became a major problem. Yvon, who was hauling that day, exhausted himself on every pitch, becoming increasingly tired as the day wore on.

In the early afternoon, we were surprised by the passing of a golden eagle across the face. Welcoming the chance for a brief respite, we ceased our labors and watched as the magnificent bird glided effortlessly high above us. Although he presented an inspiring sight, we hoped his nest would not lie on our route. In the days to come, this eagle would seem to make a ritual out of crossing the face, sometimes as often as three or four times a day, as though he were a silent guardian appointed to note the progress of the three intruders who labored so slowly through his realm of rock and sky.

By the end of the second day, we reached a group of ledges so large and comfortable that we named them the Sheraton Watkins. It was here that we were faced with the first major setback in our carefully planned route. The top of the dihedral was still some 200 feet above us. That 200 feet presented not only rotten, flaky rock and incipient cracks but also the probability of having to place a large number of bolts. Now that we were within 200 feet of the prominent arch we had seen from the ground, we could see clearly that it did not connect with the large buttress in the center of the face, but that a gap of 100 feet or more separated them. The prospect of bolting across 100 feet of blank wall so appalled us that we began searching for other avenues of approach to the middle of the face. We were in a deep corner, the left wall of which presented messy but continuous cracks leading 80 feet to a ledge on the main wall. From this ledge, it appeared that a short lead would end on the first of a series of broken ramps sweeping westward across the face. It seemed the only reasonable alternative, and we had just enough light left to ascend one pitch to the ledge 80 feet above before settling down on the Sheraton Watkins.

We were up early the morning of the third day in order to ac-complish as much as possible before the sun began its debili-tating work. From our high point, Yvon began the next lead. It was here that we began to literally walk out on a limb. We could see the broken ramps leading across the face for several hundred feet. Once we left the dihedral, retreat would become increasingly difficult. Not only would the route beyond have to be possible, but we would have to consistently make the correct decision as to which route to follow. Using every rurp and knife-blade we had brought plus three bolts, Yvon succeeded in reaching the beginning of the first ramp. Then I began the first of three leads which were to carry us 300 feet across the face. Although the climbing was moderate fifth class, it required a great deal of effort.

After nearly three days of climbing, the heat had reduced our strength and efficiency to the point where we moved at a snail's pace. Warren was barely able to manage the haul bags without assistance, and most of the afternoon was spent getting our lit-tle expedition across the traverse. Although we had not gained much altitude, our efforts were finally rewarded when the tra-verse carried us into the buttress in the center of the face. Once again resorting to the indispensable rurps and knife-blades, I led a delicate and circuitous pitch past a dangerously loose flake to a curving arch. Following the arch as far as possible, I descended, leaving what I thought would be a simple pendulum for tomorrow's climbing team. We were now situated on widely spread but comfortable ledges, and as we munched on our ever decreasing supply of cheese, salami, and gorp, we caught a glimpse of our friend the eagle as he passed on his daily rounds.

At the end of this, the third day of climbing, we were well aware of our critical situation. We had brought enough water for four days. It was now obvious that we could not reach the summit in less than five. Seven hundred feet remained between us and the giant ceiling at the lip of the summit, and the route remained uncertain. We reluctantly agreed that it would be necessary to reduce our ration of water to provide enough for at least one additional day on the face. We did not yet consider the possibility of retreating, although the prospect of facing the unbearable heat with less than an already inadequate supply of water filled us with dismay.

The fourth day proved to be one of the most difficult and uncertain any of us had ever spent on a climb. The sun continued its merciless torture as Yvon and Warren returned to the struggle. Warren found that I had underestimated the pendulum. After an agonizing effort, he finally succeeded in swinging to a ledge, and I proceeded up to haul. By midafternoon, after climbing as slowly as turtles up the central buttress, we reached the most critical point on the climb. Above us, a blank 60-foot headwall topped by an overhang blocked further progress. Warren had nearly fainted several times from the heat, Yvon was speechless with fatigue, and I was curled up in a semistupor trying to utilize a small patch of shade beneath an overhanging boulder. In an effort to provide more shade we stretched a bivouac hammock over our heads, but it provided little protection. For the first time, we considered the possibility of retreating. But even that would require another day on the wall. It seemed that those very qualities that had made the climb so appealing might now prove to be our undoing.

Warren investigated the possibility of rappelling 100 feet in order to reach the opposite corner of the buttress. However, we did not want to lose 100 feet of hard-earned altitude, especially since we could not be certain that the left side of the buttress continued to the summit. After a barely audible consultation, we decided to try the headwall above us, hoping that eventually we would find cracks leading to the summit, still 500 feet above. Warren volunteered to go up first. After placing three bolts, he came down, too exhausted to continue. I went up next and with extreme difficulty placed two more, the first direct-aid bolts I had ever placed, barely adequate, even for aid. Yvon took my place and after breaking two drills was able to place one more before relinquishing the lead to Warren. Instead of placing more bolts, the latter lassoed a small tree and prusiked 15 feet to a horizontal crack. With a magnificent display of spirit and determination, Warren continued the lead over the headwall, did some extremely difficult free climbing, and reached a ledge adequate for a belay. Refreshed in spirit, if not in body, Yvon followed the lead in semidarkness, marveling at Warren's endurance. Leaving a fixed rope, they returned, and we all collapsed gratefully on barely adequate ledges.

By the fourth day Yvon had lost so much weight from dehydration that he could lower his climbing knickers without undoing a single button. For the first time in seven years I was able to remove a ring from my finger, and Harding, whose resemblance to the classical conception of Satan was legendary, took on an even more gaunt and sinister appearance.

We slept late the fifth morning and awoke somewhat refreshed. Confident that we would reach the summit by nightfall, we ascended the fixed rope to study the remaining 400 feet. Once again we were faced with a critical decision. Continuous cracks led to within 100 feet of the summit, but it appeared they would involve nailing a long, detached flake. Yvon led an awkward pitch that curved to the left around a corner. After joining him, I dropped down and swung to the left corner of the buttress. Still I was unable to see if that corner of the buttress continued to the summit. I decided to climb the cracks above Yvon. They were of jam-crack width, and I pushed the free climbing to my limit in order to conserve the few bongs we had brought. After a fierce struggle through bushes, I was able to set up a belay in slings. That morning we had had two full quarts of water for the three of us. Yvon and I had already finished one quart, and when he joined me I was surprised to find he still had a full quart. Warren had refused to take any water that day, preferring to give the climbing team every advantage. His sacrifice was a display of courage and discipline that I had rarely seen equaled.

With added incentive, Yvon led a mixed pitch up a strenuous and rotten chimney, executing some gymnastics at its top to gain a narrow ledge. He joyfully announced that the next pitch appeared to be easy aid climbing and that the summit was only 200 feet above him. Anxious now for the top, I climbed as rapidly as I could while Warren struggled resolutely below with the bags. What we thought was a detached flake from below turned out to be a 100-foot column, split on either side by a perfect angle crack. The right-hand crack seemed to require fewer bongs, so I quickly nailed my way to the column's top, a flat triangular ledge only 80 feet from the summit. It appeared that the next lead would just skirt the gigantic ceiling at the lip of the summit.

Yvon, resorting one last time to rurps and knife-blades, tapped his way to the crest of Mount Watkins just as the sun went down. His triumphant shout told me what we had all waited five days to hear. When Warren reached the ledge, he asked to clean the last pitch, as he felt he had not contributed enough that day! Warren Harding, who had been the original inspiration for the climb, whose determination had gotten us over the headwall below, and who had sacrificed his ration of water after five days of intense thirst, felt that he had not done enough! I passed him the rope, and as he began cleaning the last pitch of the climb I settled down on the ledge to my thoughts.

In the vanishing twilight, the Valley of the Yosemite seemed to me more beautiful than I had ever seen it, more serene than I had ever known it before. For five days the south face of Mount Watkins had dominated each of our lives as only nature can dominate the lives of men. With the struggle over and our goal achieved, I was conscious of an inner calm which I had experienced only on El Capitan. I thought of my incomparable friend Chouinard, and of our unique friendship, a friendship now shared with Warren, for we were united by a bond far stronger and more lasting than any we could find in the world below. I wondered what thoughts were passing through the minds of my companions during the final moments. My own thoughts rambled back through the entire history of Yosemite climbing—from that indomitable Scotsman Anderson, who first climbed Half Dome, to John Salathé, whose philosophy and climbing ethics have dominated Yosemite climbing for nearly twenty years, to Mark Powell, Salathé's successor, who showed us all that climbing can be a way of life and a basis for a philosophy. These men, like ourselves, had come to the Valley of Light with a restless spirit and the desire to share an adventure with their comrades. We had come as strangers, full of apprehension and doubt. Having given all we had to the climb, we had been enriched by a physical and spiritual experience few men can know. Having accepted the hardships as a natural consequence of our endeavor, we were rewarded by a gift of victory and fulfillment for which we would be forever grateful. It was for this that each of us had come to Yosemite, and it was for this that we would return, season after season.

My reverie was interrupted by a shout from above, and in the full, rich moonlight I prusiked to the top where Yvon was waiting for me. Warren had hiked to the summit cap to see if anyone had come to meet us. He returned alone, and the three of us shared some of the happiest moments of our lives. As we turned away from the rim to hike to Snow Creek and some much-needed water, I caught a last glimpse of our eagle, below us for the first time. In the moonlight, he glided serenely across the face, as majestic as always and as undisturbed by our presence as he had been five days before.

Chuck Pratt's photographic masterpiece, taken at the Tenement Flats hanging bivouac: Tom Frost, Royal Robbins, and Yvon Chouinard waking up after a hanging bivouac about 1,500 feet straight up the sheer North America Wall of El Capitan during the route's first ascent in 1964.

CHUCK PRATT

ROYAL ROBBINS

Royal Robbins, Salt Lake City, 1991.

Royal Robbins on the third pitch of the Salathé Wall of El Capitan, 1961.

Royal Robbins was the leading light of Yosemite rock climbing during the enchanting 1960s when the game of big-wall climbing and the art of free climbing were being invented. He was the first to climb 5.9 in Yosemite, in 1951 as a sixteen-year-old kid. He also did the first 5.10 in Yosemite in 1960. He climbed El Capitan many times, including the first ascents of the Salathé Wall and the North America Wall. In ten days, in 1968, he made the first solo of El Capitan, via the Muir Wall route. He has enjoyed chronicling his ascents and has been a prolific and talented voice in the world of climbing writing.

In the *American Alpine Journal*, 1964, Royal wrote about a climb of the East Wall of Upper Yosemite Fall: "Some 2,500 feet below was another world, populated by creatures with their own concerns of a new day. Automobiles crept along the wet asphalt like ants. Somber and impassive, the granite walls stood as they have for millions of years, seemingly eternal, while Nature's creatures passed part of their momentary and insignificant existence between them. And what significance had our little adventure? None. Knowing this, we took it for what it was: a stimulating experience that awakened our minds and spirits to a lust for life and a keener awareness of beauty."

Such beautiful and impassioned writing has come to symbolize the great author of so many climbs, the man referred to on the cover of his biography as "Spirit of the Age."

Jack of Diamonds

*I am like Walt Whitman, a mixture of sublimity and garbage—
well not quite like the Good Gray Poet, and certainly not sublime.
In 1963 or so I wrote a short article on climbing two routes on
Longs Peak's Diamond with Layton Kor, for publication in the
Climbs and Expeditions section of the* American Alpine Journal.
*Ten or more years later, in about 1977, I wrote another piece on
the same subject, as a reminiscence for Bob Godfrey's Colorado
climbing history,* Climb! *I have selected this second version. I like
it for its economy and because I believe it captures my delightful
first visit to Colorado and the supercharged experience of climbing with that gifted, indefatigable, and swift genius of a climber
who was Layton Kor. Looking back, those were two magical and
memorable days I spent with one of the greatest climbers America
has produced.*

ROYAL ROBBINS

You asked me to reminisce a bit about the first ascent of Jack
of Diamonds that Layton Kor and I did in the summer of
1963. I remember that summer fondly. I was doing lots of
climbing, was fit, and Liz and I had saved enough money to
travel and climb as we pleased. I spent a lot of time around
Boulder that year, making the most of the rich lode of climbing
opportunities offered by the eastern Rockies. I climbed in Eldorado and Boulder Canyons, fell off Ament Routes on
Flagstaff, couldn't get high enough to fall off Gill Routes in
the marvelous Split Rocks, scraped skin on the Owls and Sun-
dance, and came to grips with the prince of Colorado walls, the
Diamond of Longs Peak.

It's a long but lovely walk up to Chasm Lake. I remember
more the loveliness, at this distance, than the length. Embed-
ded in my memory are pictures of the pines and twisted as-
pen, the fresh stream bubbling downward, the wildflowers,
and, up high, the meadows and lakes. It has always been a wonder to me that the Colorado Rockies, which appear so deso-

late, barren, and dry from a distance, can present to the visitor such an abundance of alps, wildflowers, lakes, and streams.

There were several parties camping in and about the stone shelter at Chasm Lake when Liz, Layton, and I arrived. We were ambitious to make the second ascent of D-1, because of its reputation as a Yosemite wall in an Alpine setting, and also simply because the Rearick-Kamps route was an elegant line up a stunning face. We were doubly ambitious, for we hoped to get up in a day.

I knew there was no one in the country, perhaps in the world, at that moment with whom I stood a better chance of climbing the Diamond in one day than with Layton Kor. He

Sheer 2,000-foot east face of Longs Peak (Diamond is upper half).

AMENT COLLECTION

was fast. Kor, in fact, had never developed the knack of climbing at any speed other than flat out. He was always in a hurry and climbed every route, even the most trivial, as if he were racing a storm to the summit.

Climbing with Kor, one could not remain unaffected by his tumultuous energy. It was stressful, because to climb with him as an equal required that one function at the limit of one's abilities. Layton was ever alert to a weak moment, and perceiving one, would pounce with the ever-ready phrase, "Maybe I should take this lead?"

Kor was a phenomenon. He was the first climber to break the hegemony that Californians had long enjoyed in Yosemite. Until Kor arrived, it was folk wisdom among Yosemite climbers that *everyone* who came there—no matter how they might star on their home ground—every climber on his first visit to

Layton Kor, atop Red Dihedral, above Eldorado, Colorado, 1964.

PAUL MAYROSE

Yosemite suffered a decline in his personal estimation of his climbing worth. Yosemite would inevitably take the piss out of the arrogant visitor. This was mostly due to the peculiar nature of Yosemite climbing, which tended toward holdlessness and strenuousness. But Layton wasn't daunted. He astonished us all by his ability to immediately do the harder routes in the valley, and in record time as well!

I had great respect for Kor, and this would grow during our ascents of the Diamond. But more than respect, I liked Layton. He was a climber's climber, which is to say, he didn't play to the crowd, and he climbed for the right reasons, that is, to satisfy himself. He wasn't the sort of fellow to step on a piton and later claim a free ascent, because to him that would be utterly pointless. It wasn't what others thought of his climbing, but what *he* thought, that counted.

Layton was certainly highly competitive and inwardly driven to make an impact upon climbing history. His list of first ascents of technically difficult rock climbs, both free and aid, is perhaps unmatched by any American climber. But Kor was one of the very few highly competitive climbers who never criticized the efforts and achievements of others. He was interested in action, life, joking conversation, and plans for the next climb. In fact, although he never talked about religion, Kor was a sort of natural Christian, generous when others were wrong, and not in the habit of finding fault with his neighbor. There was one exception to this. I once heard Layton express scorn for a Coloradan who had made a tasteless bolt route up one of Kor's favorite sandstone spires in the Utah desert.

During the afternoon of July 12, Layton and I left the shelter cabin and trod the fine brown granite along the south shore of Chasm Lake. We were soon on Mills Glacier and then followed Lambs Slide to Kiener's Traverse, which brought us to North Broadway and a several hundred foot descent to our bivouac at the base of the Diamond. It was comfortable, and our sleeping bags assured a good night's sleep.

Our ascent went smoothly, except for a ten-foot fall when Kor pulled an aid pin. The icy chute at the top of the wall provided interesting variety to what was otherwise a straightforward, if difficult, technical rock climb. That Rearick and Kamps had climbed this route with only four bolts was evidence not just of their technical competence, but even more of a stern antibolt discipline that had its roots in Yosemite climbing at that time; a discipline that, though occasionally violated, would later prevail in American mountaineering.

According to Bob Culp's prodigious memory, we did D-1 in fifteen hours. Sounds about right. At any rate, we reached the refuge before dark.

After two days' rest, we were back on Broadway, this time by way of the 600-foot North Chimney. This approach was shorter, but not without its dangers. We climbed it unroped with packs, and at times I felt we were engaged in a daring enterprise. There were several unpleasant passages, and at the top a steep section of loose rock. Layton swarmed up it, but I was thwarted by a hold out of reach. Kor, seeing my distress, lowered a vast paw that I gratefully clutched and used to reach safe ground. I excused myself with thoughts of a heavy pack and lack of reach, conveniently forgetting how often shorter climbers than I had managed stretches where I deemed a long arm essential. Hoping to avoid a bivouac, we started even earlier than we had on D-1. I remember Kor swarming up the first pitch, pulling off a great block of loose rock that crashed down the North Chimney.

One of the lovely things about an east face in the high mountains is that the morning sun so quickly takes the night chill from the air. For a while, everything seems warm, secure, and safe. Hard to imagine suffering from the cold in such a place. Quite different from Yosemite, where the breezeless morning sun is an enemy. But mountain weather is ever fickle, partly because we are ever foolish, wanting to believe it is being nice just for us, when it is just one of her inconstant moods.

PAT AMENT

Royal Robbins,
Longs Peak, 1963.

By noon the winds were being rude, and clouds swirled overhead.

Now, to lead was a pleasure and to belay a cold hell. Not that either of us fiddled about on the leads. We were competing against each other, yes. After all, each of our lives was given to climbing, and we both wished to excel. In this sense, each of us was an obstacle in the other's path, or so it seemed. In this sense we *were* competing—but our cooperation was far more important. Thus, it is off the mark to say we climbed the Diamond rapidly because we were competing. It is more accurate to say we climbed fast in spite of the running dog of competition that raced with us to the summit.

The east face of Longs loses its benign aspect when the sun disappears westward. The wind brings numbing cold to fingers and cheeks, and snow whirls about. Discomfort is intensified when one is in a hanging belay, becoming impatient even with the speed of Layton Kor.

I quote from a note about the ascent that appeared in the 1964 *American Alpine Journal*: "Racing against the setting sun to avoid a bad night in slings, Kor led the last pitch, a long, strenuous jam-crack. On my last reserves I struggled up this final pitch, topped the Diamond, and shook the hand of a great climber."

It was a long walk down. Mile after mile through the night I paced steadily behind Kor, through the Boulder Field—which seemed an enormous area. Kor showed no signs of weakening, and I forced myself to thrust my legs forward, long strides trying to match his. I wouldn't weaken. I would keep up behind this natural force that wouldn't slow down. Aching feet, legs, back. Mind numbed, but there was the light of the shelter; crowded, sordid, smelly, but warm and welcoming. I well remember Liz, but, oddly, I can't recall booze. Ah, I have grown so sophisticated that I can't imagine a climb like that, with a walk like that, not being followed by wine as well as love.

REG SANER

Reg Saner, Boulder, Colorado, 1995.

Reg Saner, poet and teacher, has climbed, hiked, and skied throughout Colorado's mountains and has explored many other "rough terrains," especially in the western United States. He studied English as a Fulbright Scholar in Florence, Italy. For many years a distinguished professor of English, Shakespeare, and creative writing at the University of Colorado, he has keenly observed the complexities and beauty of the mountains.

Saner's poetry has won numerous awards, including the Walt Whitman Award in 1975, the National Poetry Series in 1981, a National Endowment for the Arts fellowship, the Creede Repertory Theatre Award, the State of Colorado Governor's Award, the Quarterly Review of Literature Forty-Fifth Award, and the 1997 Wallace Stegner Award from the Center for the American West.

He is indeed a climber, and a sample of his work is fitting for this collection. Although not a severe technical climb, the ascent out of the Grand Canyon tells us as much as would any actual climbing piece about sheer rock. This is especially true when the author of such a piece is a superbly imaginative poet. Saner explores not only the idea of climbing but the idea of moving up and out of a lower consciousness to a higher—perhaps a perfect metaphor for all climbing.

Up and Out, the Myth
of Emergence

A passage borrowed from my Reaching Keet Seel: Ruin's Echo
and the Anasazi *is my introduction to this piece:*

> *Places and steps toward answering two*
> *deceptively simple questions: Why do I find*
> *these things so strangely moving? and What are*
> *they trying to tell me?*
>
> REG SANER

If you live long enough, you begin having days when it seems
you may actually be getting some sense. How to act, how to see,
what to care about. What truly matters. Perhaps your slowness
in getting wise is simply what happens to people in a consumer
culture, a car culture, a get-the-money culture. Subtle or rau-
cous voices are always nudging, blatting, or sweet-talking at
you. TV as obedience training.

"Wisdom" is a word it feels wise to hope you're walking toward, but with little chance of actually getting there. Arrival?
That seems reserved for white-clad figures spreading both arms
wide from a balcony; for hundred-year-oldsters, who from the
front porch have seen it all by rocking chair; for gurus available in a six-cassette series from a 1-800 number; and for the
gnomes of Zurich, whose wisdom is ingots softly humming to
themselves in a vault.

Retarded as you may feel about having taken so long to get
a clue, you've plenty of company, ancient and modern. Every
ethnic group preserves one or another story version of much
the same thing.

Pueblos, for example, speak of the Emergence, and for solid,
archaeologically based reasons, it's almost certain the Anasazi
did, too. Variations on myths of emergence, therefore, angle
like spokes of a wagon wheel toward the same hub, whether

71

those myths be local to Acoma, Jemez, Zuni, Zia, Hopi, or other Pueblos. As if in response to questions such as "Where were we when we weren't anywhere?" or "What were we before becoming as we are now?" they tell of a sunless underworld from which pre-human-beings issued. In the version collected by Frank Hamilton Cushing, who a century ago lived at Zuni for nearly five years, these protohumans were long-tailed creatures, muddy and cold, with scaly skins. Their bulging eyes blinked constantly, like owls, and they had webbed fingers and toes. An Acoma legend speaks of soft-bodied creatures imperfectly realized. Yet a different twist is given by the Hopi myth of subhuman "animals that somewhat resembled dogs, coyotes, and bears." Although they were furry-coated, their fingers were webbed and their tails reptilian. Unsurprisingly, behavior of these less-than-humans was as confused as their bodies, including much violence, sexual license, and cannibalism.

All that was far back, in times murky as the world's beginning, and the beginning of us, followed—whether in Zuni, Acoman, or Hopi myth—by ages of wanderings and migrations. But wandering toward what?

Not a "what" but a "where," which is also a more fully evolved body, a manner of traveling more upright than reptilian. Once there, your worries won't be over, but your phase of wrong turns and mistaken directions will be. At any rate, that's the goal. For Zuni, the aim was to locate "the middle," and for Hopis, "the center place," Thus Pueblo myth is itself centered by one long "going toward," the kind that we call Becoming; the long, often disheartening quest for the center. But aren't all our quests variations on the same thing, wandering toward the well-balanced, fully realized self? Clearly it's an awareness of parallel evolutions—bodily and behavioral at once—even if we sometimes feel we've done more aging than emerging.

With the rise of Darwinism, a slogan using three huge words grew current: "Ontogeny recapitulates phylogeny," which meant that your growth from embryo to fetus to infant to child to teen to adult made you a capsule version of our species' entire evolutionary history. You were first a water creature, had a literal tail (the coccyx), and lived in darkness; then graduated into a little animal with an intellect so unenlightened it amounted to a cry and an appetite. You then crawled and gnawed, trying your teeth. Learned a first word, then another, then how to put words together. But hadn't yet learned to control your animal functions, much less good behavior. And so forth. Those Pueblo myths tracing "the people" up from mud, reptilian tails, and webbed toes into lawless conduct, then toward a final issuing forth into sunlight and right ways amount to variants of similar things.

The fact that some tribes of the Southwest place the site of their Emergence at or near the Grand Canyon hasn't caused me to claim I share that experience with them. As a non-Indian my sharing is limited to my share in human nature, but also to the mere happenstance of having emerged, literally, and on a specific afternoon, from the Grand Canyon's display of geological strata with my sense of personal identity forever changed. Except for that coincidence of place, it had nothing to do with Native American myth. Or so I supposed. It's just that to touch with your own hands and booted feet *some* of the depths of the Earth; to ramble for miles along trails half a billion years deep in time; to descend from there even further into time's actual abyss—well, that's like breathing human insignificance into your own lungs, or inhaling the brevity of your own bloodstream and muscle.

If, on descending, you're the kind of Grand Canyon hiker to whom that can happen, you'll never climb out of there alive; that is, the "you" who went down won't be identical to the "you" who emerges. In my own case, nothing before or after, seen or done, ever caused any change like it.

As if I were climbing the ladder up and out from a kiva's dusk into sunlight, which among living Pueblos is a symbolic repetition of the Emergence myth, that ascent from the Colorado River took me from my past as blue-green algae, then trilobite, then crinoid, then reptile, then rat, then ape, then *Homo erectus* . . . till finally I climbed out onto the South Rim of now. It was an Emergence whose stages were written in stone: from the Inner Gorge of Vishnu schist, up past Zoroaster granite onto Tapeats sandstone, over the broad Tonto Plateau and up again, past Bright Angel shale, Muav limestone, Redwall limestone—upward still through the complex Watahomigi formation, the Manakacha, the Wescogame, then rising through Esplanade sandstone, Hermit shale, Coconino sandstone, the Toroweap formation—with the final few, yet strenuous, hundreds of feet up through and out onto Kaibab limestone.

It altered my view of almost everything. It altered the way I now look into another person's eyes.

My knowledge of astronomy: why hadn't that wrought the same effect? Cosmic immensities, and all. It hadn't, and for the simplest of bodily reasons. Virtually everything we know about planets, asteroids, galaxies, and the like comes to us via printer's inks on paper, or colored pixels on a TV screen. Such knowledge differs greatly from what's gained while paying for it with rivulets of your own personal sweat, one downward, jolting step at a time, grunting slightly with each footfall. Does that sound anti-intellectual? Even at Oxford and Harvard, biology and geology students, to cite but a couple of disciplines, are told by their lecturers, "Well, now it's time for a field trip." The field idea was itself a boldly intellectual reinvention: for real understanding you have to get your nose out of books and go see for yourself.

So myths of emergence describe something like fieldwork: a whole people's "hands on," trial-and-error discovering of their place, which is also a lifeway.

As for book knowledge, it's true that before and after my personal Grand Canyon "Emergence" I had delved into technical studies of rock, sand, and Europe's early attempts at dating

Earth's age. Naturally, what I learned went into what I saw, because seeing is done by the mind's eye. Bodily eyes are really the mind leaning forward. So even if the earliest humans had emerged from or near the Grand Canyon, it couldn't possibly have been the same rim of Kaibab limestone I climbed out of and onto. Their seeing would have been a world different, on all but a single aspect perhaps.

That aspect, grandiose as it may sound, might have been the mystery of human existence. From childhood I have wanted answers to a few unanswerable questions, have groped toward them without ever giving my wandering, or "migration," any such high-sounding name as "quest." It's just that, without realizing what I was up to, I had simply never stopped asking myself, "What am I? Where is this? Why?" Surely those are everybody's questions, even if few people are naive enough to keep after them.

Hopi myth includes frequent admonition by spirit beings who scold "the people" for backsliding into low, lawless impulses and forgetting the meaning of life. Such forgetfulness surely parallels the "wanderings" of Hopi tradition and the "migrations" so pervasive in Zuni legends, whereas "the center place" or "the middle" is as much how we live as a physical place. Call it a state of mind: the truest possible sense of who, what, and why we are. But whether any of the Anasazi priests or shamans, any of the Pueblo or Navajo or Ute holy men, ever got more than glimpses of such a mental landscape isn't for us non-Indians to judge.

Now comes the twist that makes endless questing for knowledge problematic. We assume that knowing what, where, and why we are is a good thing. Is it? When ignorance is bliss, the proverb reminds us, "'tis folly to be wise." Despite such sayings, don't we claim to follow "truth" wherever it leads? Or is that only a flattering mirage? In medieval Europe and earlier, certain kinds of questioning were forbidden by authorities we now call benighted, repressive, tyrannical—which they were.

That much we devoutly believe. Still, maybe the ignorance they promoted was to some extent "bliss."

Take genetic transmission of fatal diseases. If we had paid a microbiologist to mail us a profile accurately predicting, on the basis of genetic inheritance, our cancer chances or our chances of cardiac arrest, how many of us would at once rip open the envelope? While genetic markers are far from being specific enough to foretell anybody's death date, we might nonetheless agree there is knowledge it may be healthier not to have.

So just how fully into awareness dare we emerge? And at what cost?

In hundreds of versions the world over, one or another mythic or semihistorical figure looks upon a humongously powerful deity and is thereby destroyed by what he or she sees. Such tales imply that there's an ultimate level of awareness so awesome and terrible you can't stand it, a blaze of revelation turning to ash the mortal who beholds it unprotected. But what any myth or legend "says" can be variously interpreted. Influenced by my own "Emergence" from the Grand Canyon, my personal take on those death-by-divine-annihilation parables is this: There are indeed such awarenesses (calling them "truths" risks blurring into religion), ones which your old self cannot survive. If ever such light dawns on that self, it either looks quickly aside and forgets what it saw or is zapped out of existence.

In the English nineteenth century, there were people who, on reading Darwin's *Origin of Species*, went into convulsions of despair, claiming that Darwin had "destroyed" their lives. If zapped, therefore, your soul's future depends on whatever was holding you up and together in the first place. Was it something you leaned on? False values? False gods? Even if what held you together was something like backbone supported by your own two feet, nobody who gets zapped by a world-altering revelation escapes being staggered. You could lurch into permanent loss of balance, cynicism being the worst imbalance of all. Alive, yet dead.

But why should cynicism have the final say? Without stirring a foot from wherever you happened to be standing, your zapped self may "emerge" into a world more strange for being more truly known, more mysterious—and therefore more daunting, even terrible—than the best-spoken among us will ever put into words.

What can't be spoken, of course, only a certain quality of stillness can express. That sort of stillness could be found in lots of places on the planet, our high Southwest among others; but before it can be found anywhere else, it must first be found in ourselves. Only then, for example, would it be discoverable in the Southwest's cinematic fantasies of painted rock and invisible air. In the butte-haggard loveliness of its desolations, naked horizons. In its desert wisdom. Which at certain moments seem to whisper, "You wanted to know? Well, now you do."

JOE SIMPSON

Joe Simpson

Joe Simpson travels the world, climbing the big mountains, exploring cultures, relating to the ghostly and the mystical and to mysteries of each culture's people. He writes almost frenetically, it seems, as when he produced his classic and best-selling *Touching the Void* (1988), which won both the Boardman Tasker Award and the NCR Award (sponsored by National Cash Registers)—Britain's most prestigious nonfiction prize—and has been published in fourteen languages. He claims that he never read that book—only wrote it!

In the following piece, Simpson speaks about how the idealized world of climbing can intersect with the real world of human suffering, with uncomfortable results.

Guilty as Charged

By the time my next book is published I will have written over half a million words! How do you choose a few thousand!? The following is an amalgamated chapter, adding a little from the chapter that precedes it ("When Terror Came") for context. The subject is important to me.

JOE SIMPSON

[Simpson had been informed of a crude gravesite of stones "further down along the trail," where people recently had placed a woman, apparently Tibetan, who had died crossing a pass along the Tibetan border.—Ed.]

The bleak emptiness of the stony valley where she had died unsettled me. I hoped that she had died in the company of others, even the arms of strangers, rather than facing that ultimate loneliness by herself. The barren mound of rocks she had become was something to warn passing travelers and quicken their steps; a grim, lonely site, unmarked, almost indistinguishable from the surrounding rubble. I turned my back to the valley and strode toward the sunbathed mountains astride the Tibetan border.

I wondered whether she had been with a group or if passing traders had stumbled across her body as it was released from the melting winter snows. Perhaps she had been separated from her party in a storm, slowed down by her weakness until at last she succumbed to the insidious grip of winter's frost. Maybe she simply got lost in a blizzard and passed the group of shelters, never knowing how close she was to protection from the storm.

Who was to say that it was a storm or altitude sickness that had killed her? Her frailty may have already been created long before she attempted to cross the pass. She could have been a nun escaping imprisonment and torture, half-starved, staggering down from the mountain, abandoning her beloved homeland

and carrying away with her the scars of rifle butts and electric batons, broken bones and battered organs. I remembered Ama Adhe's story that gave me disturbed nights for weeks after I had read it in David Part's harrowing book *A Strange Liberation*. The mountain was rocky and snowcapped, reaching high into the thin, cold blue sky. She [Ama] said it was called Nyate Khalori. It was surrounded by lakes and thick forests teeming with wildlife. There were meadows carpeted in wildflowers, so many you couldn't name them, so numerous that they collected in your toes as you walked.

Nomadic people tended their herds of goats and sheep and cattle on the passes and the plains. In the winter her family tended their crops in the lowlands, and in the summer they drove their livestock up to the highland regions where they joined the nomads and their herds of yaks. People went up into the highlands and pitched their tents, and there was music and dancing, horse races and chang drinking, sharpshooting competitions, games and picnics.

In the early mornings all the cattle would be sent up into the hills. The yak and dri, the dzo and dzomo spent the day grazing while the people boiled the dri milk, churned the butter, and made yogurt. After that the day was free for games and fun and times of inner peace for everyone. There was respect for each other and freedom for all to do as they wished. Monks were living among them, performing *pujas* in their tents, and there were many temples and monasteries and hermitages. Life was very good. This was how Ama remembered it.

There was little violence in her world. Killing and brutality were considered dirty. The Buddhist doctrines of Karma and rebirth were an inextricable part of life, giving it meaning, and everyone had a sense of right and wrong. Present and future lives were dictated by one's behavior. Generosity, kindness, and patience in life would be rewarded with health, happiness, and security, while evil, stealing, and cheating would bring poverty and unhappiness. It was not a perfect world, but to Ama it was idyllic, full of happiness and peace. That was her memory of four decades ago. Today that idyll has gone forever.

When the Chinese soldiers came to Ama Adhe's tent she knew that they had come for her. Her role in helping the resistance to the Chinese had been discovered. It was very early in the morning. Her infant daughter was gurgling peacefully in her sleep. She was dressing her four-year-old son, putting on his yellow *chuba*. She heard the dogs barking, and looking up she saw the group of armed policemen and civilian officers walking toward the tent.

While they tied her with ropes her daughter remained sleeping, but her son became hysterical and clung to her when she was dragged outside. She pleaded for mercy, begging to be left with her children. A man hit her hard in the ear, permanently damaging her hearing, and the others began hitting her with rifle butts and kicking her, and her son became even more distraught. As the men hauled Ama away, the boy ran after her, screaming incoherently, and she saw her infant daughter laughing happily as if it were all a game. The little boy fought desperately to cling to his mother, but the men were too big and strong, kicking him hard and high into the air. He got up and came for her, and they kept hitting him and kicking him until he could no longer keep up. She glimpsed her son in the far distance as she was marched to the nearby Dri Tse Monastery, which had been converted into a prison—a tiny, hysterical figure in a yellow *chuba*, running and running and crying for his mother. She never saw him again.

Ama spent the next twenty years in nine Chinese prisons and camps. Tortured, starved, and worked nearly to death, she survived. Most of her fellow Tibetan prisoners did not. Two years after her arrest in the autumn of 1960, at about the time of my birth, she was transferred to a lead mine at a place called Gothang Gyalpo on the border between Tibet and China. Most of the women she had been with in Dartsedo Prison had died of starvation. She joined a hundred other women in the lead mine. Over the next three years all but four of the women died. In that short time Ama learned that 12,109 prisoners were starved to death in that hellish camp.

Throughout her suffering she clung to the hope that her children had been looked after and were still alive. After sixteen years she learned from her brother, Nyima, that her son was dead. Hysterical with shock and grief, the toddler had been inconsolable, refusing comfort and food from friends and neighbors, biting their hands to get away from their care, until he escaped and ran away, a tiny yellow figure lost in a sadness he could never have imagined. They found his body in the river where he had fallen and drowned.

She came back to a destroyed, denuded, unrecognizable homeland. Almost all the monasteries had been sacked and destroyed. Only nine out of fifteen hundred survived. Hardly any people remained. Her mother had starved to death, her husband had been killed, probably by poison. Her brother-in-law, who had been imprisoned with her, had been executed, his brains blown out as he stood in front of her. Ama also lost her "elder" mother, brothers and sisters, and three close relatives to the Chinese. Only her infant daughter had survived.

Nothing whatever remained of her former life. There was no place in which to practice her religion. The monks, lamas, and nuns and the entire educated class of their community had been exterminated. What remained was fear and deprivation and a police state.

Ama Adhe's story is exceptional only in that she survived the holocaust visited on her land and the Tibetan people by the Chinese. Holocaust is exactly what it was. There is no other word for the systematic destruction of a people and its culture. The Chinese claimed that they came into Tibet to liberate the serfs from their feudal slavery. In attempting to transform Tibet into Mao Tse-tung's insane ideological notion of a workers' paradise, they virtually annihilated it. His dictum had been: "Destroy first and construction will look after itself."

In the first thirty years of Chinese occupation one-fifth of the population—1.2 million Tibetans—were killed by either execution, slow torture, or starvation. More than six thousand monasteries, convents, and temples were destroyed and their precious statues and contents melted down or sold for foreign currency. Sixty percent of Tibet's literary and cultural heritage was burned. The region of Amdo has become the world's biggest gulag, believed to be capable of holding 10 million prisoners. One in every ten Tibetans was imprisoned, 100,000 in labor camps. Tibet was now China's largest intercontinental ballistic missile base.

■ ■ ■

I could not get the young boy, who had looked at me with such old and appraising eyes in the lodge at Ari, out of my mind. *Where was his mother? Was she dead too? Could that have been her heaped under the cold hard stones? Had she been with him? Is that why his eyes were so old?* The questions kept returning, and there were no answers, only a sense of discomfort.

Eventually the slow, hard grind up the lateral moraines leading to base camp pushed the thoughts to the back of my mind. The camp was situated on a bleak, desolate plateau of broken boulders. Snow lay in small drifts between the rocks. Looking back, I saw a horizon ringed with spectacular ice mountains which seemed to rear up abruptly from the barren wastes of rock rubble. The low afternoon sun cast a soft golden glow across the summit ridges of two pyramid-shaped mountains. In the foreground, almost lost amid the endless gray boulder fields, I could just make out the squat dark shapes of the Austrian tents which belonged to the only other team on the Nepalese side of the mountain.

We camped in the lee of a vast rock wall sheathed in ice that gleamed a hard blue light down on us. The sun faded behind the jagged ridges, setting them momentarily alight with dancing flames.

The temperature dropped rapidly as we cleared spaces among the boulders in which to pitch our tents. A knifing icy wind scythed across the plateau. I found the remains of an old yak shelter, a three-sided wall some six feet high with flat slabs of rock paving the floor. My tent fitted neatly inside, giving me shelter from the wind and peace from the eternal flapping and shaking of nylon.

I lay in the doorway watching flurries of snow swirling across the ice cliffs at the foot of the mountain which loomed above us. I traced a possible route up its right flank, a great sweep of wind-hardened ice capped with a serac band. The seracs hung out over the ice field ready to plunge down at any moment. I studied them warily. If a sizable section of those blocks of ice collapsed it would obliterate our campsite in seconds. There was nowhere to run, no place to hide.

"It's not bad, is it?" Mal said as he appeared framed between the stone walls of the doorway.

"Do you think they're safe?" I asked, and he followed my gaze.

"Oh, aye," he said after a moment's pause. "They look pretty stable to me. Nothing to worry about there."

"Let's hope not," I said fervently. "Listen, which one's Cho Oyo?"

"Up there." Mal pointed toward a sea of rubble-strewn glacier. "You can't actually see it from here. It's round the corner to the right, but that's the Nangpa La, there. That notch between those two peaks."

"What do you suppose they're up to?" I nodded in the direction of the distant cluster of tents.

"That's the Austrian-Brazilian Cho Oyo Expedition," Mal replied. "Three blokes and a lass. A model, I think, or was she a stewardess?"

"Really?" I said brightly.

"She's getting married to one of them in Kathmandu after the trip," Mal said, laughing at my sudden interest.

"They've already made one attempt," he went on. "Reached 8,000 meters, but they were forced back by wind. Said they'd have one last go. They look pretty wasted to me."

"Are they doing the same route as us?"

"Yeah. Apparently it's the fortieth anniversary of Herbert Tichy's first ascent by the route we're trying," Mal said. "He was Austrian. Do you want some coffee?"

I took the small steaming mug of fresh percolated coffee. "Brilliant. I didn't know we had such luxury with us."

"We don't," Mal said with a grin. "Just Rick and I have got it. Secret stash, so keep the noise down."

I sipped the strong black liquid and looked up the valley. Beyond a sea of moraines the glacier spilled down from a high bowl hemmed in by mountains. On the right there was an obvious corridor of smooth, uncrevassed snow leading up to where a small ice cap was just visible. To the left of this corridor, through the jumbled icefall, I could see a chaotic mass of tottering cliffs and crevasses with blue fins of ice poking through the gray moraines at its foot.

"It looks like quite a slog to get up there," I said. "We could easily get lost in that lot."

"Should be fun," Mal said with gusto. "There must be a well-marked trail through it. The Tibetans come across all the time."

"How far do you think it is to the Nangpa La then?"

"We'll put an intermediate camp on it because Chwang reckons it'll take six to eight hours, and then Camp 1 is way round the corner, another three hours more."

"Eight hours of staggering up scree—my legs will love that," I moaned.

"Don't worry about it. You'll soon get used to it. How are you feeling?"

"Oh, pretty good, but I haven't managed to shake off that cold. I've been coughing a lot today. Still, I don't think it's a chest infection."

"Ah well, we're taking it easy for a couple of days, so it should give you a chance to recover. By the way, Chwang says he's got some monk to perform the *puja* tomorrow. He's a cousin of one of the Sherpas. It should be a good one."

"Why? Will it be more than the usual rice throwing and offerings?"

"Yeah. There's a serious amount of prayers and blessings, and endless mantras. It'll be the full works if the monk does it, and that's good for the lads. Good omens."

"Do you believe that?" I asked in surprise. "I didn't think you went for all this spiritual stuff."

"I'll take every bit of help I can get, and actually, yes, I think it does help. It has a bonding effect on us as well as the Sherpas. I can tell you that when they have bad *pujas*, it's no joke."

"What do you mean by bad?"

"Oh, if the prayer flags catch fire or the pole falls down. I don't know what they do exactly, but there's a lot of driving away of demons and evil spirits, and calling on the sacred mountain gods for protection and help. It really freaks the Sherpas out when it goes badly. Me too," Mal added ruefully.

"Didn't that happen to that West Ridge of Everest trip a while back?"

"What? The pole falling down? Aye, and I think the flags caught fire as well." He laughed at the thought. "There was some heavy trouble after that. The Sherpas wouldn't go on the hill until they got a new pole and had another *puja*."

"Do you blame them?"

"It's all very well—where do you find a damn great pole in the middle of nowhere? It must have taken days to send someone down to fetch one. I just hope our *puja* goes smoothly. I know it sounds superstitious, but I've been to so many now that I would feel uncomfortable without one. I can do without demons on the hill."

"I know what you mean. It gets inside you after a while, doesn't it? All the prayer flags, and ceremonies. It's impossible to ignore it. It becomes part of our lives when we're here, like we've been dyed by it."

"Aye, it's a sight more real than all that lip-service religion we have at home. Here they live it all the time."

The wind tugged at the long stream of prayer flags that Jetta was struggling to fasten to a pile of heavy rocks. They arched out in a brightly fluttering curve, flying at a man's height above the ground. The altar to which they had been attached was only partly built. Chwang and Gompu were attending to the final details. They planted the central pole in the flat stone top of the altar and wedged it in place. Jetta seemed to be doing his best to pull it down. As he battled with loops of loose string and fluttering colored cotton, Gompu strung another ninety-foot length of flags away into the distance, fixing it firmly to a raised spike of rock. He jammed heavy slabs on top of the taut string to keep the flags in place. Jetta could now stretch his line in the opposite direction so that opposing forces held the pole upright. Two more strings of flags were attached and drawn off to distant moorings.

The pole had a sprig of juniper tied to its top, and a white ceremonial scarf *(khata)* streamed out beneath it. A rush mat had been laid on the ground in front of the altar facing a small hole built into the front of the waist-high plinth of layered stones. By its side lay a supply of fragrant juniper branches for burning on the altar. This practice of burning incense *(sang)* is a pre-Buddhist ritual. A circular woven straw platter laden with offerings had been placed in front of the rush mat. After the *puja*, juniper would be burned when climbers were on the mountain as a prayer for good weather and fortune. The flags flapping in the wind would send their prayers to all corners of the world. Offerings usually include five types of grain, butter lamps, and chang, but they are not restricted to these items, and I have seen anything from Mars bars to half bottles of Polish vodka on offer. Rice is thrown and water sprinkled in all directions. Water plays a purification role in the Buddhist religion. Unlike the Hindus, who indulge in ritual bathing in what are regarded as sacred waters, Tibetan Buddhists have abstracted the ritual to such an extent that they simply dab some on their heads and sprinkle droplets in all directions. There is an old Tibetan saying: "Hindus clean outside, Tibetans clean inside."

The *puja* ceremony was explained to me as an act of giving on the road toward fulfillment, knowledge, enlightenment, and peace, a benefit to mankind. It is also intended to cleanse sins accumulated in the past and expand the devotee's spiritual consciousness. On a personal level, this offers the chance of a better rebirth, an opportunity to escape the privations of the present life and exchange it for a better future. The casual pilgrim may briefly copy the actions of the dedicated *sannyasi* (one who has formally renounced all earthly ties and taken the vows of abandonment) and by so doing receive a taste of true insight.

The aim of the serious pilgrim, I was told, is to achieve spiritual merit. By enduring a series of mental and physical trials a state of awareness is reached which enables the pilgrim to follow in the footsteps of the great masters to where all existence is unified in a state of pure love. Admission to the state of Sukhavati is forever; it can never be left, for it is impossible to discover the return route.

The goal, it seems, is entry to the Buddhist "paradise" where one is finally liberated from the repeating cycle of rebirth and suffering. There are various ideals of paradise, and according to Tibetan scripts, several paradisiacal sites have been identified in Tibet as "opened" by former masters. These opened sites, or hidden valleys called *beyuls*, are believed by the Buddhists to be special places where followers can take refuge when disaster threatens the survival of mankind. They include Khembalung in Nepal, the Pemako valley in southeast Tibet, Lapchi and Rongshar on the Nepal–Tibet border, and Dremojong and Chorten Nyima on the Tibet–Sikkim border.

Perhaps the most famous *beyul* is Sukhavati, the fabulous "western paradise" of the Buddha Amitabha which Victor Chan described in his comprehensive pilgrimage guide, *Tibet Handbook*: "This fabulous retreat is full of wish-fulfilling trees, where no wish is denied. There is no suffering or sorrow; the finest silk, food, and precious stones are there for the taking. Caves have springs where milk flows perpetually, lakes bestow clarity of mind, and certain caves promote full enlightenment. While here the *budhicitta* (Buddha mind) of a pilgrim increases and ignorance is wiped out."

It is hard to comprehend the terrible suffering endured by the Tibetan people at the hands of the Chinese and how they managed to reconcile such a dreadful nightmare with the teachings of their religion. Perhaps the holiest and most devout are able to be philosophic about their fate. How many of the lamas and abbots and monks who were humiliated, tortured, and slaughtered managed to take comfort in their faith at that final defining moment of their existence? Was the unspeakable violence inflicted on them just another manifestation of the cycle of rebirth and suffering? Or was it so depraved, so abjectly inhuman, that it became impossible for them to believe that this was the life accorded to them for the sins of their past? How many of those select few, I wonder, reached the embracing sanctuary of those elusive paradisiacal *beyuls*? To the majority of the people, all those except the holiest, most precious lamas and the dedicated *sannyasi* pilgrims and *yogins*, that holocaust must have been inexplicable.

To be allowed to enter an opened *beyul* the pilgrim must have not only absolute faith in its existence but also much accumulated merit, abandoning all worldly goods and desires. Only the most devout and practiced *yogins* can enter such a place. Even then the disciple wishing to enter a *beyul* must learn the way and know the exact timing needed for entry. This knowledge is usually passed down orally by a teacher *(guru)*. A lifetime of meditations and spiritual transformation is needed to get past the many psychological obstacles set in the path.

I watched as the monk sat cross-legged on the mat before the altar, chanting a continuous stream of prayers as he performed the *puja*. Another man sat beside him, turning the yellowed pages of holy script that lay in the monk's lap. The long, narrow pages flapped in the cold wind which threatened to rip them from the silk-bound book. The monk's voice rose and fell on the wind as the prayers resonated in what sounded to me rather like the rhythms of Gregorian chant. I knew that they were distinct prayers, not to be mistaken for the ubiquitous mantras. The mantras are repeated by pilgrims as a way to reach a meditative state on their journey. They are believed to have magical qualities and supernatural effects, such as curing sickness or misfortune, or blessing a barren woman with children.

What stage of enlightenment, I wondered, had the young monk achieved? I wasn't even sure that monks followed the same path. It seemed sacrilegious to think he might just be doing his job. He certainly didn't look very impressive. He was a small man with a shaven head, dressed in simple clothes. There was nothing about his appearance to suggest great spirituality and deep inner calm.

We stood in respectful silence in a semicircle behind the chanting monk. His head nodded with the murmured rhythms of his prayers. Every now and then Gompu would step forward and take an offering from the platter and place it reverentially upon the altar. The cold wind made the juniper flare up in bursts of sparks, and the smoke streamed horizontally away from the altar. More twigs would be fed into the flames. Occasionally the sweet-scented smoke blew into my face, reminding me of past *pujas* I had witnessed, the beginnings of so many other adventures. I remembered with a pang of regret that the only time I had climbed in Nepal without a *puja* I had suffered severe injuries in a terrifying fall. I looked intently at the monk's bowed head and hoped he was having a good one.

When at last he had finished chanting the prayers and we were shivering in the icy wind that swept across the rocky plateau, rice was handed to each of us and we were encouraged to scatter handfuls in all directions. There were broad smiles all round as the gifts on the platter were handed out and bottles of fiery spirits were opened to toast our safety and success. I looked up at the flanks of the mountain above our camp with its forbidding black cliffs and the gleam of hard blue ice surging down from the summit headwall and wondered if anyone or anything had heard us. I hoped so.

A year before Reinhold Messner climbed Everest alone in 1980, Tibet was just beginning to feel the influence of a new Chinese policy of liberalization instigated by Hu Yao-bang, Deng Xiao-ping's successor. Horrified by what he had seen on a fact-finding visit, he sacked local party leaders and introduced a six-point plan designed to improve the economic and social conditions of the Tibetans. Most of the Chinese cadres were to leave Tibet within three years and be replaced by Tibetans. Private enterprise would be encouraged, taxes abolished for two years, and efforts made to develop Tibetan culture, education, and science.

For the first time in twenty years people could move up to ten miles outside their villages without a permit. People were allowed to wear their traditional clothes, the *chuba*, learn the Tibetan language in schools, and sing Tibetan songs. The hated daily political meetings became weekly. Monasteries and nunneries were reopened, some partially rebuilt. Some holy statues and relics were restored to Tibet from China. There was even talk of the Dalai Lama returning. It all sounded too good to be true—and it was.

For the first time China encouraged foreign tourists to visit Tibet in large numbers. These visitors saw, despite supervision by the Chinese, the destruction of Tibetan culture and the ruins that littered the land. The truth was all too obvious. By 1983 the Tibetans had given up believing that anything would really change. Independence groups roused themselves to action, and the authorities responded to even a show of passive resistance with enthusiastic violence. Hundreds were arrested, beaten, and tortured. Public executions increased in number, and the Chinese rediscovered their old practice of cutting prisoners' vocal cords to prevent them from crying "Free Tibet."

Tibet was flooded with Han Chinese. This method of overcoming opposition in minority ethnic regions was one that China had tried successfully in Manchuria and Inner Mongolia. Induced by offers of high wages, interest-free loans, guaranteed housing, and paid home leave, the Han came in their tens of thousands. In some areas, such as Amdo, they already outnumbered the Tibetans three to one. The Tibetan people were becoming strangers in their own land.

Despite the vast amount of land space per person, harsh birth control measures had been imposed on Tibet in the 1970s. And although they were only loosely applied at first, now strict control was introduced and enforcement teams were established throughout the country. Many forced abortions took place as late as three, four, and even five months into the pregnancy. Refugees gave harrowing accounts of fetuses being aborted at a very late stage in pregnancy, and some witnessed the slaughter of tiny babies born to mothers of two-child families. Lethal injections and drowning were often used to dispose of babies on delivery. The killing of unborn children is all the more horrifyingly traumatic for a Tibetan Buddhist, who believes the taking of any life is a terrible sin.

Seven years after I had attended Messner's lecture about his solo Everest climb, violence once again erupted in Tibet. Riots broke out in Lhasa. A new generation of Tibetans, born after the horrors of the Cultural Revolution, had never known a Tibet without the Chinese presence, yet they fervently wanted independence and freedom. The old communist orders of Eastern Europe were beginning to crumble; it was time for a change, time to demand freedom. Intensive reeducation classes all over Tibet could not erase the growing sense of unity among the people. They wanted the return of the Dalai Lama and an end to the Chinese occupation.

On 24 April 1988, five young nuns were arrested for shouting "Free Tibet" and calling for the release of political prisoners as they circled the Jokhang temple in Lhasa. For this heinous crime they suffered unimaginable humiliation. As Mary Craig recounted in her book *Tears of Blood*, one of the nuns, twenty-three-year-old Gyaltsen Chodon, described how they were beaten, stripped, and chained to a wall, how electric cattle prods were applied all over their bodies by several men at a time pressing them into their eyes, their mouths, and their vaginas. Killer dogs were set upon them, and heavy iron rods were dropped onto their spines as they lay face down on the ground. Their hands were stamped and crushed, urine and excrement were poured over them, and even their food was dipped in this filth. They were strung up by their thumbs, made to stand for twelve hours at a time in freezing ankle-deep water in the middle of winter, and as a matter of routine kicked and beaten with sticks while they were interrogated.

This happened, and I knew about it, and still I wanted to climb in Tibet.

After March 1990, after the Tiananmen Square massacre in the Chinese capital itself, there was a sense that, perhaps for the first time in forty years, they might no longer be alone. The international community was starting to take notice. China's ludicrously extravagant attempt to celebrate the fortieth anniversary of Tibet's liberation was boycotted by Britain, the United States, and several European countries. Few went to China's party. For the first time governments, including those of Britain and the United States, talked openly of Tibetan independence. In April 1991 President Bush declared his support of Tibet's freedom, and then strangely went on to renew China's most favored nation status, in the hope that trade would be a powerful enough incentive for the Chinese to improve their human rights record. The United States Senate accepted that the true leaders of Tibet were the Dalai Lama and the Tibetan government in exile in India. It was a major shift in attitude—yet the regime of Chinese terror goes on apace.

The Tibetan people are still dying, and their land and culture are dying with them. There have been many conflicts in the world throughout this century that were conducted with all the savagery that man's ingenuity could devise. The Holocaust that Nazi Germany inflicted upon the Jews, Stalin's maniacal slaughter of so many millions of his own people, Pol Pot and the Khmer Rouge's excesses in Cambodia—these three horrors stand out clearly above the miasma of other crimes against humanity. They are widely known about. The tragedy of Tibet should be added to this catalog of depravity. It is Mao Tsetung's enduring legacy, the fruit of his tyrannical rule. His Great Leap Forward, his Cultural Revolution, his megalomania, evidence of his insane lust for power, were imposed upon his own people with appalling consequences, but what was meted out in Tibet is both China's enduring shame and our own. For we in the West simply turned a blind eye and allowed it to happen.

I knew a little of Tibet's history, and for my own convenience I chose to ignore it, or at best I made excuses for myself. I wanted to play expensive, dangerous games on big mountains. It was about adventure and excitement, vicarious thrills, toying with the idea of being an explorer. There are no explorers any more. Most of us on mountaineering trips are simply credit card adventurers.

JOHN LONG

John Long

John Long was a young, untamed lad in Yosemite in the early 1970s, under the inspiration of an even more untamed rock climbing talent—Jim Bridwell. Here Long writes about those early years. He soon progressed and became one of America's most powerful climbers. His instructional books have made him a best-seller in the outdoor industry. His recent book *Advanced Rock Climbing* won the 1999 Banff Mountain Book Festival Award for best mountain exposition. His literary short stories have been widely anthologized and translated into many languages.

Long's legendary achievements include the first one-day ascent of the 3,000-foot face of El Capitan, with Jim Bridwell and Billy Westbay, and the first free team ascent of the east face of Yosemite's Washington Column (Astroman), with Ron Kauk and John Bachar. Other adventures include an expedition from Baffin Island to the North Pole; the first coast-to-coast traverse of Borneo; discovery and exploration of the world's largest river cave in the Gulf Province, Papua New Guinea; the first descent of Angel Falls, Venezuela; and the first land crossing of Irian Jaya, considered the most primitive region on earth. Long attended LaVerne University as an undergraduate, then studied philosophy at Claremont Theological Seminary and clinical psychology at Antioch University.

The piece below speaks of a wild time in a wild place, in and around Camp 4, the vagabond climbers' campground of Yosemite, with young souls looking to climb and sort out their lives.

The Bird's Boys

Some folks have roasted me for writing this piece, and one (in a scathing personal letter) referred to it as an "insolent celebration of shameless conduct." On the one hand, it's hard to argue that point. Just the same, doesn't shameless youth appeal because it's raw and without guile, and doesn't it endure, however briefly, because it accepts no order but its own? For me, this incident highlights the folly and rascality inherent in everything we humans do. In the heart of the "just and devout" is a bumbling charlatan, and it is this charlatan that holds out the chance for joy. Just maybe this whole business of life is neither dire nor reckless nor (fill in the blank). It's just life. Ultimately, the evangelist and the climbing bum belong together, or at any rate, they are drawn together by unseen hands. Side by side, they confound and enrich each other and form a wondrous whole.

JOHN LONG

I first went to Yosemite Valley when I was seventeen years old and continued to spend every summer there till I was twenty-five. The first thing I remember of the place was the Camp 4 parking lot, an oily acre crammed with the proudest medley of heaps and rust buckets imaginable. Among the really prime rigs were an ancient British step-van that must have been parked on the street during the blitzkrieg; an old dented, salt-pocked Cadillac, now a convertible thanks to a cutting torch; and a VW van, broadsided, rear-ended, and rolled, not a window in it, Vise-Grips where the steering wheel should have been. Few of these ran without priming and a push start, if then. There wasn't a treaded tire in the whole lot, and a live battery got passed back and forth like a gold brick. The license plates were from Canada, Colorado, Wyoming, New York, most of these junkers having been babied down the road with little chance of reaching Yosemite and no chance of ever leaving it.

Beyond the parking lot lay dozens of colorful tents, scattered like a fistful of jelly beans over several acres of shady forest. In

97

the summertime, between two cinder-block bathrooms at both ends of camp, many of the world's greatest climbers called this place home. Back then, "official" campsites were marked with a tin stake or a number stenciled on a splintered picnic table, but there was never anybody to enforce this, or anything else. Other legitimate campgrounds, full of scrubbed tourists and RVs and screaming brats, featured kiosks full of rangers, who were full of silly rules, but during the first three summers I spent in Camp 4, I never saw a ranger. The Park Service had essentially roped the place off. Only climbers stayed there. With no rangers and no rules, we were in hog heaven. In the almost complete absence of any women to sow some shame and keep discipline, the whole place was, in fact, an international ghetto.

Jim Bridwell—"the Bird," as we later styled him—was de facto lord of Camp 4 and everyone in it. He had a vulpine smile and a gymnast's frame and was the biggest name in American climbing. In a manner, a rope ran from Jim back to the beginnings of the sport—for he'd climbed with Kor, who had climbed with Robbins, who had climbed with Wilts, who had climbed with Mendenhall, who had climbed with Clyde, and for all I knew, the only thing separating me from Edward Whymper and the first ascent of the Matterhorn was the chance to rope up with the Bird. And that was no problem because the Bird needed climbing partners, which left him to pull a couple of us up to his level—no easy trick, since Jim Bridwell was probably the finest all-around rock climber on the planet.

His method was unadorned: he'd snag the most promising kids in camp, climb them till they couldn't climb anymore, then tie them back in and climb them some more. He wanted to find our maximum effort, how much we could take. And he got it all. He never eased us into anything, and he never worried about teaching us more than we could learn. In this manner he was able to sift the sands of daydreams until he produced the solid stuff—the best climbers and the greatest ascents of the era.

Within a week after I'd first stumbled into Camp 4 (school was now out across the country), every campsite was packed. Of the hundreds of climbers, about six or seven others, of roughly my age and ability, had gone through a trial by fire with the Bird, and we sort of fell in together. Aside from my southern California partners, Rick Accomazzo and Richard Harrison, there was Mark Chapman, with his poet's soul, simian strength, and a voice like Frank Sinatra, and Eric Shoen (aka Mellow Brutus), who was strong enough to rip your head off at the waist but never would, since he got weepy over stray dogs and kids on crutches. And, of course, Rick Reider, a flame redhead with a cowlick his barber didn't understand. He had the talent to change climbing forever, but his career was cut short the following year when a rockfall on El Cap fractured his skull. God only knows what Rick would have accomplished had he lasted a couple more summers. And then there was Dale Bard—one part anorectic brat, two parts dynamite, three parts climbing fanatic. Despite a strict diet of wild honey, hot chocolate, and Snickers bars, Dale was so lean and whey-faced you wanted to ask about his embalmer. Over the next ten years, Dale would climb El Capitan more than forty times. (Dale once told me, "There's more to life than climbing, you know." "Yeah, like what?" I asked. "I don't know," he said, "so it can't be much.") Later came Kevin Worrall, Ed Berry, Billy Westbay, and others. We were all the Bird's boys.

For that first month, most of us slept on the ground. The Bird, however, had a tent—a sprawling green-canvas affair, the kind Ike used to tenant in the European theater. When the Bird was handling some personal business inside, he'd hang a cardboard sign on the zippered door: KEEP OUT. This went for tourists, fellow climbers, park rangers, the president of the United States, and Jehovah. By morning the sign usually was gone, and in the faint musk of perfume and tawny port, a little group of us would hunker down inside and discuss various climbs, getting the Bird's feedback as to routes particularly germane to our curriculum. We broached other topics besides climbing, though the Bird did most of the talking because he was just enough older than we that he seemed to know everything.

Much has been written about the climbs of that era, and the Bird (and whoever of his boys happened to be holding his rope) has been properly lionized for his pioneering ascents up the dreadful faces of El Capitan, Mount Watkins, Half Dome, Washington Column, and Sentinel. Though exciting in a fashion, most granite chronicles are your standard "slugging up the impossible cliffside" fare. But "standard" did not apply to the other things about life as one of the Bird's boys.

Love

Day-to-day living in Camp 4 was coarse business. Over time, our typical lodging became a four-man expedition tent, often "on loan" or bought secondhand from another climber who had either borrowed it himself or gotten it as a perk for some expedition. No one I knew had actually gone to a retail store and bought one. Even twenty-five years ago, high-tech tents cost hundreds of dollars—which none of us had—and you simply had to have one to safeguard your few possessions against squirrels and flash thunderstorms. Understand that "four-man" refers to an area sufficient to allow four beanpoles to sleep on their sides, with not space enough between them to drive a knife-blade. So in fact a four-man tent was just big enough for one climber to inhabit with some elbowroom.

We didn't much care what we slept on, so far as padding went, but if we had any hopes of luring a girl into our tent, we had to have a mattress. These were acquired from girls who worked as maids in various park hotels, lodges, and tent cabins. Since we could rarely pinch the precious mattresses outright, we normally had to barter for them, and such transactions took many and curious forms.

My buddy Ron rebuilt a girl's carburetor in exchange for a mattress. Tim guided a lady up the East Buttress of Middle

Cathedral, got pinned on the summit in a thundershower, and had to bivouac with no gear, starving and freezing in the rain, the girl cursing him through the livelong night—all for his feather bed (from which he got crabs). And then there was a maid, one Tina, a vinegary debutante who weighed well over two bills, had about three teeth in her head, and "bucked like a mule and snored like a chainsaw," according to Howie.

Howie was the only climber (that I know of) desperate enough to swap a long night with Tina for a secondhand mattress, after which his back looked like he'd been attacked by a black panther and his peter "felt like it had rifling on it."

Since it was summertime, the valley was always full of girls, and our craving to get laid cannot be overstated. Furthermore, sex, and plenty of it, was an indispensable aspect of our training routine—according to the Bird. The perilous climbs demanded steadiness and a Zenlike acuity impossible to achieve when freighted with "urgent fluids." They encumbered the "terrestrial body" and distracted the "astral body" so essential for the truly grim leads. The fluids had to go. But the Yosemite climber worked the field at a disadvantage—ninety cents away from having a buck, ragged as a roach, eating the holes out of doughnuts, and trying to woo Helen of Troy. That we might end up with someone a little less was to be expected; that we ended up with anyone at all was a miracle. But kids somehow manage to strike up the band no matter the circumstances. Occasionally we got lucky. I often wonder how the girls felt about a bunch of rogues who understood it was their pleasure that counted.

Many climbers put substantial effort into trimming out their tents in the hopes of creating a tender atmosphere. Some had "stereo" sound systems, consisting of various two-bit radios, tuned to the same station and positioned about the tent. Others had pictures of schmaltzy sunsets or portraits of Pan and Venus de Milo or even pink cupids taped and stapled to the nylon walls. Still others hung bead curtains and small mirrors, burned incense, or had fancy bedding (Bernie fleeced the purple satin sheets and pillows from a whorehouse in Blue Diamond, Nevada—swank merchandise, save for the stains). Of course the crux was always getting the girl into the tent in the first place, and more than one would-be darling found the decor so ludicrous that the amour never got past the rain fly.

VITTLES

The business of eating was, remarkably, even more important than getting laid. The Bird's boys were appallingly hungry young men. Food was fuel, and we burned immense amounts of it, judging all meals by quantity, not quality. Ninety percent of our money went for food, the other ten percent for intoxicants. Every "campsite" had a trashed old picnic table usually shared by four climbers. Each table bore a smattering of pots and pans—black as stovepipes—plus a Coleman stove that broke down so often and so entirely that every Camp 4 climber could rebuild one with a screwdriver.

Meals were one-course affairs. The standard entrée was a sort of goulash consisting of rice and spuds as the principal ingredients, enriched with whatever else we had to chuck into the mix—canned vegetables, tuna, acorns, even pie filling—anything to sweeten the pot. The trick was to keep the stove going and to keep stirring the bubbling gunk so that it didn't burn. Once the fare was judged "done," we all tore into it and would eat till we felt ready to explode, rest for a bit, and then eat some more. Several of us were typically found lying on the ground following a particularly wholesome graze, so bloated we couldn't hope to stand.

A favorite stunt was to frequent barbecues and picnics put on by various religious groups that swarmed into the park for weekend retreats. These were strictly private gatherings, though strangers were sometimes tolerated so long as the spirit of the thing was close to their heart (if you could suffer through a sermon and the singing of hymns and so forth). Acting pious and playing along was our ticket to the chow. And so we'd all turn out in our finest gym trunks and T-shirts, smiling through a torturous homily and crooning along with the righteous, the whole time licking our chops and growing increasingly restless until we could finally break for the vittles like wolves. These celebrations were generally large, and our numbers were comparatively so small that we could eat like we'd just gotten down from a two-week wall climb and no one ever cared. Or almost never.

I have no idea how the Bird learned of these affairs, but he did, and so frequently that Dale Bard claimed a tourist couldn't not so much as roast a couple of marshmallows without the Bird catching wind of it. He usually tried to keep our numbers down to three or four of his hard-core little band, but one time the word had gotten out, and about twenty of Camp 4's hungriest showed up for a stiff affair put on by the Four Square Pentecostal Church out of Modesto, California. We were as out of place as Oakies at the Louvre, and everyone knew it.

The pastor, a vast southern windbag possessed by his own drift, sailed extravagantly on about the Good Book. When he started in with the flood and the tower of Babel, we were right there with him, following his traveling hands and the rampage of his fractured drawl. Drifting to Leviticus now, and the law of holiness, I noticed an uneasiness moving through our group—not from our butchering of said law so much as the fact that we were now well over an hour into it and the aroma of spareribs was endangering our concentration. We traversed the plains of Moab, then on to Babylon and Nebuchadnezzar, and the boys were starting to openly sigh and fidget. He touched on the eight visions, and Daniel in the lion's pit, and by then we wanted to chuck that preacher in there with him, heckled as we were by the smell of those ribs and the fact that the maniac seemed to be catching his second wind. By and by we met the Apostles, Saint John came and went, Judas Iscariot threw his silver pieces, and as dusk stole over the valley we suffered a regular crucifixion as the man bent our ears to perdition and back. Solomon spent twenty years building the house of the Lord and, around half past eight, when we finally rose for a closing prayer, that hayseed seemed to take forty years before his voice box finally failed him and he squeaked out an "Ah-Men."

Straightaway the climbers stampeded over the congregation and entire tabletops of ribs and burgers and fried chicken vanished in seconds. Guys were plunging their bare hands straight into great vats of beans and potato salad and shoveling huge and sloppy loads into their mouths. Punch was swilled directly from the jugs, faces were stuck right into layer cakes and pies, and all this before the proper crowd had eaten so much as a carrot stick.

I don't remember what set the thing off, only that one of us crashed the line for the tenth time, reaching for a last drumstick or something, and someone angrily grabbed his arm. Words were exchanged; there was some pushing and, as the shocking news spread that the food was all gone, we scattered into the surrounding forest. I had so many franks and ribs and rhubarb pies on board I could barely walk. I caught up with the Bird in the darkness of the forest, and we both leaned against a tree and glanced back.

The dust had cleared and the big pastor was up on a picnic table, sweat pouring off his bald pate like the rivers of Damascus. He glared down at the great mountain of bones and rinds and corncobs strewn about him. Then looking at the starving faithful, he threw up his hands and cried, "Christ Almighty, folks. The famine is sore upon the land!"

"Stolen waters are sweet," said the Bird, stumbling away.

TREASURE

Climbing consumed most of our daylight hours, and we were generally so exhausted afterward that our few idle hours, and the things we filled them with, were seldom remarkable. Until "the Wreck." Twenty years later, a shamelessly embroidered version of the event would provide the basis for Sylvester Stallone's hit movie *Cliffhanger*.

In short, one of the Bird's boys—call him Woody—was shacked up with a gal who worked as an operator on the Park Service switchboard. By mistake, she cut into the chief's line and overheard a conversation concerning a plane that had crashed into Merced Lake, sixteen miles away from valley central, in the rugged and then snowy backcountry. Over dinner that night, she casually mentioned to Woody what she'd heard. Woody saw some potential here, for the plane had been identified as a Lockheed Lodestar, and he knew the nickname for such a craft: Smuggler's Special. The next day, Woody's girl was eavesdropping the chief's line in earnest.

She quickly learned that the previous morning two rangers had been dispatched to go scout the wreck (it was never known how the Park Service discovered the wreck in the first place). The pilot and copilot were found dead. Given the waist-deep snow and sixteen-mile trudge from the valley floor, the chief chose to wait till winter thawed a little before conducting a recovery operation, expensive even in perfect conditions. The two stiffs came out on sleds, and the case was put on ice.

Following a confab with the Bird, that night, freezing their asses off in Levis and tennis shoes, Woody, Buzz, and Skillet trekked up to Merced Lake to find the Lodestar augered into the frozen surface. With the aid of spelunkers' headlamps, they picked through the debris inside the plane, their legs stemmed out on twisted struts above a maw of icy slush (the nose of the plane was pointing straight up). When Skillet reached down into the slush and heaved out what looked like a hay bale, the headlamps converged. They hauled the stuff outside into the moonlight, studied it under their headlamps, sniffed it, ate it, and still couldn't believe it. They scrambled over one another and back into the plane, and sure enough, the submerged fuselage was bursting with five-kilo bales of high-grade Colombian weed.

The trio made three trips in as many days and weren't able to put the slightest dent in the vast payload. Each time they hauled out a bale, another one would bob to the surface. Since there was obviously enough for every rascal in Camp 4 to get quickly and shockingly rich, all of the Bird's boys and all of their friends were recruited. (If nothing else, Woody needed a few dozen strong backs to hump his plunder out.) In a matter of hours there was a virtual mule train of climbers making withering loops to and from the lake. Woody had his load out by the first day; then it was each for his own (though most climbers worked in teams of two and three). Some returned with upward of 150-pound loads of the "red-haired" weed, a burden that fetched roughly $50,000 on the open market. "Hiking for dollars," we called it, and in a week's time, more than half a million dollars' worth of booty had been hauled to light.

The plane had broken up, and many of the bales were lodged under the ice some distance from the wreck. After the easy pickings were plucked from the slush, locating the remainder was written off—till another Camp 4 rogue we'll call Hugh schlepped in a chainsaw. For several days Hugh skipped around the rink, boring the ice with the whizzing saw. If a blizzard of green stuff shot from the chain, they knew where to dig. By the time the lode was played out, the lake looked like it'd hosted an ice fishing convention.

What followed the strike was right out of a Fellini film. My friend Upton was one of the first ones on the site after Woody's initial sortie. He probed the wreck for one minute, found a wallet containing nearly $10,000, turned around and walked—and kept walking, right out of the park. Forty-five days later he staggered back into the Bird's tent with a full beard, a shiner, and two bucks in his pocket. Gene found a little black book with Italian names scribbled throughout. He burned it on the spot. On the last day, Steve returned from Fresno with a diving mask, flippers, and a wet suit. After standing by a roaring fire for twenty minutes, he lashed a rope round his waist and dove through a hole and into the bowels of the fuselage. Good thing, because in ten seconds, his limbs went dead in the ice water; but when they pulled him out, he had a death grip on an attaché case full of greenbacks.

The fuel cells had burst on impact, and some of the weed was drenched in av gas. If you couldn't smell it, you'd find out the second you stoked a pipeful, when a flame like a blowtorch would leap off the hooch. The Bird (who throughout acted as a sort of ombudsman, shipping manager, and logistics director) said not to worry, that the tainted goods could be peddled off at top dollar. In fact they were, and that's when things got crazy.

Tim left for Berkeley in a wheezing DeSoto crammed to the shattered windows with soggy hemp. Ten days later he tooled back into the valley driving a candy apple red convertible Lincoln Continental with fleecy dice hanging from the rearview mirror. Butch rolled in on a chopped Harley with more chrome than the Las Vegas strip. Hank showed back up in a three-piece buckskin suit with a Scandinavian hussy who spoke almost no English and wore almost no clothes, fawning over him like he was the Second Coming. He spent $800 in the bar the first night—even bought the rangers a beer. Climbers who a few weeks before hadn't had two dimes to rub together streamed back into the valley and were spending cash money with all the nonchalance of a Saudi prince. Good-bye Top Ramen. It was steak dinners forever and cognacs all around.

When the rangers put the pieces together, most of the Bird's boys cleared out to avoid the grill. The months that followed for all of us are best illustrated by the "climbing" trip undertaken by Buzz and five others.

They took a charter to New York and the Concorde to London en route to Chamonix and the French Alps. They had big plans: the north face of Les Droites, the Walker Spur on the Grandes Jorasses, to name a few. Later they'd swing by the Eiger, once they'd dusted off the French Alps. They got hung up at a whorehouse in Bordeaux, however. A week stretched into two weeks. They were still there after a month. In fact, they never made it to the Alps at all. The next spring the six returned to the valley, flat broke and about thirty pounds overweight.

AND SO IT GOES

I saw Buzz—now a land developer—last year and asked him if he regretted not banking a leaf or two of the long green instead of pissing it all away in a French bordello.

"What, are you crazy?!" He laughed. "You can always make money."

Much has changed with the original group, which numbers attorneys, no-accounts, dentists, carpenters, photographers, and felons among the ranks. But one and all, we'll always be the Bird's boys.

Jim Bridwell (arms folded), Bev Johnson (there were a few Bird's girls also), and champion boulderer Barry Bates, Yosemite, about 1969.

PAT AMENT

PAUL PRITCHARD

GEORGE SMITH

Paul Pritchard

British climber Paul Pritchard epitomized the "dole climber," the soul who financed his climbing with unemployment checks in a time when jobs were scarce in England's Peak District. When Paul moved to North Wales, he began to make a name for himself through his climbs on the Anglesey sea cliffs. In 1987 he and another youngster, Johnny Dawes, free climbed the continuously overhanging Sron Ulladale in Scotland. His beginnings as a climber on slate quarries in Wales eventually led to expeditions to exotic locales such as Patagonia, where he and several friends completed a major new route on the east face of the Central Tower of Paine. His book *Deep Play* won the Boardman Tasker Award, as did his second book, *Totem Pole*, which talks about his recovery from a serious head injury he suffered when a rock fell on him. The reader may momentarily puzzle over Pritchard's colloquial Welsh English, for example, "jumper" for "sweater," and "no fifties for the leccy meter," which refers to a fifty-pence pay-as-you-use electricity meter.

Rubble Merchants, Slateheads, and Others

I chose "Rubble Merchants" because it was a special time for me. We all have a magic summer in our lives, just one, that we look back to. This was my "Fernhill."

The mid-1980s were an economically depressed time for Britain, with over four million people on the dole. It was quite easy to avoid work, because there wasn't any. Unbeknownst to us, we were spending our days creating a leisure facility. The giant Dinorwic slate quarry had lain dormant since 1969 when the last of six thousand men lost their jobs. By forging hundreds of new routes up their derelict faces, we were transforming these quarries and enhancing the tourist industry. We had no idea back then that the weekenders would come in droves to climb in these huge holes in the ground!

PAUL PRITCHARD

Wales, 1987.

Cigarette butts, crumpled beer cans, the Captain's been on the sofa for weeks. The carpet's still damp under stocking feet since the pipes burst in the winter. No gas, no fifties for the leccy meter,[1] no window in the front door, hardly any food in the cupboard, and no one's washed up for a month. But there's thirty bottles of spirits in the kitchen. Sell some of them and we'll have some dosh. It's daft having all those bottles of evidence in here, though. The house is dark and smells of sweat and breath and mold. A muffled cough comes from upstairs. I creep up there for the bog.[2] The door to Carlos' room is lying on the floor. That's it, I remember, Gwion kicked it in last night to make him go and sort out Karen, who had put a bottle through the front door window and was making a scene in the street. The broken glass crunches under my All Stars as I step outside. The sun's been up for ages and pricks hot needles into my eyes. Spring's doing its thing now, and the Snowdon railway whistles good morning. Its sulfur smell catches my nose. I'm uneasy on my feet down the steep hill of Rallt Goch. I spit as I turn into Goodman Street and ruffle my hair. That wakes me up a bit. The kids in the park slide and swing with their young mums. There's the professor. He makes me shiver as he stops and watches the children through the mesh fence. All those things you hear are only rumor, though. You've not to forget that around here.

I grind the gravel of the pavement under my shoes. It feels real—more real than anything that happened last night. In Pete's Eats the tea's too hot for my lips. I hunch quietly and watch the others through the steam. There's the Fly, bent over his plate. He's called that because he sometimes throws his food up and then eats it again. But I don't think he'll do that this morning. The Lobster looks as though he's had a long night. I try and avoid the Lobster, all red and shiny, short in his long robbing coat.[3] He'll get anything for you, dead cheap. Give him your order in the café and he comes back half an hour later with the goods. Pulled two ice axes out yesterday and dropped them on the table. They say he's the most well endowed man in the village. I rub my eyes and try and push the hideous image out of my mind. The jukebox is playing Jimi Hendrix too loud and the smell of burnt liver makes me gag.

"Number twelve. Fried egg and beans."

"Yeah, that's me."

Women, aged before they should have, sag at the next table and push Embassy Regals into their mouths, tired of it all. Their husbands are in the betting office. They'll meet up at the chippy and chatter in a high-pitched Creole of Welsh and English. Dafydd Chips, the second biggest boy in the village, will scoop their deep fried offerings into newspaper packets for them to rush home with up the steep side of Llanber'. Meeta comes in. Looking happy, she snaps her tobacco tin down on the table top. I have to hang on her words at this hour to decode her Swiss accent, and she entrances me with tales of

Bolivian jails and Indian mystics. I gaze outside and imagine distant places.

Rain is spitting onto the glass now. Looks like another slate day.

The slate's best when it's showery, it dries in minutes. It's where it's all been happening of late, why I came here. I saw a picture of a mustachioed, muscley guy manteling these tiny edges, trying to put both feet next to his hands, grinding his nose into the purple rock, and not a runner in sight. Now I'm living with him, Carlos they call him because of his Spanish waiter looks, and Gwion. They're letting me doss there till I find a place of my own. No luck yet though, and I've been there six months. We did have an ace place before, but we got kicked out after we got caught with a pin in the meter.

I asked Carlos about the photo, and he told me he'd fallen off just after it was shot and went sixty foot. When I got here the slate scene was already big. The days when the mysterious Rainbow Slab was spoken about in hushed voices, a top secret location, were near since gone. The falls you could take off the hard slate routes were already legendary, and I wanted to take one. I didn't have to wait long before I was emulating Redhead and Carlos by falling eighty feet off a new route I was trying, drunk on the Rainbow. When I came to a stop, four feet off the ground with my nine ripped nuts stacked on the rope at my waist and Gwion higher up the crag than I was, I was content, and later bruised. I need to buy some chalk.

The sky is sagging and dark now, and the village seems to be resonating at a low frequency. The Lard's new van is throbbing to house tunes, and he's sat inside his shell suit[4] on double yellows, menacing (he's the biggest boy in the village). Last week he knocked Manic Ben over, right there in the street, in front of everyone. I don't return his stare. I must take care not to tread in dog shit on the pavement. There's Tatan on the other side of the street, "Hi, Tat." He looks ghastly. The other week on the way back from a day trip to Dublin, lashed up,[5] the lads ripped his clothes off him and threw them overboard into the Irish Sea. He's always the brunt of their jokes, but they love him really. When he showed up at customs starkers and the officials had to kit him out with a too-small pair of nylon football shorts, they all had a good laugh. Climbers in yellow and pink tights and ripped jumpers[6] are in the street; some live here, some are visiting. They pace around like peacocks, too colorful for a dark Welsh village. The old quarry men don't know what to make of them. The young locals react against them. I got pushed around in the street after hours a couple of times, but Gwion's a good man to know. He's a local himself, one of the few who hasn't gone the other way and doesn't want anything to do with the mountains. He's our mediator. He let the guys know I was OK, and now I can drink a pint with the same blokes who hated me before. Outsiders aren't always accepted here, especially big-time climbers with inflated egos. I've become the same, wary of newcomers, safe in our group.

Some try too hard to be accepted. One guy—the Weird Head we called him—who appeared for a while, said he'd base jumped the Troll Wall. He just wanted to fit in, that was all. When Bobby confronted him and told him that we knew he hadn't, he broke down and sobbed. There's a lot of crazy people here, people who can't sit still. The place is like a magnet, and for some there's this perceived pressure to be crazy too. The ones that try too hard don't seem to last long, they disappear. This old slate mining village has many good people. It just seems unavoidable that it should make winners and losers.

There's a distant brass band and a voice from a tannoy. It's carnival day. I'll run up the hill and wake the guys and head across to Vivian or up to the Lost World maybe. "Yahoo, guys. Who wants to climb?" Gwion's psyched. Carlos isn't moving—he's turned nocturnal, stays in his room all day reading horror stories. Gwion apologizes for hitting me last night (I was only trying to stop him from slashing his wrists on the broken glass), and then we're back out on the street. The carnival floats by, children in outfits with paint all over them looking self-conscious and, at the head of it all, this year's carnival queen. Graham Sis they call him, a fat man, very effeminate in his long red halter-neck. He drifts by waving in his lipstick, his dream come true. The village is heaving now, and we hurry across the fields toward the big holes.

In the quarry they're all there; new routes going up all the time. Things getting repeated and talked about. The Captain's having a tormegamite experience on something loose as hell, sweeping as he goes. The Dawes is trying a horizontal double dyno with his tongue sticking out the side of his mouth. There's JR creeping up the rock, thinking about genitalia. Nicky is psyching up for her ninety-foot leap into the steel black water of the pool, and Skeltor is wrapping his vast ape index around the purple rock. The Giant Redwood is on a rope, trundling blocks to uncover a modern classic. Harms the Stickman prances up the Rainbow looking unhealthy (how can he do this on his diet of chip butties and Newcastle-Brown?). The Horn pops in and flexes his tattooed biceps on Colossus Wall. Moose is soloing like a maniac 'cos his girlfriend's left him, and Bobby's bouncing around like a thing on a spring. And there's the Tick, recording all these antics through the lens and turning them into history. Uncle Alan watches from the bridge and reminisces about the thirties, when he was blasting and pulling the slate out of there. He warns us of the dangers, the giant rockfalls, but he's glad to see the quarry alive again. It's why Llanberis exists and why it had prospered for a hundred years, until the sixties, when it shut down and all the men had to look elsewhere. That's why, now, so many shops are boarded up around here. But this is a real village, with real struggles, not tarted up, making concessions for the tourists.

There'll be teams out on the island today, it'll be baking out there. I feel like I'm missing out teetering around in this manmade scar, and for a moment I want to be above the sea, brushing lichen off crimps with my fingertips, searching for ways through uncharted territory, studied by seals. But you can't be two places at once, and it could be worse. I could have a job. Big G and the Waddy will be out there with car inner tube knee pads on, barring their way across some incomprehensible ceiling with sea-reflected sunshine dancing on their backs in a dark cavern. Pengo and Manuel could be taking a trip to the moon on the Yellow Wall, and the Crook will have invented new jargon to describe an obscure nook or cranny which will be the scene of an even more obscurely named new route. Tombs the mathematician could be with him. "No money, no job, no girlfriend. Might as well be dead," he had said. Ben and Marion will still be on Red Walls, moving in and out of the quartz, smooth and solid after all these years. And there'll be Craig, making his name in a splash of color as the sun sinks into a receding tide. Up in the mountains Cloggy is turning gold, and Mr. Dixon will be up there doing his own thing on the cathedral of rock.

So as hands tire and blood sugar levels drop in the twilight, the climbers home back to Llanberis, to eat badly and rush for last orders. In the Padarn they're all drinking—the farmers, the girls from the chemist and the Co-Op, the hairdressers and the builders, the walkers and the climbers. That builder I've seen doing one-arm pull-ups on a door frame at a party and laughing at the supposed climbers who couldn't get near it. And there's big Tommy forcing his weight against the bar, as if trying to stop it toppling over, as he sinks his pints. Gabwt's standing on a chair shouting "Hash for cash" with his nunchukas[7] in his hands, terrifying those who don't know him, as merrymakers sneak out to the Broccoli Garden for some extra stimulation. That's Dewi playing pool. He killed the vicar with the end of a snapped-off pool cue that looked very much like the one he's holding now. Once he was beating Bobby at a game when Bobby remarked without thinking, "Bloody hell, Dewi, you're a killer with a pool cue!" We all stepped back and waited for the explosion, but he mustn't have heard 'cos he just missed the black and sat down. Those climbers over there are standing cool and not talking about routes and moves, even though they want to. I ask Johnny for the numbers on some route or other up the Pass. "Three, five, two, eight, one," he says, and makes me feel about this small. But me, Carlos, and Gwion are buzzing. We downed a load of our spirits before coming in 'cos we haven't any cash to buy drinks. Those Giros[8] only seem to last a day or so and then you're skint for a fortnight until you post your next slip in. Tonight's dinner was a rotting cauliflower that we got from the Co-Op for 10p, boiled up with five strands of pasta and a stock cube we found in the bottom of the cupboard. We called it cauliflower surprise. But Carlos has usually got some scam or petty crime worked out to keep us in food and other stuff. Never mind. Tonight people will be queuing to buy vodka and gin, and tomorrow we can eat full sets in Pete's. As "last orders" is screamed out Kenny the Turk erupts in a fury and starts spinning a cast iron table around his head. The crowd sweeps backward in a wave and tries to paste itself to the nicotine-stained walls of the room. The guy who has fallen out of his wheelchair in the crush pulls out a baseball bat and lashes out at anybody who tries to help him. For a moment things are completely out of control until Ash the barman, five ten and thin as a rake, gets in there and calms the Middle Eastern stand-up comic's temper. Just another night in the Pad, really.

Out in the street drunks mumble to themselves, dossers look for dosses and the partyers want to know where "the scene" is. So it's off to some terraced house under an orange street lamp to try and prolong the day, wishing sleep would never have to come. The house is throbbing with the beat, and those inside are giggling and dancing and you can tell by the look in their eyes that some people will be up all night. But if you eat those 'shrooms you won't get to Gogarth tomorrow, you'll sit around and waste your day away. Next to some hot knives on the stove we swap our stories of bricking it miles out, or talk of the moves on some slate horror and how you should try it like this or like that next time. But some of the others are bored by your keenness and wish you would shut up, and you suddenly feel self-conscious as the herbs take effect. You realize you've overdone it and are incapable of speech, and the girl you've wanted to work up the courage to ask is talking with that other guy. So you leave for home without saying your goodnights, tripping over your own feet as you head down the hill. In the dark house you get into your pit, lie on your back, and drift off, your head swimming, dreaming about tomorrow.

NOTES

1. Fifty-pence piece for a pay-as-you-use electricity meter.
2. Toilet.
3. A long coat to facilitate pilfering items from a store.
4. Storm clothing.
5. Drunk.
6. Sweaters.
7. A weapon made of two sticks connected by a chain or cord.
8. Government checks.

PAT AMENT

BETSY SWAN

Pat Ament, Flagstaff
Mountain, above Boulder,
Colorado, 1968.

Pat Ament was born in 1946 and started climbing in Boulder, Colorado, in 1958. He is author of thirty books and a hundred or more published articles. Fifteen of his essays have been included in various anthologies of best climbing writings. His books include the biographies of America's two most legendary rock climbers, Royal Robbins and John Gill. Two of his books have been short-listed for the Boardman Tasker Award. Ament graduated from the creative writing program at the University of Colorado and is a poet, editor, illustrator, photographer, and lecturer. His "Renaissance path," as John Gill has called it, includes a black belt in karate, two filmmaking awards, hundreds of published photographs, a "cult" career in piano and songwriting, an expert rating in chess, and an award for fine-line ink drawings. In 1967 he was a gymnast at the University of Colorado and set the standard for difficult bouldering around Colorado and in Yosemite.

In *Climbing: The Complete Reference to Rock, Ice, and Indoor Climbing*, Greg Child writes about Pat Ament: "He is a mentor influencing some of the outstanding climbers of three generations. He opened some of the first 5.11 routes in Colorado. Supremacy Crack, Vertigo, Northwest Corner of the Bastille, Super Slab, Country Club Crack ... are still respected classics. With John Gill he developed extreme bouldering around Boulder in the late 1960s."

Reflections on Being the Best Climber in the World

I chose this piece because I had fun writing it. One of the more recent of my writings, it also is one of the least known, and thus I think it deserves more exposure. I have shortened it somewhat from the original. The piece is a playful extended reflection.

In Climbing in North America, *Chris Jones wrote of my sixteen-year-old self, "Ament announced that in two years he would be a better climber than Kor and set out to make good his prediction." What a humorous thing for me to have said! Indeed, I was a humorous young creature, but never was I so gauche or ridiculous as to have actually said such a thing. Kor was my friend. To attribute such a statement to me was calculated, it seemed, to irritate anyone who admired Kor, which was almost everyone, and thus perform some malicious act upon my name and character. Yet perhaps it was an effort to portray me or the way I came across. I was shy and insecure, and highly uneducated in the ways of the world, and I needed acknowledgment.*

The following piece is my take on the process of growing up, a study of who I truly was and am, apart from the speculation. It is also a small perspective on that dreamy breath wind of years, so few and so quickly gone, that were so magical and that we gave the name "climbing."

PAT AMENT

From the moment life called on my spirit to make things interesting, there was rock. At first I was as awkward as an infant, as against the world as a cripple. Yet I was able to imagine that I was the best climber in the world.

Such a feeling was created in me perhaps to help me get past fear or rise toward the exaltation I sensed climbing to be about. In my thirteen-year-old heart, the slightest places of exposure bore terrible implications. Thus there was a disparity between what I felt and what I did. My eyes and spirit went upward, while my body only tentatively comprehended that it should

121

follow. I was impressionable, easily owned by fear. Yet because my imagination also could cast me into the image of a great climber, there was a possibility that I might overcome my fright and physical weakness and one day arrive at some actual level of ability.

People took collective issue with me from the beginning. I was concerned with my looks, as young people are. I held my shoulders squared back. I was confident, even though I lacked confidence. T-shirts I wore expressed the mildly developing muscles in my arms and chest. I kept my head upright and level. I was lean and light in those days, the late 1950s and early '60s, and more or less presented myself for acceptance to the community of climbers around Boulder, Colorado. I sometimes was careless with words. I tended to talk the talk before I was quite ready to walk the rock. Yet to speak about my climbs, as on occasion I did, was not bragging. It was youth. It was enthusiasm. The small air of dignity I communicated, however tenuously based on a rather imagined reality, was to suggest to myself, as much as to others, that in climbing I had made a wonderful discovery. Climbing instilled in me a sense of strength, spirit, and bearing, and its mysterious beauty was in command of me. To climb was a way to embrace the world and pay reverence to it. It was to recognize the worth of life and treasure the beauty and greatness of things.

By some marvelous spiritual chemistry, I happened into climbing. Or rather, it happened into me. I turned, it might be said, to the revelation of rock (which need not stand independent from the rock of revelation). Had there been no fear or apprehension, perhaps I would not have been lured up into the rocks to explore them. Even something so moderate as the Third Flatiron—the 1,300-foot sandstone slab that looms above the city of Boulder—seemed, when I was thirteen, to be huge, formidable, and full of terror. That rock was also wonderful, beautiful, magic, and sacred. As an experienced climber, years later, to recall these first feelings of mystery and mystique would be to apply them. I could project into climbing, as it became less new and magic, some of the elation of my first years. As a seasoned climber, it would become a peripheral task on almost any ascent to feel the primal exhilaration of when I was young and when I was the best climber in the world.

A beautiful self-worth tends to flow to one from the rock. Climber and rock meet somewhere in the air, and friendship hails from the edges of terrain. The rock has an energy, a spirit, if you will, that flows outward and into a climber. For as long as I have been at it, having spent a few thousand days on many thousands of climbs and boulder problems, I have been aware of such an interaction between my being and, call it, the inner spirit of the rock. The spirit of the rock, at least on occasion, does seem to receive me as a friend. Many evenings on Flagstaff Mountain, above Boulder, with cloud formations full of color and quiet faces, the bouldering hour (as opposed to the happy hour), I was filled with an appreciation of the beauty of life and of nature. I took whatever small beauty I myself might chance to possess as part of the wider grandeur of the mountains and the world. That wasn't an egotistical thing to do. I simply made a point to hear pines, to feel air through them. Those were precious times. Places of climbing were provided, along with friends, and I had a spark of ability that I was excited to develop.

Among the spiritual presences of forest, sky, and rock formations were climbers, people I knew and many of earlier generations of whom I could only be told. Ghosts—friends alive and dead—inhabited the pines and sandstone. Climbers leave in rock the air of their time and something of what they felt. Who they are, in their hearts, comes to reside forever in the rock.

No one ever can, in an objective sense, be worthy of such a valuation as the best climber in the world. In a relative sense, however, in a spiritual sense, it is possible for almost everyone.

In addition to all the spirits of climbers and forest and rock are quite a few spirits within oneself, various qualities of eager-

ness and uncertainty, an urge to go upward, an impulse to retreat, a recognition of danger and mortality, along with a few
odd impressions of indestructibility. . . . The light suddenly im-
proves among pines in late afternoon. The meaning of the light
exists, somehow, along a border of imagination, among the
mysteries of the sacred. It is a kind of sentient stomach, to begin to name it. Or perhaps the feeling is higher, in the shoulders
. . . or head.

I have touched now on something that may, or should, be
of the greatest importance to climbers. At the heart of a
climber's life is a gorgeous, deeply inner feeling—a notion that
holds the entire meaning of the universe. One holds to this feeling as much as to any ledge or crack in the rock. Sandstone
soars above. The soul is pulled upward. The rock puts a taste
in the mouth . . . of dirt or lichen. A morning, wet shrubs, a
river, clouds in a new, ethereal array. . . . There is a cloud of
which the climber is aware, perhaps to the right or left, at the
edge of vision. It has in it, as he has in him, an understanding,
a fulfillment, an exaltation. Revealed in the solitude of a forest
are secrets of oneself. Something mystical and "inner" is shaped
in the movements of a climb.

A previous night's rain imparts fresh atmosphere. The rock
has a damp smell yet quickly becomes warm in sunlight. Such
things memorialize a life. They give to one a sense of the body's
freedom. To use a set of holds is to reach with care toward
things that only can be felt in the heart and soul. Sometimes
the moves are straightforward, other times bizarre, even forced.
At other moments the effect is a series of graceful, creative
moves, discoveries of balance and judgment, inspired by some
lovely quality of rock. Climbing speaks so well, so truthfully,
of life. At the beginning, when all is discovery, one feels, thinks,
and moves up into the happiness of it all. Sometimes the feeling moves away to a higher or lower set of holds. It seems to rest
in a pine at a certain moment and later as the memory of a
friend or the smell of rope. Sometimes I stand on a foothold for

the length of a few breaths and think, "Look how beautiful the light is in the canyon right now."

I have a special memory from my early childhood. I awoke after a long sleep, looked out a door, and saw a large cloud breaking open at the end of a storm. The cloud was filled with light. There was a smell of rain, and a tremendous, spiritual feeling came over me that only now, in retrospect, am I able to somewhat understand . . . or very partially describe. I now tie that memory to much of my experience as a climber. To behold something beautiful in nature is to marvel quietly at the great bounty of existence and feel close to it, virtually a part of something so deep, and so amazing, that I am powerless to know it closer than in glimpses. I always seek, however, to get close, to find the feeling and the imagination to delve deeper.

The most beautiful rock does not lose its mystery, and you don't want it to. As time and age allow a person to begin to get over himself, he grows to appreciate even more deeply forests where hidden sandstone boulders flash with light from behind trees and where places of solitude inside clouds invite one to be.

It was given to me to be a climber. It was a gift I brought with me to this life, or so it feels. Among the work to which I was called in life was to save myself, save my friends, discover a route, and search out a descent. It was for me to get to secret places that somehow I believed were vital to my salvation or the salvation of others, the hold that no one yet had found. It felt almost immediately as though I carried in my soul the power of the rock.

Much of my life as a climber has been triumph. I do not mean to overstate things, and I speak rather of strange, inexplicable secrets of experience. Such triumph, properly, is significant only in the hidden places of one's soul. My sense of the world was adequate enough when I was young to know that there were climbers elsewhere and everywhere in the world who possessed or would possess more expertise and competence on rock than I. Yet with the rock in my face, so immediate and rushing and filled with the energy of its presence, and the fearful feel of the upward moves of my body near the tops of pines, as air brushed past the rock, thoughts of other climbers did not trouble my soul. I imitated those people and imagined what they might do. I did not know them, yet they were examples. I was especially appreciative of those who had gone before.

I was my own realm of experience, my own domain of real weaknesses and imagined strengths. The only actual strengths I possessed were desire and a love of life. These were enough. The life that I had been given and had accepted was, as I saw it, the only one I was to be given, and to have its mysteries and terrain was to feel, imagine, think, believe, and embrace . . . with a perfect liberty. There was nothing wrong in the notion that what I was doing was important. As shy and careful as I was, as terrified, the jubilation that resulted and imagination that was conjured were proportionately fantastic. Thus for the most part I *was* the best climber in the world, even though every friend with whom I went up on the rock was braver and had more ability to climb. I could match them in imagination or in some personal way of which only I had the ability to know.

As I grew older (I will not say "up"), I began to take upon myself a mantle of true ability. Such a term, "ability," is based on my day and on fellow climbers who were, more or less, the pioneers of rock climbing in America, around Boulder, Colorado, and in Yosemite in the 1960s. To be accepted into the small Boulder order of friends, a band of individuals, occurred for me as a result of their generosity. Baker Armstrong, Dale Johnson, Larry Dalke, Layton Kor, Bob Culp, Dave Rearick. . . . When I hear or think the name Rearick, I see the dark, mysterious Diamond of granite, an extremely sheer wall a thousand feet high on the snowy east face of Longs Peak. I am carried back to 1960 when Rearick and Bob Kamps were the heroic two of the Diamond's first ascent. How I admired them! How much awe I felt when, from a window of my parents' car, I looked up from the road at that huge, sinister mountain wall!

Pat Ament, Yosemite, 1967.

LARRY DALKE

The acceptance and guidance I felt among those few Boulder climbers helped me form in my imagination a notion that I was important and unique and that my presence might benefit the world. I believed there was a use for what gifts I possessed— most of which I had yet to discover. The manner in which my fellow climbers looked at me gave me a sense that they expected me to grow, to learn of those gifts, and to be worthy of climbing—at least of a few of its secrets. I expected climbing to reveal to my friends the person I imagined myself to be at my greatest. It must have been a surprise to my friends to discover how quirky I was.

On any of those jingle-jangle mornings when I came following Kor, there was, for me, a perception of my own strange characteristics and adolescence. I was concerned about a small expression of acne, and there was something going on along the lines of an appreciation of girls—not quite yet sexual desire. I think I envisioned myself as being able to marry. I indeed would be engaged briefly to a schoolmate, in 1964, when she and I were both seventeen.

While sincere, much of what I said had the look and sound of odd or inappropriate. There were a few minor occasions where I exaggerated my achievements, as though to force the recognition that I deserved but that others were not naturally inclined to give. Young and somewhat hopelessly inept at the keener requirements of social interaction, I found also that I had an artist's idealism and a sense of aesthetics. I was able to recognize beauty with the best and oldest of them. The Zhivago in me began at an early age to look up into clouds and hear air through pines. A face of rock that seemed to others as though a mad artist had thrown paint at it revealed to me design and beauty. Young, strange, chaotic ways that I looked at the world became mingled with poetic contemplation.

It was impossible to do anything about a God-given gaucheness. Yet while I was unable to save myself from such things, and from inexperience, a sense of something sacred and quiet remained as a guiding companion to my climbs. Strangely, climbing has the power to balance and blend, if not harmonize, the diversities of soul. The great, sounding distances of sandstone or granite sharpened my senses and awakened my soul. If I never would completely escape who I was, I would know, as I grew, that life, after everything, is beautiful.

Kor was the best climber in the world. Six foot seven, filled with energy and madness, he made his climbing partners laugh so hard it hurt and also made them shudder and feel veritable fear. The thought of his falling and the wonder at where he might lead us were intriguing under-spirits of each experience on rock. His recklessness in the earlier days of his climbing, or in a car, or wherever, was something we tolerated, out of a desire to be in his overwhelmingly enjoyable presence.

Layton, Larry Dalke (my school friend), and I were in our own worlds. We stood beside each other yet absolutely were different from one another. I believe this is true of every person in relation to any other person. Dalke was a gifted climber, intense and uncertain about life. Inexplicably tormented, he rode his motorcycle wildly through the night, sometimes chased by police. Kor climbed, it seemed, because he was possessed by the demon of climbing. His wild, compulsive reaction to so much fun and beauty made him instantly (and outrageously) good at it. I, with my reflection and aspiration, gaucheness, and occasional glorified claims, was an equally ridiculous creature. Each of us was given the charge of too much rich life to know exactly what to do with it.

I must have appeared to the world as possessed with a larger than average degree of confusion. To add to the bewilderment (and perhaps it was an innate desire to sort it out), I carried with me a kind of announced intention. It might be said that I verbally processed my goals, feelings, accomplishments, and worries, and sometimes—heaven forbid—within earshot of others. I soon began to sense in the general establishment of climbers chords of turmoil, suspicion, and jealousy. People were offended by my rough edges and, it seemed, by the effrontery of my achievements. As they detected defects in character, they could dismiss me as flawed. They could scorn me behind my back. To them, my young age was no excuse. That I took as my friends individuals of the caliber of Rearick and Kor perplexed them all the more. A few looked at me as though I would marry above my station. Such a marriage was impossible. I was too young, too rough, too poor in spirit.

Climbing, I began to find, was a place of elusive triumphs. If you fought your way to some high ground, there were critics. There was the observing public. Time was passing, and it would not be easy for me to get on top of such things. Life, I began to realize, is a short-lived appointment, and the only hope was to fill it with a variety of everything.

I must get back to the mildly apocalyptic idea that I was the best climber in the world. Such a thought strikes at the core of what climbing is about. And I *was* the best, second only to whomever was with me at the time. And getting back to that notion of announced intention. Almost everyone must have been aware by now that I wanted to be a good climber and that I loved to climb. Not everyone liked it or my assumption that I would succeed at my hopes and dreams. I think I acted as though I already had succeeded. Quickly I began to rise into a new, even more able elite.

I did not know about humility. That was an advanced idea of which I would begin to get a sense later. I felt it in Rearick, and it would take the likes of Robbins, Gill, Frost, and others to help me grasp the idea and want it. None of those four climbers I just named, by the way, was or is perfect in his humility, but to modestly assess their climbing achievements was among their natural inclinations. It was hard for me to suddenly develop such a flair, what with being the best climber in the world—second only to those souls who went before and second only to whomever was my paramount inspiration at the moment: Kor, Rearick, Robbins, Pratt, Higgins, Gill, Bates, Barber, Breashears, Bachar, Croft . . . to name a few. The gods always would put a high standard out there for me to observe.

The climbers with whom I spent the most time were able to tolerate (or forgive) my gaucheness. I think it was a blessing to be gauche. The quality was sincerity combined with naïveté and inexperience (a Laurel and Hardy mix). I could not help it and probably would have been less interesting had I been otherwise. Each time I tried to show humility, people acted as though such an attempt made me less humble. They had defined me already and were not about to allow me to change—and thus meddle with their preconceptions. If I accidentally demonstrated humility or modesty, they responded as though the young demon was being someone he was not. They did not want any air of saintliness.

Friends, on the other hand, watched and took note of whatever point along the gentle slope of progression I attained or pretended to attain. They did not want to intervene much in the process. They knew it would be difficult to change the irreducible, creative incorrigible into a universal. Some of the rest of the climbing community, meanwhile, read into me impetuosity, what with how I went up on their inviolates, such as the Diamond, at age seventeen. Certain of those people undoubtedly would have imagined some sinister comfort in my demise. I was discovering the paradoxical nature of civilization—how easily one could find a friend or become a foe to others by no more than to reach upward with an arm in sunlight for a hold in a dihedral. Climbing, I would learn, was formed of goods and evils. Yet like poetry, it was "a place where contradictions do not destroy one another" (Howard Nemerov).

It would have shown more respect had I been less overt with my imperfections. Others kept their imperfections concealed. My rougher qualities were apparent. I wore them on both sleeves—which prevented some of the people around me from seeing that I actually was a friendly soul and was kind and gentle behind the facade. I had a proper share of intelligence and perception at the heart of the Laurel and Hardy performance of my daily affairs. I was attentive, at a young age, to pores and textures of stone, to the spirit alive in rock and in pines, and in people sometimes, in the sandstone, leaf, or grass blade, and in exposure that electrified me as I gazed down or outward from the rock.

I had no intention of offending other climbers. It never really did feel good when I was able to climb harder things than others were. Ability, I wanted to believe, was relative. I mean, 5.8 in the 1930s was probably more difficult than 5.10 in the 1960s. I didn't want to take anything from the experience of others or negate any individual. It was not difficult to show up other climbers, especially on the boulders, what with the gymnastic strength I was beginning to develop. Yet they climbed less often than I. So how could I compare? The average climbing populace would never lead the scary, unprotected, second pitch of Psycho on a frigid Eldorado day, or lead the Crack of Fear above Estes Park, yet it was something that gave me only the smallest pleasure to know. I preferred to see friends and my climbing students succeed. I loved to help a friend discover climbing and show him or her how to make a difficult move that at first seemed impossible. I wanted them to share in the good feelings of climbing.

Yes, there was the competitive impulse in bouldering now and again, and I was conscious of the standard that I sought to push as a free climber, but even the most serious efforts had a spirit of play. My mind was given to higher concerns than whether I was a better man than someone else. Why would the best climber in the world wonder about such things?! I simply wanted those holds not to shear off. I wanted the little knife-blade piton to stay in its crack when I put my weight on it. I wanted to kiss a girl. I wanted the pine limbs to shake and wind to blow. I wanted to hear the fabric of my pack scrape against rock and for there to be a metal jingle of pitons and carabiners inside it when I walked upward toward rock over crackly needles of pine. I hoped the lightning would avoid me and that the sun would shine. I wanted the rope not to get stuck around a flake. I wanted to smell the rope and let the memories that inhabited those smells bring to me the beauty of climbing and all that was good to breathe among the rocks, timber, and air. I wanted to find ways not to have to work at some regular job. I wanted to fulfill a vision of uniqueness my mother had of me. I hoped to be able to do something that would honor, if not impress, my father. He was not easily impressed, and he was not inclined to admit it if he was. I hoped to excel at climbing, because if I did I would like myself and people would like me. Of most importance, I wanted to be with a friend and share something sacred, beautiful, and ours alone.

In Eldorado, and I mean an older Eldorado, when there were few people and more sun, almost anyone at any given moment could be the better man. The yellow red, beautiful rock, against bright green pines and even brighter blue sky, made it easy to know that you were unique, great, and good-looking and that everyone else was also, even those less friendly gargoyles who taunted from below and from the sides. Somehow they also were of value to life, and you would be, you hoped, in the final appraisal, valuable to their lives.

I was, if I dare say, part of the in-crowd—that ill-fated comedy of people who are, in reality, outside everything and who rely largely on the adrenaline of themselves. To be one of the elect group required that a person have the inner climbing. That is, you had to have gone through a few types of difficulty and solitude. You had to know certain climbs, each hold of a number of specific, classic places on rock, the key position of each of the better, more mysterious climbs. It had to be understood in your eyes, or your feel, that you knew such places and what they were . . . and in a number of kinds of light. That light changed from move to move and was imperative to salvation. It was vital that it be remembered.

The entire Eldorado Canyon was, in two words, light and salvation—full of secrets, deep with tasks of a sacred kind, and very brightly rich with answers to the universe. I was determined to get to the meaning of my surroundings. At a glance, it might be nothing more than to squeeze, pull, and use my shoes the best ways on small, sloping holds. There was depth in just that.

I wanted what I was doing to matter to others, and thus I knew what others did had to matter to me. This might have been a form of true modesty, or humility. I did love my friends. Arrogance would have been not to care at all about anyone, to manicure my fingernails, put a ring on each finger, and a chandelier on the piano. I climbed into the air and sun of my feeling, with light all around and thoughts of friends. The sandstone was warm. I wanted to show even my enemies the beauty or at least show them I had shown it to myself. I did feel contempt for a few—those that felt contempt for me. That tended to be my simple-minded criterion. If they detested me, for no good reason, then I detested them.

My frail feelings—they really were tender and grand—were hurt more than occasionally. Two or three times, as a result of not wanting to set myself up for criticism, or not wanting to be rejected, I gave myself the benefit of the doubt that I had free climbed something when in fact my style was some point below perfect. Things are not easy for the best climber in the world. I would go on to do the first climbs of a 5.11 grade. I would give several hundred climbing lectures, illustrated with my slides. Twice I would be guest speaker for the British National

Mountaineering Conference in England. I would write many books, have many articles published in magazines. I would teach climbing to a few hundred people, several of whom would become the best climbers in the world. I would save a few lives. My spirit would become fused into the rocks of Boulder. My best boulder problems still are right there. They have not (like their master) gone the way of the world.

One can do only so many boulders and climbs before the memory of climbing becomes as strong as, and in some cases stronger than, the reality. The two realms intertwine until they are indistinguishable. I found after enough years that I was able to have the deep, inner feel of climbing when I did no more than look at my slides or walk up the road in Eldorado Canyon on an afternoon as sun hit the Yellow Spur. This way of climbing, to not actually climb, unfortunately began to be a good sister to an ever-decreasing motivation to stay in shape. To have a genetic disposition to gain weight, to burst at the seams, so to speak, I took myself out of the physical picture altogether. I went from Laurel *to* Hardy, through the years. I found myself unable to produce the old gymnastic strength. The person once described by the *Estes Park Trail* as "formidable area rock wizard" was now "the old sage"—a charitable phrase intended to acknowledge my technique, experience, and wisdom at the same time it permitted me to gracefully exist in a removed dignity.

Once able to do slow, straight-body hollow-back presses off the floor or 125 fingertip pull-ups in ten minutes, and having invented the one-arm mantel, I now had weak arms. They were at least atrophied. Combined with my growing irresoluteness, I was too weak to pull the extra weight I rather suddenly put on. I was not grossly overweight, just fifty pounds or so—which is a lot to a former university gymnast who in his prime was about fifteen pounds below ideal weight and could lose his routine on the parallel bars by eating a second helping of spaghetti.

Now and then I still could show a spark of that old lightness and ease of movement on rock, which really are the love of climbing. I still do climb, and not without at least a small sense of the art of past years. The memory of experience lives in my skeleton.

I see climbers today who feel they are the best climbers in the world, or else they are able to identify those who might be. They *are* the best—second only to whomever is with them at the time. A girlfriend of mine once said, "It is a spiritual gift to be able to recognize the talents of other people." That is one of the most important things ever said. Often we climbers seem to negate the achievements of others. This is because it feels that to acknowledge another implies some kind of concession with regard to oneself. The majority of climbers today, and most of those I ever knew, are fair candidates for those adjectives, "best climber," each person good and gifted in some individual and specialized way. In the case of today's climbers, it is not because he or she knows how to do those hard new things so much as it is because he or she is ready to embrace the weather and light and the beauty of the rock. So many of our modern crew are beautiful young spirits, coherent, exact, and focused on what it is they wish to do. Each has a beating heart and a recognizable personality. Many of them do not have, as yet, a vision that is their own. They know only that they are the best climbers in the world, and we can be sure they will, for at least a brief spell, or even a moment, indeed be their best.

I wish climbing magazines would stop publishing articles such as one I noticed in 1997 (I think) that had the title, "Why the Europeans Are Better Than the Americans." How crass, cold, and uninsightful such a statement is. It turns out they were talking about competition climbing. The important qualification was left out of the very general title. In their way, the Europeans *are* the best. In the spaces between their minds and their rock exist some of their own kinds of gifts, electrical clouds, and holds.

For me a beautiful world is to climb. It is a sunlit, somewhat fairy-tale world I have gone to more than a few times, of concord and discord, of atoms and ethos, an all-powerful place that produces peace and order at the same instant it inspires fear and a sense of its strangeness. Moves on rock, like souls of people, are too personal to be timed or graded. Rembrandt or Da Vinci? Which one was better? Who painted faster? Every climber worth his or her salt has some talent that is individual. It is ludicrous to think, as the media often would have us, that we are to be compared, that it is possible for us to move along identical lines or be on the same path. I feel the compulsion to tell all my climbing students, from novice to intermediate, that they are great, even if such a notion suddenly complicates in a slight way their immediate experience and unduly causes them to imagine. More of them than not will, in time, or in the end, find something in their climbing that is the incarnation of that beautiful idea. A person's gift sometimes proves simply to be that he or she loves climbing to such a degree as to stand out, above and alone, regardless of ability on rock. The person may give friendship and knowledge to others in great ways.

We only get into trouble when we use our gifts or our successes to negate the efforts and worth of others. Each of us must struggle through life on his or her own terms. When I look in the mirror now, I think, "Some settling of contents may take place during shipping." I bought a T-shirt not long ago that said, "The older I get, the better I was." I am no longer a climber—an interesting affirmation that I have allowed to creep into my psyche.

One climb I did lead in my older age, in the mid-1990s, was Curving Crack, a 5.10 finger lieback of which I made the first free ascent in 1964 in a snowstorm. It felt good now to ascend this ancient little prize, although my body was murmuring, "This would be easier if you would exercise even once in a rare while." Below, two climbers walked past under the route. They had no expression on their faces and glanced up at me. Perhaps they wondered who the unidentifiable, slightly jaundiced duffer was above who had placed so many more wire nuts in the crack than ever should be needed. Those people below were, in symbol, the entire, stoic climbing world, the sordid whole of the complex panorama of climbers—whom I admire in large part, and recognize for their talents, and to whom I have, to some magnitude, given the parting handshake in a spiritual and secret sense.

An important tool of a person's progression is to be reduced. It has been, over the years, a peculiar form of growing to watch students—and I mean dozens of them—find a way to outdo me on rock, surpass me in biceps strength or leg strength, and mock me with some form of physical or mental prowess. At least two individuals, to whom I dedicated countless hours and days, even disavowed any benefit from my influence (apparently out of a desire to stand in their own light). One has since realized the error and apologized.

In any case, I was going down, down into the dust of the distant, dreary darkness of dear and delirious old age and obscurity, and a few of my friends and protégés—to whom I have given so many riches of ideas, so much technique, and gentle gems of genius—have been, as a fine way to thank me, agents of that fall. A tear should well up in your eye now. In any case, to see an article with that title ("Why the Europeans Are Better") was to feel as though I was going down and my country down with me. What a state of affairs, until one of those sparks of light, one of those fast clouds through blue, entered the side of my head and I remembered.

I am told I will always be an important part of the mythology of a number of individual lives, yet it does not alter the impression that I have faded into the obscurity of pines.

I love to reflect on the achievements of others. In the mid-1990s, Peter Croft and his partner, Dave Shultz, did El Capitan twice in a day. Lynn Hill did the Nose of El Cap free. Chuck

Pratt in 1965 led on-sight, with no chalk and no protection, Yosemite's 5.11 off-width Twilight Zone. For shoes, he wore crumbly old Cortinas. Was there ever a bolder lead? When Gill in 1961 did the first 5.12 route in America, the Thimble, in South Dakota, and a few of the first 5.10 routes on Teton buttresses, he was the best climber in the world. He still is the best—second only to me.

I think of Whillans and Brown in the 1950s doing English routes in tennis shoes in rain, a sling around a stone wedged in a crack as their protection. Royal's solo of the Muir Wall of El Cap in 1968, Higgins' lead of Jonah at Tahquitz in the mid-1960s. . . . To think of these people, and their climbs, is as vital as to breathe. I celebrate them in the corridors of my being. There always have been and always will be climbers who are able to dangle from the pinkie of one hand on an overhang while they scratch their ribs with the other hand, but they are not Whillans or Brown, not Robbins or Gill. . . .

I think of Henry Barber's lead of Butterballs in the early 1970s and his two-and-a-half-hour solo of the Steck-Salathé on Sentinel. . . . I envision Yosemite pioneer climber John Salathé up on those big walls, a man armed only with crude pitons he forged. In memory are those *Alpine Journal* photos of Oliver Perry-Smith, an American who made his show in Dresden and other places of Europe. He was the greatest climber in the world—second only to Fritz Wiessner when Fritz led his off-width on Devils Tower. When in 1975 David Breashears climbed Perilous Journey—a 150-foot vertical wall without one point of protection—he did a route that no climber ever will do again, even if they ascend the very line of those holds. Bachar's route, the Bachar-Yerian in Tuolumne, continues to amaze me for its imposing, vertical nature. I think of Derek Hersey, one of the best of all. His guardian angel was the only one Derek was unable to keep up with.

At the semiannual outdoor trade show in Salt Lake City, in 1998, Alex Lowe told me I was an inspiration to him. Robin

Erbesfield won the World Cup with a smile, then one day hugged me and said I was one of her heroes. I love the honest, happy smiles that play over the countenances of these people, although no one of them is more beautiful than I in my younger years with all that young good hair, thin body, and muscles. How beautiful the rock was and the sky. How natural it felt to be driven by confusion and love, haunted and gauche.

The years passed. I became a father. At least it did not happen until I was fifty. I love my daughters. They are the best daughters in the world—second only to my wife and my mother and grandmothers (and a few former girlfriends).

I will offer another quote from Howard Nemerov. He was the best poet in the world. But this is not a poem. It is from his essay "Speculation Turning to Itself" (from his *Figures of Thought*) in which he seems, as always, to express something that will change your life and that tomorrow you will not remember. It has something akin to my own words and the thoughts I struggle here to form:

> For the sight of the eye the world is evident, it is there, it is a surface. For the sight of the mind the world is a secret to be probed, and the fascination of the mind, the fearsome pleasure that holds it to the world, comes from the belief that what we see is never what is there, or never only what is there, but always stands in some shadowing, reflecting, distorting, hinting relation to what is there. What the eye sees, the mind holds to be appearance, and sometimes it seems as if the mind's great ambition would be to declare the whole show a false appearance, and to behold it fade into invisibility even as the beholding mind itself swooned into unconsciousness. But that ambition has so far seemed unable to be satisfied short of death, for the appearance, in the mind's

myth about it, can never be altogether and only
false, because it is only by seeing through it to
something else, something beyond, beneath,
above, that the mind can delight itself for a
moment with the discovery of what it was that
the appearance tried to satisfy. For a last turn of
the screw, you have the mind's deep suspicion
that the reality concealed and hinted by all the
appearances of the world is the mind itself, which
can obtain no view of itself save by going forth
into the world and becoming itself an appearance
of itself.

Now will you repeat that back? What I remember is the part
about going forth into the world—as I did when I was a boy
scared but somehow attracted to the constellations. What I
remember about the Nemerov quote is what I remember about
the word "knife-blade," or "bugaboo piton," my eyes blinded
by sun, the clarity of vision in so much agency and light. I
was willing to suffer the fear in order to get to the secret. I
must have been the best climber in the world. I had assigned
myself something so large and various as rock.

I must forgive those Europeans, with all their conquest and
domination. I must allow them their greatness, and they will
take it—provided they are not asked to do the Twilight Zone
unprotected, with no chalk, and only crumbly Cortinas, provided they do not have to do El Cap twice in a day, and provided it does not require one of Gill's one-arm front levers or
my one-arm mantel, and provided they stay within the palette
of their gift, their understanding, their beauty and genius. I
admit that I paint against the grain of today's competition
climbers, but to their credit they may be far more in the moment than I was. As I say in a poem, "We suffer for the fragile
beauty / Of the moment— / So intense that it cannot reach farther, that, / Created, finds its life is near the end."

This is one of the things my story is about: time and the way it passes. The context of our lives. How we fall into the realm of comparing, in our efforts to keep and paint what we feel. Layton, Larry, Dave, and I knew we had discovered the lost gold. We were not about to turn it over to anyone. It was ours, the feeling of those few years. Don't tell me there is nothing new under the sun. I knew something that truly was new. The feelings possessed by people who came after were different. Perhaps the deepest part of climbing began for me with some type of latent realization that I was unable to hold on, to those days, that I would spend them, and spend those colors of Eldorado before I knew them fully. I never was the best in the world at holding on, to things, except small holds on hard moves in my prime.

In 1997 I took my wife, Robin, nine-year-old son, Cody, and infant daughter, Maren, to the base of El Capitan where, thirty years before, in 1967, I had done the first 5.11 climb in Yosemite. It is a small route, and a block has broken out of the crack to provide hand jams now where once there were finger jams. It no longer is 5.11, so some say, but rather 5.10c or d. My family and I gazed upward at the enormous spectacle of trees, granite, clouds, and sky. My wife and son held the rope, their first attempt at a belay, as I made the thirty-year-anniversary ascent.

My announced intention today is that I will continue to enjoy beautiful places and people of the world. I will continue to climb, even though I no longer am a climber, and my daughter has a perfect right, if it is her desire, to be the best in the world—second only to her father and the ant that she notices on the rock that has noticed her. At the base of El Cap, I held my daughter up to the granite. She touched and slapped the white stone. She laughed and looked at me as though to ask what she was to make of this large, smooth, hard presence of white. Already she had gotten the essence.

Just when climbing has gone by me, or I think it has, some-one gives me a boost in morale. Just as I move away from the need for acknowledgment, I get it. In the later 1990s Peter Croft complimented me for a certain difficult boulder route I did in the late 1960s. He said he'd struggled for quite a time but finally one day made Ament's Arete in Yosemite's Camp 4. I wanted to say, "There were other routes of mine much harder than that." I bit my tongue. I know more about humility now. I am not the most modest person in the world, but I have gained height (even when I think to be modest a few times and, by thinking so, am not). It made me feel good that someone from the new generation should be so decent as to respect someone from an earlier generation.

In a newspaper article advertising a climbing show I was to give, there appeared a photo of John Gill I had sent the paper. This was a classic, famous bouldering shot of him on the un-derside of the Scab in the Needles. The photo never would be mistaken for me—except by the newspaper editor who, to my chagrin, captioned it "Rock Climber Pat Ament." I had very much surpassed the normal definition of out of shape and been that way for years. In fact it would require a trampoline for me to arrive at that set of holds on the Scab, and it would not be certain then that I could hold such a position the time it would take for someone to snap a shutter.

John had chastised me for letting myself get out of shape. On occasion he had sent me one-line e-mails that said, for example, "Now get down and do five pushups." Why should I need to, if I am able to get newspapers to put my name under a photo of him? Soon after my lecture, I sent John a copy of his photo with my name under it. I wrote, "I've gotten a lot better since you last saw me."

It's just that kind of coincidence of fate that one of the more frightened boys in Boulder should be drawn to the power of rock. Had I not been the right kind of person, at least in some ways, I would not have gotten the holds right in as many ways as I did. That I am the best climber in the world is to say that a certain simple, pure, innocent joy I found when I climbed remains my model of thought, although I have discovered a few new kinds of space between the rock and myself, and I shall master them, and they shall master me.

It is interesting that the rock does not diminish after we go everywhere up it we desire. Spring comes, summer, or . . . I want to climb. During the last ten or so years, I have enjoyed a few secret areas that almost no one but me would see as worth the trouble of a visit. These places have sun and holds. At the place I have gone the most, there is a stream below. Air is in the pines. There is a small rock, enough to work with. Always there is some new, old grain of light. There are splotches of color in the rock, as yellow as a banana, as orange as a tangerine, a few kinds of green that shade into grays. . . . A climber becomes, at least for the length of a short time, an airy being, like Shakespeare's Ariel. His mind and soul are infused by something liberating, light, and beautiful. The likeness to Ariel lessens as one gains weight. As I arrive at what John Gill tells me is "the youth of maturity" (have you heard a better euphemism for fifty-four?), nostalgia more than anxiety is aroused. I am perhaps more like Prospero (the antithesis of Ariel), who stands out in a wind some afternoon, who looks upward at clouds and rock, and bids farewell to his magic.

GREG CHILD

Greg Child, Water Holes Canyon, Arizona, 2000.

Greg Child won the American Alpine Club's Literary Award in 1987. He climbed as a teenager in his native Australia and established numerous climbs on the rocks there. Moving to the United States, he made the first ascents of Lost in America and Aurora, two big-wall climbs on Yosemite's El Capitan. He has made a number of significant and serious ascents in the Himalaya, including Shivling, Broad Peak (of which he writes below), Lobsang Spire, Gasherbrum IV, Trango Tower, and K2.

Greg is an excellent writer, contributing to various magazines and publications. The piece he has chosen speaks of how deadly the Himalaya can be.

On Broad Peak

"On Broad Peak" is a story that has already appeared in several publications, but I think it is one of my best.

GREG CHILD

We were stepping over yak dung in the streets of Askole that summer of 1983, trying to act as inconspicuous as a pair of Westerners can in this village of mud-walled houses and warrens that treads a line someplace between now and the Stone Age. Neither Pete Thexton nor I was having much success in photographing the brightly dressed, goiter-ridden local ladies. Like startled cattle, they would run from us down alleyways or giggle and chatter behind shuttered windows. The few we did aim our lenses at screeched and threw themselves down in the gray dust, covering themselves with their many layers of ragged dress.

An open window invited us to peer into someone's home. Through the dust motes that eternally rise from these earthen floors we could see the straw bedding and blackened pots around a blacker fireplace. A goatskin sack hung on the wall, as did a few pictures. One was a charcoal drawing of a helicopter, that mysterious beast that sometimes hovers up the valley of the Braldu. The second was a poster of Bhutto, the ex-president of Pakistan, ousted and eventually executed by General Zia. In the corner of Bhutto's portrait a candle, freshly extinguished, symbolically wafted its last puff of smoke. Above both of these presided a photograph of the Ayatollah Khomeini, his cheerless countenance seeming to stare through the dim, dusty light and directly into our eyes.

In this almost lawless frontier of Pakistan it is odd to see a portrait of a past leader but not surprising to see the face of Islamic fundamentalism. While politics means little to the Balti, Islam is everything. Tied to the land as they are in this desolate place, perhaps a notion of God is all that they have. Of Bhutto, our liaison officer says evil genius. Of Khomeini, evil idiot.

We turned to the street again and soon confronted another cluster of women, threshing a heap of grain with green branches. Poised for purdah, they seemed ready to bolt, but Pete had another strategy. He emptied a bottle of bright red multivitamins onto the palm of his outstretched hand. The women inched closer and with doe-eyed temerity submitted to our cameras, gently taking the magic medicine from Pete's hand as if it were diamonds.

As doctor of the expedition, Pete's was the face that all the villagers knew. At each village along the approach he would no sooner arrive than the sick and ailing would mill around him, as if an Identikit picture had preceded him. To these people medicine was more magic than anything else, and Pete was held in particular reverence. Each night he would spend a couple of hours doing what he could, even making house calls when asked. To us, nothing could have seemed more unlikely than hiking a long day in hundred-degree heat and finishing the day's consultations with a candlelit gynecological examination of a Balti woman in her dusty home, with children, chickens, and husband gathered around. But to Pete it was just another curious experience for a doctor in the Third World.

"If there is such a thing as reincarnation," I remarked, "and your past deeds are accountable, and you were to find yourself reborn into a place like this, then you could say with a fair degree of certainty that you had previously blown it."

"One could do worse," Pete replied.

I found it hard to imagine a station in life much more difficult than this, save for such hells as warfare or prison, which man contrives for his own kind for the sole purpose of misery. Pressed, Pete elaborated.

"Well, you could come back as an Askole chicken, for instance," and he pointed to a brood of bedraggled and scrawny birds rooting about in the gray muck of a culvert.

That fate, we agreed, must be reserved for the really bad eggs of society.

A month later, after our twelve-member expedition had marched to the end of a buckling swell of ice called the Baltoro Glacier, we divided into smaller teams and set off to climb the west face of Broad Peak, a 26,400-foot mountain with a summit that rose 10,000 feet above our base camp. Just outside base camp, as we walked toward Broad Peak, Pete and I came to a zone of crevasses covered by a thin layer of snow. I poked my ice ax into a suspect snowpatch to test its strength. The very moment I assured Pete it was safe to cross it, the surface gave way and I dropped into a crevasse. I felt the foolish surprise one would feel standing on a glass-topped table that had suddenly shattered. More surprising was that the crevasse had a false floor and I had stopped just a few feet down.

"Crevasse," I stated in the quiet that follows smashed mirrors and glassware.

"Thought I'd lost you already," Pete said as I extricated myself. Then he added, "You'll be pleased to know you've got an audience." Some trekkers on this well-traveled tract of wilderness had seen the whole display from their camp a few hundred feet away.

"Don't worry," he said with a grin, "no one from our camp saw it."

The sun was setting on one of those rare Karakoram days when there is not a breath of wind from glacier to summit, or any cloud or snow plume streaming from the giants. The rock on nearby K2 took on an orange glow.

By the time we were in the first couloirs of Broad Peak it was night. The snow was firm underfoot, and shortly the full moon rounded the south flank and doused the west face with bright light. We reached 19,000 feet, rested a while, and then carried on in the moonlight.

Step after step, breath after breath, every hour the atmosphere became just a little thinner. Behind us the first hint of dawn was turning the horizon every shade of blue imaginable, while the moon sat great and white, refusing to evaporate. All the mountains glowed, every minute changing color like chameleons.

Daylight revealed relics of other expeditions: shredded tents, bits of fixed rope, an old oxygen cylinder. The path was already pitted with the tracks of four members of our group above. I briefly pretended to myself that I was following the tracks of Hermann Buhl back in 1957, the year of his first ascent of this, the twelfth-highest mountain on earth. Fifty-seven was also the year of my birth, and the year Buhl died while climbing on Chogolisa, a snowy pyramid that lay to my right.

At about 20,500 feet we met Alan Rouse, Andy Parkin, Roger Baxter-Jones, and the Frenchman Jean Affanassieff, the four members of our expedition who'd set off up Broad Peak a day before Pete and me. Returning from their ascent of the previous day, they looked tired. Alan told of the damnably long ridge at the end of the climb and of the windless hour they'd sat on the summit.

We reached 21,000 feet an hour after passing our four friends and fell into a deep sleep inside the tiny tent we pitched on a small clearing in the snow. Doug Scott and Steve Sustad— two others of our group—caught up to us in the early afternoon and shared the same camp. Our tired minds were alive with fantastic dreams, and as we four set off together the next morning we compared the places these dreams had taken us.

At 22,800 feet we rested again. After rehydrating ourselves with cups of tea brewed over a small gas stove, we set out just as Don Whillans and the Pakistani climber Gohar Shar—the final members of our expedition—arrived. Those two bivied here while we climbed higher, gaining height for the next day's summit push.

Pete and I pitched a tent beneath a small ice cliff at about 24,500 feet, and Doug and Steve bivied 400 feet above it. It was late into the night before we finished melting snow to drink, and even then we felt we could have drunk a gallon more.

During the night the altitude crept into our heads, and by morning it was bashing away from the inside. We'd chosen a very high spot to bivy—the highest I'd ever climbed. Waking was a long and difficult process. While brewing tea I heard Pete mumbling in his sleep.

"What about this rope then?" he asked.

"Rope? Our rope is in the pack," I answered.

"Noooo, not that rope," he chided.

"Then what rope?"

"This rope we are tied to."

"We're not tied in, Pete. We're in the tent, on Broad Peak."

"Noooo, you don't understand," he said, and I began to feel like a thick-headed schoolboy giving all the wrong answers. I plied him for more clues to his sleepy riddle and got this:

"It's the rope that all of us are tied to."

"Fixed rope?"

"Noooo," he whined.

"Umbilical cord?" Any wild guess now.

"Noooo!"

"Then you must be speaking of a metaphysical rope, eh, one that everyone is tied to but no one is tied to?"

But before I got an answer to this, the smell of sweet tea had woken him and we were trying to force breakfast down our throats. A few aspirin later we were moving.

A short step of vertical ice to round a serac got our blood flowing. Doug and Steve were already close to the snowy notch that divided the rocky cappings of the central summit and main summit of Broad Peak when I caught sight of them. By the time we surmounted the steepish final chimney to the col, at just under 8,000 meters, a strong wind was blowing. Suddenly we could see into China, where the wind was coming from. Rust-colored peaks and valleys contrasted sharply with the blinding white of the Godwin-Austen Glacier.

On the final ridge to the summit—a rise of 400 feet but a length of a quarter mile—lay the hardest climbing yet: endless short steps of steep snow interspersed with rock. At perhaps 1:00 or 2:00 P.M. Doug and Steve passed us on their return from the summit. "It's even windier and colder up there, youth," Doug said, "and the top is two hours away at the rate you're moving."

Moving at this altitude was like wading through treacle. I became aware of a peculiar sense of disassociation with myself in which I felt as if part of me was external to my body and looking on. I felt this most acutely when setting up belays or making a difficult move; it felt like having someone peering over my shoulder keeping an eye on me, or as if I had a second, invisible head on my shoulders.

We went on for another hour to a dome of snow and cornices, where we rested. The sense of disassociation had begun to be punctuated by feelings of total absence, momentary blackouts, when neither I nor the guy over my shoulder seemed to be around. I would wake from these blackouts a few paces beyond where they had struck me, which led to a concern about stepping off the narrow ridge. "Like a dream," I murmured to Pete, but the wind snatched my words before he heard them.

Ahead, the ridge dipped down and curved left in a long, even slope to the summit, perhaps a half-hour trudge away, yet just twenty vertical feet higher. But here my fears about what was happening to me doubled. A vicious headache gripped me, and a tingling in my arms grew so intense that my fingers curled tightly into a fist, making it hard to hold on to my ice ax. To articulate this to Pete was difficult, as speech and thought seemed to have no link in my mind; in short, I didn't know what was going on.

Exhaustion I can accept, and given that alone I might have crawled to the summit; but something alien was going on within me, and I wasn't prepared to push my luck with it. I got it out that I wanted down. Pete knelt beside me, tried to talk me into going on, and his ever-present determination nearly got me going. There is a state of mind that sometimes infests climbers in which a particular goal achieves a significance beyond anything that the future may hold. For a few minutes or hours one casts aside all that has previously been held as worth living for, and one's focus falls on one risky move or stretch of ground, which becomes the only thing that matters. This state of mind is what is both fantastic and reckless about the game. Since everything is at stake in these moments, one had better be sure to recognize them and have no illusions about what lies on the other side of luck. This was one of those times. I had to weigh what was important and what was most important.

"It'd be nice to reach the top, you and I," Pete said. And so it would have, to stand up there with this man who had become such a strong friend in such a short time.

"Didn't you once say that summits are important?" Those were my words he was throwing back at me, shouting above the wind and his own breathlessness. Something I'd said a few weeks before on a granite spire called Lobsang Spire. I'd said it to encourage us when the rock turned blank and it looked like drilling bolts into the cliff—a tiresome process—was necessary to get up. I struggled to compose an intelligible sentence.

"Only important when you're in control. . . . Lost control. . . . Too high, too fast."

Pete nodded. I could see that he was feeling the strain too. We just got up and began the long path down. When I looked toward those red hills in China, I saw they were now covered in cotton wool clouds that lapped at Broad Peak's east face. We were so far above them. In two and a half days we had gone from 16,100 feet to 26,250 feet. It was the limit of what our bodies could do.

Three hundred feet below our high point I blacked out for twenty minutes. I woke momentarily during this period, trying to force myself awake, and recall seeing Pete next to me, observing my state, as a good doctor should. When I regained control of myself, Pete put a brew of grape drink into my hands. I drank it down, then promptly threw it up.

"See. . . . Told you I was . . . sick." The purple stain I had made in the snow formed intricate arabesque designs that grew onto the snow crystals glinting in the afternoon light. Hallucinations.

Once we were moving I began to improve, when suddenly something else happened. Pete appeared over a crest, lagging on the end of the rope. He took short steps and looked stressed. Speaking in a slow whisper, he told me he suddenly couldn't breathe, as if his diaphragm had collapsed. His lips were blue, a sign of oxygen starvation. We had to get down, and fast, but a snail's pace was the best he could manage in this thin soup of air.

At perhaps seven in the evening we reached the col and rappelled 60 feet to the start of the snow. Wind had covered any sign of our tracks. Dragging the rope behind me, I began plunge-stepping down, making tracks for Pete. After 400 feet I turned and saw that he had barely moved. By the time I crawled back up to him through the soft snow, it was dark. He had his headlamp on, shining out into the windy night. When I turned to the glacier I could see a light shining back from base camp. It was Pete's girlfriend, Beth, giving the 8:00 P.M. signal, and Pete was returning it.

Conversation was superfluous. We knew that we were going to be on the go all night, very high, and the wind was rising. I tied the rope around Pete and began roping him down, length after length, till his strength began to ebb; then I began to talk him down, ordering and cajoling every step out of him. At about 10:00 P.M. he slumped in the snow and whispered that he could no longer see. So I guided him by direction, telling him to traverse 45 degrees right, or straight down. With no tracks it was all instinct anyway, and the bastard moon shone everywhere but on the upper slopes of Broad Peak. And all the time, wind and spindrift blew.

Somewhere near was the band of 60-foot ice cliffs we'd surmounted that morning. We had to find the low spot in them, but where that was . . . was anybody's guess. Pete had gotten too weak to walk, so I was dragging and carrying him and both packs. The sensation of being outside myself was more prevalent than ever, my watcher checking every ice ax belay and every decision. He must have lent a hand in carrying Pete too.

At some point in this nightmare, I recalled reading about the first ascent of Broad Peak's central summit, made by a Polish team who were caught in a storm on the descent. The account, recorded in a climbing magazine, described what ensued as a "struggle for survival." Accompanying this story was a photo of Broad Peak, littered with crosses where four men had perished from falls and from the biting blizzard winds. Those crosses were now underfoot. I felt as if the ghosts of history watched in the shadows.

Around the lip of the seracs the angle steepened. Pete and I linked arms and shuffled along in the dark to what I hoped was the low spot. The wind howled. It became too steep to blunder about as we were, so I began making 20-foot leads, shoving my ax into the soft snow and pulling Pete in to me. At the last belay he let go of everything and swung down to the lip of the serac. The shaft of my ax dropped alarmingly. I lost my cool and yelled a mouthful of curses at him as I hauled him back up.

"Sorry," he whispered calmly. Throughout this ordeal he had stayed composed, seemingly reserving his energy for matters of survival, rather than letting fear or emotion take hold. I clipped him to his ax and wrapped his arms around it.

"Just don't lose it now, brother. Please."

The wind seemed to attack with unprecedented malice, burning our faces with thick clouds of spindrift. Somewhere nearby in the black at the bottom of this serac was a tent, and if things had gone as planned, Don and Gohar were in it. I called till my throat was raw and shoved my ax into the snow as deep as it would go to lower Pete.

So much was confusion in the minute it took to lower him. Pete was so disoriented that he couldn't tell where he was, I was blinded by spindrift, and the ax was again shifting and coming out of the snow. I wrapped the rope around my arm to distribute some of the weight while pushing the ax in with my knee. There was no way of telling if Pete was down, but he came to a stop anyway. I rappelled off my second, shorter tool, moving quickly before it slid out. Pete could barely move. We again linked arms to negotiate some broken ground and then reverted to piggybacking, when a light suddenly appeared.

"We've got a sick man here, Don," I called to the bobbing light. Pete crawled a few feet along a crest and then stopped totally. Gohar arrived, himself groggy, awakened from a deep sleep. While I sat Pete on my shoulders and slid us down the last 50 feet to the tent, Gohar belayed us with a rope. At the bottom, Don helped drag Pete into the tent, where we began warming and rehydrating him. It was 2:00 A.M. We'd been moving for twenty-two hours.

All of us lay crammed in together in the quiet of the tent. It took a long time for feeling to return to my hands and feet, and Pete's were ice cold but remarkably not frostbitten. Warm liquid seemed to perk him up.

"How are you, Gregor?" he asked, his voice regaining its familiar, impish tone.

"Done in. Rest a couple hours till dawn; then we'll head on down." My eyelids closed under the weight of exhaustion, and I dreamed of grassy places.

Those were the last words that we spoke together. At dawn Pete awoke to ask Gohar for water. A few minutes later Gohar pressed a cup of warm liquid to his lips, but Pete would not drink it. Don and Gohar looked at each other for a few seconds, then called me. "Dead," they were saying. But no one in my dreams was dead. We were making it.

Then sense prevailed like a sledgehammer. I tried to force life into my friend, through his mouth, with mine, breathing my own thin and tired air into him. His lungs gurgled loudly—pulmonary edema. And we pressed our palms against his chest to squeeze a beat out of his heart, but he would have none of it. He would only lie there with an expression of sublime rest on his face, as if dreaming the same dream I had.

We sat in silence for a while, our heads full of sad thoughts. Suddenly I hated the mountain. Over and over I muttered, "It's not worth it," till I couldn't talk for the tears. And what about the people below and at home who loved him, what about them? Outside the day was clear and calm, the Karakoram ablaze with light.

"Notice how the wind suddenly dropped?" asked Don. "Not a breath. It's always the same when death is about, always a lot of noise and wind, but as soon as it gets what it's after, it quiets down. I've seen it before and it's always the same."

I'm still thinking about that one, still wondering.

The wind rose up again a few minutes later, even stronger than before, and threatened to tear the tent apart with its claws, like some predator searching for us. I knelt beside Pete, incredulous and oblivious. Gohar took my arm and with a look of natural fear said, "Greg Sahib, we must go." We left everything as it was, zipped the door shut, said good-bye in our different ways and turned into the maelstrom. It was a long descent, every step full of a great sense of loss, and perhaps a foolish feeling of guilt at having to leave our friend as we did.

But the snow would soon settle over him and set him firm as earth. The snowfield would inch inexorably toward the ice cliffs and peel away in bursts of avalanche to the glacier, which would carry him within it to the fast-flowing Braldu River. His journey would outlive us, and no ashes could be scattered more thoroughly nor a monument exist more lasting than Broad Peak.

The terminus of the Baltoro is a huge black tongue of rubble and ice that lolls rudely across the breadth of the valley and gives birth to the gray Braldu River. I had left the expedition early with Don to get word to Pete's family. As we stepped off the end of the glacier I began to feel like some harbinger of terrible news, and my body felt wrought and knotted, like some piece of gristle that the glacier had spat out, indigestible and bitter.

Ahead lay the rotting villages of Askole, Chongo, and Chokpo, places lifted from the pages of some Graham Greene tale of Third World purgatory. Behind, the others had chosen to stay and attempt K2. All along our way were reminders of Pete: places where he had sat and gazed at the mountains; boulders at Urdokas that we had tiptoed upon and sheltered beneath.

Though I had only known Pete for the span of this expedition, we had become fast friends, seeing the same joke in this or that, moving at the same speed in the hills, and talking, always talking. Javid, our Pakistani liaison officer, between his sobs, said that according to his religion every move that we make, from beginning to end, is predestined by a higher force. But others would talk about the randomness of death, its fickle whims and unpredictable chaos. All that was sure to me at that time was a nagging uneasiness in the pit of my stomach and a certainty that it is just as poignant and terrible to lose a new friend as to lose an old one.

Gray skies followed us for days, sweeping us out of the mountains, disguising the fact that they were there at all. No last glimpses of the Karakoram, no summits through the clouds, nothing to tempt us. Good. We walked fast. There was no reason to turn around. Nothing to look back on.

MARK SYNNOTT

Mark Synnott on Shipton Spire.

Mark Synnott has climbed more than fifty big walls worldwide, including major first ascents in Baffin Island, the Karakoram, Patagonia, and the Bugaboos. One of the first climbers to explore Baffin Island's remote east coast, Synnott has initiated four big-wall first ascents there, including a grade VII on the 4,700-foot north face of Polar Sun Spire. Most recently, Synnott made the first ascent of the northwest face of Great Trango Tower in Pakistan with Alex Lowe and Jared Ogden. The forty-four-pitch big-wall climb was over 5,500 feet tall and topped at 20,500 feet. It stands as perhaps the tallest big wall ever climbed. In 1997, with Jared Ogden, Synnott completed a grade VII first ascent on Pakistan's 19,700-foot Shipton Spire—only the second climb of this difficult peak. The following winter in Patagonia, Synnott and Kevin Thaw ascended Cerro Torre's Compressor Route in a twenty-seven-hour push.

Closer to home, Synnott pioneered a grade VI in the Bugaboos in 1994 and has done more than twenty-five big-wall climbs in Yosemite. He currently holds the record for the fastest ascent of El Capitan's Lost in America, which he completed in just over twenty-four hours. His big-wall activity has also been concentrated in Colorado's Black Canyon, where he made the second ascent in winter of Paint It Black and the first winter ascent of the Painted Wall by the Dragon route.

In the mixed realm, he recently completed the second ascent of Cold, Cold World, one of the hardest mixed routes in New England. When he's not on a wall, Synnott, a contributing editor to *Climbing* magazine, works as a freelance photojournalist and is a member of the North Face Climbing Team.

The Maestri Enigma

When I was a young climber, there were mountains that caught my imagination and inspired me to become a better climber. For some reason I was not drawn to Everest or other lofty Himalayan peaks. Instead, I found myself dreaming of sheer-walled rock spires. The bigger, steeper, and more remote, the better. Of the world's most stunning rock spires, none is more elegant or inaccessible than Cerro Torre. I've had a picture of it since high school that I always pin up where I can constantly look at it and dream about one day standing on top. In 1998, after years of training on the big walls of Yosemite, Baffin Island, and the Baltoro Glacier, I decided I was finally ready.

You can't follow in Cesare Maestri's footsteps without getting sucked into the story of his epic and controversial first ascent of the peak. I was inspired to climb this peak, but I also felt compelled to learn as much as possible about Maestri. That year, we had planned to attempt the second ascent of the Maestri-Egger route on the Torre's north face. We found that the route climbs directly beneath a massive mushroom of snow that consistently scours the face. We didn't want to meet the same fate as Egger, so instead we chose the technically easier and less committing Southeast Ridge (which incidentally was also first ascended by Maestri). Strictly speaking, I still haven't climbed the peak. My partner and I were turned back about 30 feet below the true summit by an overhanging mushroom of snow. Next year I plan to return. Like Maestri, I have an obsession with this peak.

MARK SYNNOTT

[Forty years after the controversial first ascent of Cerro Torre, the question remains: Was this the greatest climb of all time or just an elaborate hoax?—Ed.]

At a picnic table outside his mountain shop in the Brenta Dolomites, Cesare Maestri crosses his hands and lets a wry smile crack his lips: "I have a dream," he says. "In my dream, a big earthquake hits the Torre, breaking it into millions of

161

pieces." Maestri chuckles, relishing the image of Cerro Torre laid flat against the pampas. Like Captain Ahab, who also had a famous nemesis, Maestri, sixty-nine, has paid a bitter price for an obsession. The mountain has cost him his reputation and the life of his friend and partner, Toni Egger. Had Egger lived to substantiate Maestri's story, the first ascent of Cerro Torre in 1959 could have gone down in history as the climb of the century.

The story goes that on the evening of February 1, 1959, after six grueling days of fighting their way up and then down the north face of Cerro Torre, Maestri and Toni Egger were separated by only 300 feet from their fixed lines leading to the glacier. But with darkness nearly upon them, they would have to spend one last night on the mountain. Egger asked Maestri to lower him in search of a sheltered ledge. Suddenly a huge avalanche burst out of the clouds, "with a whistle of death," as Maestri later described it. Egger tried to scramble back to the belay, but the massive slide severed the rope and swept him away. The camera and all film were also lost in the avalanche.

Maestri returned to Italy to find himself a national hero. The climbing community readily accepted his word as to the first ascent of Cerro Torre. Fitzroy first ascensionist Lionel Terray even called it "the greatest climbing feat of all time." Indeed, rising more than 5,000 feet from the edge of the continental ice cap, and subject to the unobstructed fury of the Patagonian tempests, Cerro Torre was considered an impossible prize to mountaineers in the 1950s. To the north, south, east, and west, this needlelike tower was defended by ice-encrusted walls bigger than El Capitan.

Maestri was invited to countless press conferences, parties, and civic receptions. He also published lavish magazine spreads and wrote a very popular book called *Climbing Is My Job*. He made a respectable living from his postclimb fame.

Skepticism did not publicly surface until more than ten years after the ascent, when Maestri's chief rival, fellow Italian Carlo

Mauri, published a magazine article in which he referred to Cerro Torre as unclimbed. Mauri had recently returned from a second failed attempt to climb the peak by its west face and had been beaten so badly that he vowed never to return. Mauri wrote: "The mountaineer who succeeds in photographing the ice-cream-like formations of the summit will be able to claim truthfully that he has gone beyond the limits of *extremement difficile.*" He never explicitly mentioned the Maestri-Egger route, but his article opened the door for other skeptics.

Ken Wilson, editor of Britain's *Mountain* magazine from 1968 to 1978, was one of the first to pick up on Mauri's cue. For the past thirty years, Wilson has been the driving force behind the Cerro Torre controversy. He has written or published most of the articles on the subject, all of which are suspicious of Maestri's claims. Wilson's biggest criticism is that Maestri has declined to discuss, in anything resembling proper detail, his "greatest" climb. "If you had done the hardest climb in the world," he asks, "wouldn't you want to talk about it? Why is it that Maestri refuses to discuss the 1959 climb? The fact that he refuses to answer any questions about 1959 damns him to utter darkness. He has destroyed the historical record." Wilson doesn't believe that Maestri's reticence is justified by hurt pride or a reluctance to revisit trauma, explanations put forth by some of Maestri's supporters. He notes four separate interviews when Maestri avoided or attempted to avoid discussion of the 1959 climb.

When I interviewed Maestri in Madonna di Campiglio in September 1998, he acted as if the 1959 climb had never occurred. Beforehand I had been warned by his friends to avoid the subject. In fairness to Maestri, we have to consider the detailed reports he has already published in Italy. In a 1994 article in *Mountain Review*, even Wilson acknowledges: "The 1959 climb was accompanied by a very full expedition report, a technical route description, and several magazine articles. If there is a hoax or conspiracy it is a very elaborate one indeed, but then again, past and present incidents show that hoaxes can be extremely cunning."

It is curious then, that during our meeting Maestri was so eager to discuss his other controversial ascent of Cerro Torre— the 1971 Compressor Route. This notorious ascent, on which Maestri used a gasoline-powered compressor to drill more than 350 bolts, has also met with criticism because of the excessive drilling and his choice to forgo climbing the summit mushroom.

And yet Maestri spent most of our two-hour interview happily discussing the particulars of this climb. "Our winter attempt of Cerro Torre's Southeast Ridge was one of the greatest climbs of all time," he said through an interpreter. "It is not valid that I am known only for using the compressor." Yet the 1959 climb would have been in an entirely different league, light years beyond the Compressor Route in terms of difficulty and style. Why is he not more proud of it? This inconsistency on the part of Maestri has certainly raised eyebrows, even among his supporters.

To date, nearly twenty separate attempts have been made to repeat the north face of Cerro Torre—no one has even come close. Until recently, vestiges of the Maestri-Egger route had not been found higher than 1,000 feet above the glacier, and this led to further doubts. But after thirty years of intense investigation, there is still no hard evidence to suggest the climb is or isn't a hoax. And the only new evidence that has surfaced supports Maestri.

Last November, during an attempt to climb a new route on the 5,000-foot north face, the Italian Patagonia veterans Maurizio Giarolli and Elio Orlandi purportedly found one of Maestri's rap stations just below the English Dihedral—2,500 feet up the wall and just below the Col of Conquest. The handmade piton that they brought home is reportedly from Maestri's era, and the strands of rope tied through it match the cord found with Egger's body, which was discovered in 1976. The question of how this relic went undetected for so many years is still a mystery, but if it is authentic it raises the possibility that more evidence of the ascent may be unearthed in the future.

On a large scale, the Maestri controversy forces us to question how to treat the word and honor of a mountaineer. Should we heed Wilson, who claims it's the responsibility of every magazine editor to question the veracity of ascents? Or does mountaineering still function within an honor system? A closer look at the Maestri controversy may help you decide.

THE SPIDER OF THE DOLOMITES

Born in 1929 in Trento, Italy, Cesare Maestri as a child lived an itinerant and bohemian lifestyle. His father ran a traveling theater. His mother, an impulsive and deeply religious woman, died when he was seven years old. In 1943 the Germans invaded Italy, and Maestri watched them burn entire villages. When they took over Trento, Cesare's father became an enemy of the state for his involvement with the Italian underground during World War I. Sentenced to death, he fled Trento with Maestri and his sister and wandered the plains around Bologna for almost a year. When young Cesare returned to Trento, he immediately joined the Communist Party, because it was the strongest force opposing the Germans. Joining the Italian underground himself, he soon developed an anarchistic political ideology, which he exercised by occasionally shooting at the Germans. When the war ended, his father convinced him to begin university studies in Rome. He made it through two years before escaping his books to search for something more exciting and dangerous.

Mountaineering became the perfect avenue for Maestri to test the toughness he had developed during the war. He made his first climb in 1946 and immediately decided that it was his calling in life. "I designated myself *an athlete who practiced the sport of climbing*," Maestri later said in a 1973 interview with Ken Wilson. "I followed a rigorous diet, went to bed at 8:00

P.M., and exercised the whole time, whatever I was doing. Even when I made love to a girl, I did it in a press-up position to strengthen my arms."

By his midtwenties, Maestri was making a name for himself in the Dolomites as a bold free soloist (long before the days of rock shoes and chalk). A self-proclaimed antitraditionalist, Maestri saw climbing as a way of life and a means for expressing his strong personality. Proud, opinionated, hungry for recognition, Maestri was not a particularly popular figure among Italy's top climbers, and this may have had some influence on his development as a soloist. When Maestri did team up for a climb, it was almost always with a subordinate who would strictly follow Maestri's lead. His rule was that no one led but himself, and if you didn't like it, he'd find someone else—or solo. He first made headlines after free soloing the Solleder Route on the Civetta, a 1,300-meter 5.9 that is still considered a committing ascent due to the difficulty of retreating—even with a rope. His ascent of the Solda Route was the first free solo of the 3,000-foot limestone Marmolada—the biggest cliff in the Dolomites, often likened to El Capitan. On the 1,100-foot southeast face of Cima D'Ambiez in Maestri's home turf in the Brenta, he became the first person to free solo up (and down) a grade VI (5.10).

A handsome, barrel-chested man with gleaming blue eyes and an engaging smile, Maestri sought out and thrived in the limelight. After an article in the Italian press dubbed him "the Spider of the Dolomites," Maestri became increasingly well known for his rock-climbing accomplishments. His skills as both a climber and a shrewd self-promoter helped him quickly realize his goal of becoming one of the first professional climbers in Europe. He was one of the first climbing superstars in Italy, a country in which mountain climbing is revered like baseball is in the United States.

While Maestri was making a name for himself in Europe, Patagonia was also making headlines, with Lionel Terray and

Guido Magnone's 1953 first ascent of Fitzroy, the region's tallest peak (11,355 feet). From their awe-inspiring perspective of Cerro Torre from the summit, Terray commented, "Now there's a peak worth risking one's neck for." Cesarino Fava, an Italian living in Argentina at the time, was one of the few climbers besides the Fitzroy ascensionists who had actually laid eyes on Cerro Torre. An accomplished climber with experience in both the Andes and the Alps, Fava had never seen a mountain as awesome or beautiful. But he suffered from the handicap of having no feet, which he had lost to frostbite on Aconcagua in 1950. Fava had spent three days trying to bring down a group of Americans who had been deserted by their guide, high on the peak in a full-blown storm. The Americans didn't make it, and Fava, who barely did, ended up in a crude hospital with severe frostbite on both feet. The doctor, not realizing that Fava's feet were alive under a layer of blackened skin, amputated them both one evening without Fava's consent.

Nonetheless, Fava was eager to give Cerro Torre a try, provided he could ally himself with an exceptionally gifted partner. The Spider of the Dolomites, whom he knew only by reputation, seemed the perfect candidate.

In 1953, he posted a letter from Argentina addressed only to: The Spider of the Dolomites, Trento, Italy. The letter eloquently set forth the challenge of the Torre. It eventually found its way into Maestri's hands. Maestri's obsession with Cerro Torre began.

The Rivalry: East versus West

After accepting Fava's invitation, Maestri began organizing an expedition under the leadership of Bruno Detassis, president of the Trento chapter of the Italian Alpine Club. Among the Italian climbing community, Terray and Magnone's first ascent of Fitzroy had created a frenzy of interest in Patagonia. Maestri's archrivals, Walter Bonatti and Carlo Mauri, were also planning to attempt Cerro Torre the same season. Bonatti was from Milan, Italy's financial capital, and Mauri was from Lecco, a wealthy town on the banks of Lake Como and home to the famous Lecco Spiders climbing club. The Dolomite crew, of which Maestri was part, and the Lecco Spiders had long been rivals. Although the two groups lived relatively near each other in northern Italy, they were culturally and economically worlds apart. Mountain towns like Trento, Maestri and his cohorts' home base, had little industrial development before they became hubs for tourism, so their economy was quite depressed compared with places like Milan and Lecco. What's more, the climbers from the two expeditions did not often mix, because they practiced their craft in different mountain ranges. The Lecco climbers usually traveled to the granite ranges of the western Alps, where they developed into masterful ice climbers. The Dolomite climbers practiced exclusively in their home range of limestone cliffs and spires, where the focus was more on hard free and aid climbing.

The national Italian Alpine Club offered its official stamp of approval and a hefty sponsorship to Bonatti's expedition. The sponsorship was probably offered to Bonatti as a form of payback for his role during the first Italian ascent of K2 in 1954. Bonatti, who was one of the strongest members of the team, carried oxygen for the successful summit climbers but was forbidden by the team's leader from going to the top himself. After careful study of Cerro Torre photos, Bonatti and Mauri decided that the easiest route existed on its remote and exposed, but heavily iced, west face. Accompanied by a small support team, Bonatti and Mauri flew to southern Argentina while their rivals, who were on a tighter budget, went by boat. Bonatti and Mauri's team arrived in Patagonia late in 1957 and immediately set forth across the continental ice cap for the 40-mile approach to the west side of the Torre.

After establishing a spacious snow cave for base camp, Bonatti and Mauri climbed straightforward snow and ice slopes to a col separating Cerro Torre from the Cerro Adela massif. Above the col, vertical walls covered in a frosting of unconsolidated sugar snow halted their progress 1,600 feet short of the summit. They named their high point the Col of Hope, planning to return for a rematch the following season.

Meanwhile, Maestri's crew had set up camp in the beech forest below the Torre Glacier, scheming to tackle the mountain from its steeper but relatively dry and sheltered east side. The team's leader, Bruno Detassis, was taken aback when the spire finally appeared out of the clouds. After one look he called the expedition off. Maestri and Fava scouted the approach and possible bivy sites but never set foot on the mountain.

The only time the climbers of the separate expeditions even saw each other occurred during a simultaneous attempt to make the first ascent of Cerro Adela. Climbing from the opposite side of the peak, Maestri spotted Bonatti and Mauri near the summit but was unable to overtake them. When Maestri got to the top, he says in a *Mountain* article, "We found the snow all yellow where they had pissed. That was their greeting to us."

1959: THE FIRST ASCENT OF CERRO TORRE

During the 1958 expedition Maestri also made an aerial reconnaissance of the peak and determined that a route up the north face was feasible, noting that the col between Cerro Torre and its neighboring tower (later named Torre Egger) would be a perfect staging point for a summit push. Maestri and Fava had become good friends during the expedition and agreed to return the following season. Knowing how much ice climbing the ascent would involve, and realistic about his own limited skills with this medium, Maestri began searching for a third team member. He soon found what he was looking for in a short, powerful young Austrian named Toni Egger. A superb and widely recognized ice climber, Egger was equally well versed on rock. He had distinguished himself with many difficult ascents in the Alps and also an early ascent of the east face of Jirishanca in Peru. Blond and blue-eyed, Egger was a good-looking fellow, a ladies' man like Maestri.

After meeting briefly at the Lavaredo hut in the Dolomites, Egger and Maestri immediately hit it off—here was one of the few climbers in Europe whom Maestri could respect as an equal.

Maestri and Egger met Fava in Buenos Aires in December 1958 (Bonatti and Mauri had hoped to go back the same year, but their plans fell through). They had planned to fly to Patagonia from there with the Argentine air force, but Maestri had somehow lost the letter from the Italian ambassador asking for this favor. Instead, he spent the money for his airfare home to hire a lorry for the seven-day journey to Chalten (the closest village to Cerro Torre and Fitzroy). Early on in the expedition Egger had an infected cut on his foot, so Maestri and Fava tackled the job of ferrying loads to the base. Lacking feet, Fava had a particularly tough time, but with an indomitable spirit he hobbled along with specially made boots over his stumps. In ten days they established and stocked camps 1, 2, and 3 and even fixed the first 450 feet of the route.

When Egger's foot improved, he and Maestri worked for another week fixing ropes on the initial 1,200-foot groove, which ended at the prominent Triangular Snowpatch. They got within a pitch of the snowfield before the weather deteriorated into a sustained blizzard that raged nonstop for the next ten days. When it finally cleared, the three climbers returned from Chalten to find all of their gear buried under meters of snow. After digging like dogs from sunup to sundown, they finally found their stash of one hundred pitons.

Maestri's written account of the claimed ascent, published shortly afterward in an Italian magazine, describes how the weather made a miraculous transformation on the morning of January 28. The three climbers agreed that this was the chance they had been waiting for. Loaded down with three fifty-pound rucksacks, they ascended their fixed lines to the Triangular

Snowpatch. Here Maestri had thought they would bivy, then fix more ropes above. But Egger insisted they could make the top in five or six days if they committed to a lightweight, Alpine-style push.

Egger's plan eventually won out, so they continued across the snowfield into an obvious crack system leading straight up. This crack system was really more of an iced-up gully-chimney, exposed to objective hazards but offering the trio rapid progress with crampons and ice axes. The crack eventually ended at the base of a gigantic dihedral cleaving the right side of the east face. To reach the col between Cerro Torre and Torre Egger, Maestri, Egger, and Fava began a long rising traverse along a ramp system running below the overhanging north pillar. These pitches were some of the hardest on the route so far, Maestri later said, but they dispatched them without too much trouble and reached the col by late afternoon. Maestri had previously named this place the Col of Conquest. ("In the mountains there is no such thing as hope, only the will to conquer. Hope is the weapon of the poor." Maestri's comment, which appeared first in an Italian magazine and was then translated into French and republished in *La Montagne*, was interpreted by most as a jab against Bonatti and Mauri's naming of the Col of Hope.)

To give the more highly skilled climbers the best possible chance at success, Fava decided to descend. In the following account, written only a few months afterward, Fava describes his impressions from the col: "Shut off to the south of the Torre and to the north by another no less imposing peak, this col is truly a cyclopic window. Facing us below is the immense sweep of the 'Hielo Continental,' a veritable sea of ice."

Maestri and Egger helped Fava back across the traverse, then Fava made a series of long rappels back to their fixed lines at the Triangular Snowpatch. Fava claims to have reached the glacier while "the topmost peak of Fitzroy was still golden with the last rays of the sun."

Amazingly, he had climbed and descended 3,000 feet of difficult big-wall terrain in approximately sixteen hours. The next day, Maestri and Egger awoke to cold but clear skies and immediately set to work on the ice sheet 350 feet to the left of the Northwest Ridge. Breaking his custom, Maestri asked Egger, who was the better ice climber, to go first. Except for when Maestri was learning, Egger is the only climber he ever followed. Maestri seconded each pitch with the heavier of their two packs, while Egger belayed him on a tight line.

"At each step, the whole crust made a dull noise like a low whistle," wrote Maestri in *La Montagne*. "It made cracking noises and split into large segments. The ice pegs went in like butter and gave us only an illusion of security. At each pitch we made a platform, so that we could dig through to the rock, where we found not the slightest trace of a crack; so we had to drill holes for expansion bolts, and each hole needed five hundred hammer blows."

They covered nearly 1,000 feet their first day above the col on a wall that averaged between 50 and 60 degrees. Maestri later attributed their efficiency to Egger's small stature and catlike quickness while scampering across the fragile crust, which varied from 10 inches to 3 feet thick.

On the third day, with Egger still in the lead, they followed the line of least resistance, mostly staying in ice gullies gouged by the wind. They used every trick they knew, which included Maestri taking the sharp end and tunneling through an overhang too unconsolidated to hold ice pegs. When the north face became increasingly steep, the route wandered across the Northwest Ridge onto the west face. In the evening they followed a series of couloirs leading directly to the huge overhangs of the summit mushroom.

They hollowed out a spacious ledge 500 feet below the top and unroped for the night.

The morning of January 30 dawned with a strong, warm wind, and Maestri's altimeter indicated a precipitous drop in pressure. Egger quickly led up the fluted ice face, finding that the cornices on the summit mushroom overhung every aspect but the north—a lucky break. Belayed to an ice ax on top of the mushroom, Maestri and Egger shared an embrace, then took several photos. They left their names written inside a tin can and stashed it in the snow. At 4:00 P.M. they rapped off "without the least bit of emotion and without the slightest trace of disgust or fear," according to Maestri.

Three rappels off ice bollards got them to the site of their previous bivouac, where they had left their packs. The unseasonably warm weather was causing the mountain to melt out from under them, and the ice crust, which had proved so handy on the ascent, was now threatening to pummel them. As the avalanches poured over them during the night, Egger commented, "Let's hope we don't die a white death."

In the morning they chose the wrong gully to descend, leading them directly down the north face. Not realizing their mistake until it was too late and knowing that reversing their line of ascent would be difficult at best, they continued down the north face in a diagonal, easterly direction. The wind was so fierce that normal abseils were impossible. Instead, Maestri lowered Egger on a double-carabiner brake, then Egger held the ends of the rope while Maestri rappelled. When the ice ended, they were forced to place bolts, laboriously drilling while hanging on the rope. After eleven rappels they found a sheltered bivouac under a small mushroom, where Maestri placed more bolts for their fifth night on the mountain.

By the next afternoon, they had finished rappelling the north face, joining their ascent line approximately halfway across the "great traverse" from the east face dihedral to the col. Their 200-meter rope had enabled them to rappel past the final overhanging section of the wall above the col. By now the mountain had come completely unglued, and ice chunks were raining out of the sky almost constantly. Not far above the start of their fixed ropes at the Triangular Snowpatch, Maestri found a small ledge and tried to convince Egger they should spend the night there. Egger felt this spot was too exposed and insisted Maestri lower him to look for a safer spot. That decision cost Egger his life. The avalanche that claimed him also swept away both rucksacks, so Maestri spent a grim night in the open, with no bivy gear.

In the morning, Maestri continued down with the tattered remains of their ropes, "like a condemned man, who, indifferent and worn out, goes forth to the execution chamber," wrote Maestri in *La Montagne*. Shortly above the glacier, he slipped on some verglas and fell the final few meters to the ground. He doesn't remember anything from this point on, but he must have staggered down the glacier to Camp 3. Fava found him on the afternoon of February 2, lying in the snow 300 yards from camp.

"I just jump for joy," Fava wrote a few months afterward. "Only three words escape through his teeth and the thick crust of ice on his beard: 'Toni, Toni, Toni.' Toni Egger, your name will, on the face of that impossible peak, remain engraved throughout time."

THE AFTERMATH: SKEPTICS AND SUPER SKEPTICS

Seventeen years later, in 1976, an American team consisting of Jim Donini, Jay Wilson, and John Bragg retraced Maestri's approximate line to the Col of Conquest on their way to making the first ascent of Torre Egger. They found relics of Maestri's team, including a small equipment stash and a rope clove hitched into an entire pitch of fixed pieces. Curiously, the remnants from the 1959 climb ended at a point just below the Triangular Snowpatch, only 1,000 feet above the glacier.

Ultimately, their findings split the doubters into two camps. In an article on the Maestri controversy published in *Mountain Review* (no. 9) in 1994, Mike Bearzi, an American who with Eric Winkelman made the first free ascent of Cerro Torre via its west face in 1986, called them "the skeptics and the super-skeptics." The skeptics didn't believe Maestri and Egger could have climbed from the Col of Conquest 2,500 feet to the summit in two and a half days. The super skeptics speculated that the entire climb was a hoax. Ken Wilson spearheaded the argument, focusing the discussion on whether Maestri, Egger, and Fava had even reached the col. He and others speculated that Egger may have died early on, somewhere below the Triangular Snowpatch, then Maestri and Fava hid out for a week in a cave on the glacier, where they concocted their story.

Even if you believe Maestri would have lied to advance his career, what motivation did Fava have for backing him up? Wilson, who maintains he has debunked no fewer than eight hoaxes in the British climbing community during his career as a magazine editor, simply refused to take the climbers at their word. He claims there is plenty of precedent: "I submit that there has never been any tradition in mountaineering of believing someone's word. Every ascent is in effect checked by somebody, at least subconsciously or subtly. As editors of magazines and journals, we should never accept anybody's word on its face value. There are people out there, dreamers, Walter Mitty types, who try to get away with the wildest claims."

Duane Raleigh, publisher and editor-in-chief of *Climbing*, disagrees: "Here we have a tradition of taking climbers at their word. We try to reflect the sentiments of our readers, and they still want to believe that climbers are inherently honorable. That's how it's always been, and that's how it will remain unless something changes drastically in the future. Almost all of us have gone out and done things that no one saw. I've done it, and I expect to be believed."

Wilson has since changed his mind about whether Maestri, Fava, and Egger reached the col. He personally interviewed Fava in 1994: "Although the super skeptics still believe the gear dump below the icefield marks the general high point," Wilson told me during a recent telephone conversation, "I think Fava is pretty convincing and [we can] place them on the col.

176 • Mark Synnott

The most likely scenario nowadays is that they put in a bloody good attempt."

So why did it take more than thirty-five years for Wilson to interview Fava?

When I interviewed Fava in the Dolomites in September 1998, Fava, clearly frustrated, asked, "How can Wilson really know what happened there if he never talked with us? How can he judge a climb from what somebody told him, and these guys haven't been on the actual climb? Well, sometimes inquisitors should be inquired about themselves."

In 1976, after he had written several articles on the subject, Wilson did write a letter to Fava asking for further details of the ascent to the col. Fava, feeling he had long been snubbed by Wilson, would not cooperate. He wrote back to Wilson: "On this whole quagmire of suspicion, ill faith, and speculation I have only one comment to make, that it is *shit*. Because that is what this whole damned business is about."

Even after the recent discovery of the rappel anchor by Giarolli, some experts on the Maestri controversy still have questions about apparent inconsistencies in Fava's account. The Italian Ermanno Salvaterra has been on nineteen expeditions to Patagonia, including two attempts to repeat the Maestri-Egger route. He has a house filled with notebooks, photos, and correspondence relating to the Maestri dispute. Salvaterra has been one of Maestri's most ardent supporters over the years, and until recently he has always been outspoken in Maestri's defense. Still, he's skeptical of how Fava could have climbed all the way to the col and then rapped back to the ground while the summit of Fitzroy was still in the sun. That's 3,000 feet of ascent and descent in about sixteen hours. Having covered this same stretch of ground himself, he finds it hard to believe that anyone, even today, could have gone up and down in one day. Jim Donini agrees.

In regards to the climbing above the col, Salvaterra has still more reservations: "How could Maestri have found 50- to 60-

degree ice climbing anywhere on the north face? This wall is closer to 75 degrees, and usually not completely covered in ice, even after a storm. I don't think anyone could climb it in two and a half days." This evaluation of the north face is also shared by Donini, who had studied it while climbing Torre Egger.

Despite the fact that it has been more than twenty years since his climb of Torre Egger, Donini's recollections of Cerro Torre's north face are clear: "Above the col, the north face is a typical granite big wall. There are beautiful diagonal corner systems leading into a section of weird and very difficult-looking ice formations. The wall is at least 75 degrees and would require a substantial amount of aid. It would be a beautiful climb, but very difficult and dangerous."

Unlike Wilson, Donini is still not convinced that Maestri, Egger, and Fava ever reached the col. He has always been troubled by Maestri's description of the "great traverse" from the east face to the col. Maestri's written account of the climb described this section as very difficult, whereas Donini says, "The traverse is by far the easiest section of the entire climb to the col—very, very easy climbing, totally at odds with what Maestri said." Donini is suspicious because he thinks Maestri's description sounds too much like how it appears from below. On the other hand, Giarolli climbed this same section of ground on his recent north face attempt and reported difficulties up to 5.10.

In 1994, during an eight-day Alpine-style ascent of Crystals in the Wind, a new route on Cerro Torre's west face, Giarolli gained his own insights into the possible line followed by Maestri and Egger above the col. He observed that the Northwest Ridge is much more heavily iced than the surrounding terrain, and it is also significantly lower angled. Crystals in the Wind reached a high point 700 feet below the summit, where it intersected with the Northwest Ridge (and presumably the Maestri-Egger route). From here, Elio Orlandi rapped 50 meters down the ridge and pendulumed around, searching for Maestri relics. He found nothing. Since Maestri did not rap-

pel the same route he ascended, Giarolli, Orlandi, and Ravizza
(the third member of the team) believe that he and Egger were
probably trying to remove all their pins for use on the descent.
The Austrian Tommi Bonapace is another Cerro Torre devotee
who has come to know the north face well over the course of
his fifteen attempts to climb it.

Bonapace is from the same town in Austria as Egger, and a
local bank has sponsored him on several expeditions to try and
confirm the 1959 first ascent. Always climbing Alpine style,
without any fixed ropes, Bonapace's best effort with Toni Pan-
holzer in 1996 saw him up twenty-seven pitches, to within
1,000 feet of the summit mushrooms. The Austrians couldn't
find any logical route in the area of the north face that Maestri
claims to have scaled.

Instead, they traversed from the col past the Northwest
Ridge onto the west face, where they followed a system of broken ledges that eventually led back onto the Northwest Ridge.
Over the course of their many forays to the Col of Conquest
and beyond, they did not uncover a single new relic from the
1959 ascent. From his firsthand experiences with the difficulty
of climbing Cerro Torre from the north, Bonapace has become
extremely skeptical of how Maestri and Egger could have completed their route in the short amount of time Maestri has
claimed.

Salvaterra, Giarolli, and Bonapace all seem to agree on one
thing: If Maestri and Egger did in fact climb from the col to the
summit in two and a half days, they must have been on the
Northwest Ridge. Nothing else on the north or west face looks
remotely feasible in their time frame, or anywhere near the low-
angle climbing Maestri reported. Is it possible that Maestri
was simply confused about where he actually climbed? Giarolli,
for one, believes this to be the case.

Even more doubts have been raised about Maestri's vague description of climbing the summit mushroom, particularly by
the Brits Tom Procter and Phil Burke. In 1981, the two came

within a rope length of Cerro Torre's summit by way of a new route following the major dihedral system on the right side of the east face (now called the English Dihedral). From their high point they had a clear view of the top of the north face, and they didn't see anything resembling the 50-degree couloirs Maestri had reported. But if Maestri and Egger were actually on the Northwest Ridge, then Procter and Burke were not looking in the right place. According to the line that Maestri described to Wilson and that appeared in the photo in *Mountain* (no. 23), the 1959 route followed approximately the same finish through the mushrooms as that used by Casimiro Ferrari on his first ascent of Cerro Torre's west face in 1974. (Many experts on the Maestri controversy, including Wilson and Donini, believe the Ferrari Route was actually the true first ascent of Cerro Torre.) Mike Bearzi, who made the first free ascent of Cerro Torre via the Ferrari in 1986, substantiates that the last few pitches of the west face did in fact follow low-angle couloirs, and even more telling, he describes a break in the mushroom's cornices above the north face that allowed relatively straightforward access to the summit. "Our experience of the terrain was very similar to that of Maestri's description," he wrote in his *Mountain Review* article.

THE REMATCH

In 1970, shortly after Carlo Mauri published the article that declared Cerro Torre unclimbed in the Italian magazine *Corriere*, Maestri decided it was time to become proactive in his defense. What better way to silence his critics than by going back to Cerro Torre? In his 1973 interview with Ken Wilson, Peter Gillman, Alan Heppenstall, and Leo Dickinson, Maestri revealed just how seriously he had taken Mauri's implied criticism: "Suppose you worked in a bank and, just before you were to retire, you heard a rumor that you had walked off with [a pile] of the bank's money. What would you do? Would you go to court and try to prove your innocence or, if there was some way you could clear your name by one theatrical gesture, would you choose that? Even if it involved a certain amount of danger to yourself, wouldn't you take the latter course?"

The latter course, for Maestri, began in May 1970 at the start of Patagonia's winter season, on Cerro Torre's Southeast Ridge. This time Maestri was climbing with a take-no-prisoners attitude. The expedition was sponsored by Atlas Copco—a mechanical air compressor company—to the tune of $12,000. In return for hauling the company's 160-pound air compressor and publicizing its use as a new development for drilling rock climbing bolts, Maestri was given enough money to have everything helicoptered to the base, including a wooden hut. The winter attempt ended about 1,300 feet shy of the summit, but only after Maestri had spent seventy days on the mountain, single-handedly leading every pitch. Rather than abandoning the climb and flying home, the team moved into a nearby town to wait for summer. Five months later, in November, the team moved back to their hut and began the tedious job of hacking their fixed lines out of the ice. Within three weeks they had regained their high point. On summit day, Maestri, Ezio Alimonta, and Carlos Claus reached the base of the headwall but realized they had forgotten their pitons at the base. Rather than retreating and possibly losing their only chance, Maestri drilled an 800-foot bolt ladder to the summit. At the last belay, Maestri forbade his partners from coming up, feeling they did not deserve the high point, since he himself had led every pitch. On his way down, he chopped the last pitch on rappel, so that "I would at least compel my successors to bolt those few meters." He also chose not to climb the final ice mushroom to the real summit, rationalizing that it wasn't a true part of the Torre. "It'll blow away one of these days," he said. Maestri came back from Patagonia having drilled more than 350 bolts into the side of Cerro Torre, more than any climber had ever used on any mountain in the past.

In the early 1970s, excessive bolting on the so-called Direc-tissimas in the Alps had created a bitter controversy in Europe. Maestri's heavy-handed tactics in Patagonia couldn't have hit the press at a more volatile or unfriendly time. Rumor had it that the Compressor Route was the impetus behind Reinhold Messner's famous article, "The Murder of the Impossible," a philosophical treatise that put forth ethical arguments against the use of bolts.

Ironically, the bolting debacle also raised new questions about Maestri's ability to have pulled off the 1959 climb. If he needed hundreds of bolts and months of time to climb Cerro Torre's Southeast Ridge, how could he have completed the more technical north face, with a hand drill, in only three and a half days? There were also some questions as to why he had blown off climbing the mushroom.

To this day, there is still no consensus on whether this climb was a legitimate ascent of Cerro Torre. Jim Bridwell, who made the speedy three-day second ascent of the Compressor Route in 1978, reinstated the final pitch that Maestri chopped, and then climbed the mushroom to the true summit of Cerro Torre. Many give him credit for being the first to successfully com-plete the Compressor Route. Near the top he noted that Maestri's final anchor appeared to be significantly below the summit shoulder, more than 100 feet from the summit. De-spite his best intentions to clear his name, Maestri's theatrical gesture backfired, and his stock in the climbing community sank to an all-time low.

When I interviewed Maestri in his hometown of Madonna di Campiglio in the fall of 1998, I asked him why he chose not to climb the summit mushroom. He said, "In my opinion the mushroom is not really part of the mountain. I personally never stood on the top of the mushroom on Cerro Torre. If you still have technical difficulties, you didn't do the summit, but if it's very easy, it doesn't matter. I've never left a mountain unfinished." I was shocked by Maestri's confession to have never reached the summit. But what I didn't realize at the time was how thoroughly Maestri had divorced himself from the 1959 climb. When he said "never," he was really trying to say he "never summited in 1971." Several months later, to clear up the confusion, my translator asked Maestri again if he had ever summited Cerro Torre. This time he said, "Yes, I did summit in 1959, or at least where I was appeared to be the summit, in the bad weather."

His sentiment regarding summits is shared by many Dolomite climbers. Many Dolomite climbs finish with long slopes of low-angle, loose rock, so local climbers have developed a tradition of forgoing the final steps to the highest rock outcrop. The truth is, the question of whether or not he stood on top of the mushroom in 1959 is a moot point. If it could somehow be proven he was anywhere even near the mushroom, it would all but dissolve the controversy.

Other notable controversies, such as Frederick Cook's fraudulent claim to have stood on the summit of Denali in 1906, have been more easily settled under the scrutiny of modern investigators. The Cerro Torre mystery has been more problematic and frustrating, due to the simple fact that the mountain's north face is perhaps one of the most remote and inaccessible locations on earth. To this day Maestri maintains that he and Egger left more than a dozen fixed pins and bolts on the north face above the col. As Giarolli, Salvaterra, and Bonapace can attest, finding this evidence is akin to finding a needle in a haystack.

Still, the Italians, led by Giarolli and Salvaterra, are determined to find these relics. Next year [2000], in the Dolomites, Giarolli will host an international climbers' conference to which all of Cerro Torre's chief protagonists will be invited. He plans to unveil a model replica of Cerro Torre on which climbers can map out their various routes on the mountain.

Maestri will be on hand to answer questions and meet face-to-face with his detractors. There is even some hope of obtaining sponsorship for a helicopter-assisted abseil exploration of the Maestri-Egger route.

When it comes right down to it, there really isn't much hard evidence to prove a case against Maestri. So we have to ask: How much of this controversy has been feeding on hype? How far would this have gone if not for the fervent investigations of people like Ken Wilson, who have pursued it obsessively? Just mention the controversy to Wilson, and within a few minutes he'll have worked himself into a frenzy. Looking beyond the events of 1959, we do know that Wilson, an ethical purist and antibolter, feels strongly that Maestri's Compressor Route desecrated Cerro Torre in 1971.

The compressor certainly raised the level of Wilson's indignation. One thing is clear: Take away all the articles and investigations spearheaded by Wilson, and there isn't much left to the controversy. Although some skepticism was raised in the Italian press subsequent to Mauri's article in *Corriere*, little or nothing has been published on the subject in Italy since.

We also need to take into account that Wilson's interest in Cerro Torre is purely academic. He has never personally been to Patagonia. Other climbers, with more intimate knowledge of the mountain, have been more hesitant to judge. Giarolli, who has been on twelve expeditions to Patagonia, including two attempts to climb the north face, is still willing to offer Maestri the benefit of the doubt. Subsequent to his 1998 attempt on the North Pillar, he went on the record to tell me: "It's clearly possible that Maestri and Egger in 1959 could have climbed *easily* those difficulties. We shouldn't forget at that time . . . in many circumstances Maestri and Egger had climbed, descended, and soloed [routes that] difficult; I mean many times and consistently."

Most climbers do expect to be taken at their word, so it's not hard for them to extend the same standard to their peers. Would things be any better, any more honest, if our claims were always subject to the skepticism of editors? Liars are going to be liars, and there's nothing we can do to stop them. A verification system might even make the liar's job easier: photos can be manipulated, details fabricated. Do we really want to lay a blanket of suspicion over our entire community to keep this lowest common denominator from getting out of control? As Jeff Lowe once said regarding the Maestri controversy, "You just can't go taking away something like this from a man without having hard evidence."

Even the most die-hard skeptics will say, when pressed, that yes, it is possible Maestri is telling the truth. For this simple reason, many feel that Maestri should be given credit. Otherwise, we are basically operating under the assumption that everyone is lying until proven otherwise. Among those who know or even care about this episode in mountaineering history, little ambivalence exists. You either believe Maestri or you don't, and it has a lot more to do with romantic notions of honor than any detailed analysis of the facts. Skeptics must live with the reality that they will probably never prove conclusively that the climb is a hoax. Maestri's supporters have to accept the sad fact that Cesare Maestri, who has cancer, may die without ever having received the satisfaction he may richly deserve.

TOM HIGGINS

AMENT COLLECTION

*Tom Higgins (left),
with Pat Ament, Yosemite,
1976.*

Tom Higgins has been too grounded in profession and family to pursue writing to the degree that undoubtedly would have established him as one of the best writers in the climbing world. It surely would have happened, for every spontaneous scribbling by him has been wise, witty, deep, and filled with imagery. He has written a number of playful articles, including an imaginative piece about a famous climber whose fingers broke off and were placed in the Smithsonian Institution.

A typical excerpt from a Higgins letter: "Eldorado must be bursting now into flame, as our little lives stray away again, some to write, some to teach, to sing, even to preach. Leaves stray down to a million graves. Look at your hand—imagine it in the grave, moth-like, light, with substance gone. We hardly understand but know it is right, like the sad and true song. Hold the tree! Let the golden rain cleanse and teach who are we, we bound for black ground, but for springs, maybe forty more, when we rise up on rock, alert to the water and the wind sounds" (fall 1995).

Higgins has been a natural poet, as he was a natural rock climber who set the free-climbing standards at Tahquitz Rock, in southern California, and in Yosemite and Tuolumne during the 1960s. Especially appreciated for his strict adherence to a rigorous honesty of style, Tom has refused to place bolts unless they were absolutely needed. He did not place bolts from rappel. He was against even the slightest nuance of "cheating." His climbing has been well described: "He charms the rock."

In the following piece, Higgins likens himself and his companion to Fred Flintstone and Barney Rubble. Indeed it was a time when harnesses were not used and climbers instead tied to a rope with one strand of rope around the waist, or the rope attached to some waist loops—stone age!

186

Soarks

I remember "Soarks" as a fun and funny little piece, revealing at least a little bit about our passion for climbing and some of the oddities of the game.

TOM HIGGINS

Sometimes a first ascent teaches us several lessons. "Soarks" teaches that a short climb can be long on satisfaction. A mistake in equipment can prompt innovation. A fear of falling can ground all our pride and make us wonder who and why we are. And a simple printing error can capture an important essence.

For the past several years, I have come from my native state, California, to climb in Eldorado Canyon, Colorado. The sandstone of Eldorado fascinates me. The rough and colorful rock presents a wonderful contrast, if not relief, to the slick granite of Yosemite, Tuolumne, and the Sierra domes. Feet and hands feel so much more sticky here, and preposterous ceilings, arches, and blank planes of vertical rock are actually climbable.

The Flatirons are also composed of good sandstone and located just north of Eldorado. Until the summer of 1978, I had not climbed on the Flatirons but thought these should be more feasible than anything in Eldorado. As seen from Boulder, the Flatirons are a series of sandstone slabs side by side for several miles. Each slab sits like an iron, tilted gradually westward. In the middle of my most recent visit to Colorado, Pat Ament suggests we look at the Third Flatiron, particularly the western walls of a ridge of slabs running southward below the main summit. On July 4, in 95-degree air, I get my first endwise look at the Flatiron. It presents the profile of a ship sinking to the stern—the east slab a gradually sloping deck, as I had expected, but the west wall an awful, overhanging prow.

The route Pat selects is under the prow. The crest of the route overhangs its base by perhaps 20 feet. And all around the base, except where the route begins, is a tangle of poison ivy, swarthy, deep, and shining. Ament has spied this overhang in his wanderings among the Colorado Flatirons. He wants to play on it. I'm not certain I do.

And so he begins, working with some new, small, and golden nuts that seem to work in tiny bottoming cracks. For the moment, I'm protected from the hot sun by the shadow of the wall. As Pat proceeds, the shadow recedes. Soon the only shadow is on the wall itself. The big band of sun follows Pat up the wall like jaws.

"Did we finish the water?" I ask, fumbling in the pack with one hand.

"I think we did."

We had drunk it all. I feel a little depressed at the prospect of no water and the probability of a day spent with nothing to show. I fall into a sullen mood, trying to avoid discouraging remarks. To my eyes, the climb looks impossible. Pat is not discouraged and methodically moves higher.

Not far from me is an island of shade under a small tree. I shift the belay and tie in there while Pat anchors briefly to a protection nut. From this vantage point, I better see the climbing line. Pat has climbed several short bulges and indentations in the otherwise overhanging plane. Atop a couple of bulges is a good resting stance or pocket. The route lies generally from left to upper right. The finish appears to be a slanting flake shooting diagonally right, to the skyline. Pat has climbed cautiously to the pocket, taking plenty of time with slightly fragile holds, and now feels the need for a bolt.

As I lean back, I hear a barely audible flutter. I look up to see a hang glider cruising in a long, slow arc about 100 feet above. There is an exhilarating similarity in position between the person under the glider and the character under the overhang. Or are they both just hung up?

Pat locks his left elbow and arm between two planes of rock. This allows him to keep his balance on the bulging wall while his left hand remains free to hold and twist the drill. He pulls the drill from the small bolt kit clipped to his gear sling, puts the drill in his hand, analyzes the position, and compliments himself for his ingenuity.

Suddenly he says, incredulously, "I don't have the hammer. We forgot to bring the hammer!"

His head falls slowly forward against the wall. First we are silent, our minds momentarily acting as computers trying to refute this illogic, then the canyon around us reverberates with our laughter. Far away and below, on a trail leading south, some hikers seem to mimic our noises. In another minute or two, all falls silent. There is no good anchor from which Pat can lower, so to retreat he would have to climb down, and the way up without a bolt looks out of the question.

"Tie a rock onto the rope," Pat says.

"A rock?"

"A rock."

Silence. Soon, with one hand Pat is lowering a loop of rope.

"This would make a good picture for your upcoming book on safety, Pat."

I scout for hard rocks.

"How do you tell a hard sandstone rock from a soft one?" I ask Ament and myself aloud. More silence. I put a few flat stones in the pack, clip it to the lowered loop, and Pat hauls up the pack.

Blam, blam, blam. Slowly, primordial man emerges in the figure of a modern climber. Pat pounds on the drill holder with a rock like a large brick. After what must be thirty minutes, a couple of bricks have broken and fallen into the ivy around me, but the hole is ready.

"Now the fun part," Pat croaks. The sun has long since seized him. I'm back at the tree, huddled in the shade. Pat tries to hit the small bolt top with a rock and drive it into the hole. I'm amused, imagining a Flintstone cartoon on nude, natural climbing styles, rhino horns for drills, rocks for hammers . . .

"Think I'll rest now and lower down, let you have some climbing for a while."

Pat holds the rope running through the protection as I lower him, so that he will keep close to the rock and land in from the poison ivy.

"Is your bolt good?"

Soon enough I'm confronting it. The bolt looks very solid. The climbing to this point is no more than 5.8 or 5.9, but the heat makes everything sweaty and seemingly more strenuous. I feel weak at the core. The sun, the overhanging sensation, something is draining me away. Pat is quiet below, resting in the tree shade but set with a strong belay. Out to the right of the pocket where I'm standing are a thin, shallow crack, some pot-holes, and the bulging, rounded flake leading around the edge of the wall. As I look at the flake, I notice a girl sitting in the woods far beyond, watching us.

"Hey, Pat, there's a girl out there," I say as softly as possible, imagining some luscious nymph.

"What?" Pat's voice cracks upward.

"Never mind," I say, trying not to let on to her that I know she's looking.

My first attempt at gaining the flake is a disaster. I can't hold on long enough to get the protection I want. I return to the pocket and rest. On the next attempt, I get a good nut in the flake and then climb back again to the pocket. What's she thinking now? thinks my banal brain. . . . On the next go I reach the flake and begin the jiggling, jagged dance up and along it, my arms feeling strong this time. Then, midway up and out the flake, the nut pops out! I envision a sweeping fall. I'm stopped for a moment watching myself spill away. I look back and down, below and under, toward Pat.

"Good show, you've got it."

I think, if he believes it, maybe it's true. But I can't see the way off the flake. A split second passes like a minute. Damn it, do it, I tell myself. In one or two crossover reaches with my hands and arms I grope around the edge, find good holds, and haul around. Suddenly there's Boulder and the gentle, down-sloping deck of our Flatiron. The rock frightens you, then is your friend. I steal a look to the forest. She's still there. I set the belay at the edge so Pat and I can talk. By now the late afternoon sun is streaming directly onto the face. The breeze of the earlier part of the day has stopped. Pat arrives at the bolt. He is glistening wet. Soon he's chalked to the elbows. Without a nut in and with the one sling (around a flake) between the bolt and me removed, Pat now faces the worst swinging fall possibility of his life.

"This makes the Supremacy swing look like nothing," Pat says, referring to the 60-foot top-rope fall off Supremacy Crack in Eldorado.

The problem is that the rope runs out and diagonally for 20 feet, so that at first the fall would be down and sideways, then out and around a corner into the canyon void. The canyon below to the south makes for a great sense of height. Then there is the prospect of being lowered almost a hundred feet directly into the ivy. I think of the darting hang glider and the airy emptiness in which it sails. I don't believe in portents but throw in an extra anchor nut anyway.

Pat is not sure he wants to try this. We discuss the consequences of his falling and whether I will be able to lower him without burning myself. I set up a type of brake bar on the belay line to help me in case he does fall. We talk in circles about which is better, the fall or five days of poison ivy, welts, and pus. Pat waits in vain for a small cloud to shade the face. Each new cloud hope is evaporated the instant it casts a shadow. He scolds himself for the delay. The girl is still watching. She must be realizing the trapeze show is grinding to a halt, or is it just beginning? Does she know climbing can be a deadly stalemate with the rock, the weather, and above all yourself? I tie Pat off. We wait for the sun to go behind a ridge. I fear he's lost his momentum. Pat is stronger in the arms and chest than I am, and I know he can do it. I tell him it's not bad, probably mild 5.10. He wants to wait. We wait. I look back to the forest.

There is no one there. Good, I think. This should have been our show all along.

It is a strange climb and final hour. The situation is so much ours, so simple. If Pat does it, we go. If he doesn't, we go, except he sails around and gets poison ivy. Either way, we will be alive, unless the rope breaks. We will eat in Boulder tonight. How can such a simple crystal of human events be so pivotal, so charged and intense? I am not in outer space. I am located on the globe, on this plate of rock and earth. Yet I sense we both feel the same thing, as if all the atoms in this wall have halted their vibrations. If our man-made rope parts, Pat dies. If the nuts pull, I die. If all holds, I lower him and we walk away. The stone has nothing to do with what happens next, unless it breaks under our pulling. We are riveted here by our own doing. The Third Flatiron towering above points west, hour by hour, century by century. There is not a modicum of care in it. There are no birds calling. The trail is empty. The air is still. I doze off to no dreaming.

"Here goes," says Pat.

With the sun behind a ridge, the temperature drops a little. Pat begins. I brace as if for a mighty marlin. I can't see the creature below. It is behind and under me somewhere, beneath the curve of the wave, with me on the crest. Awakened from my momentary nap, I've lost the sense of Pat's climbing. Instead it feels as if there is something swimming below me, as part of the rock's interior rather than skimming its surface. Then there are deep spouting sounds. Any second I expect to see Pat flying below me, like the view of a dolphin sailing forward from a ship's prow. Before the image has time to set, Pat has bounced up over the edge, barely huffing. We shake hands and laugh at our elongated adventure.

In another moment the strangeness of the place and hour dissolves. The stillness intensifies, then smooths and calms our brief descent and long walk away. The lights of Boulder will soon be on. How glad we will be for liquid and a simple dinner later to come.

That night, the bursting and booming of July 4 inspires the name "Sparks." Months afterward, *Mountain* magazine notes the climb and misprints it as "Soarks." Pat and I giggle on the telephone about the new name, and both of us like it. As with the coincidence of the hang glider, the word has a feeling of haphazardness and flying about it. The word zips back and forth on the telephone wire from Boulder to Oakland, sounding more preposterous and fitting with each saying of it—Soarks!

IAN McNAUGHT-DAVIS

Ian McNaught-Davis (right), with Don Whillans, Buxton, England, 1984.

Ian "Mac" McNaught-Davis, a longtime British climber and humorist with a searing wit, has produced a steady flow of playful writings over the years, including his hilarious "Climb Only When You're Ready," a treatise on the noise and absurdity of climbing signals. One gets a sense of Mac's humor through a comment he made in 1984 before a large audience at the National British Conference in Buxton, England. About competition climbing he declared, "I will compete with anyone who is as old as I am, as heavy as I am, as out of shape as I am, and who drinks as much as I do, but I'll be damned if I'll compete with some anorexic fag in tights."

Joe Brown, the great English rock climber, writes in his book *The Hard Years* that Mac was "in the forefront of postwar university climbers, having made first or early ascents of routes like the Pear Buttress of Mont Blanc and the north wall of the Cima Grande in the Dolomites. His reputation for apparent recklessness with motor cars was well known." Mac's 1956 ascent with Brown of the Mustagh Tower in the Karakoram was a major achievement in mountaineering.

McNaught-Davis has appeared many times on radio and television, sometimes with Brown, and he became a senior executive in the computer industry.

His introduction to his piece is typical McNaught-Davis wit—dry, humble, and succinct.

The Mustagh Tower,
Climbed 6th July 1956

This little piece might seem too trivial, but it does show how casual we were back in the 1950s. The piece may or may not have been published somewhere. I can't remember, and anyway there are more important problems to consider, such as those that arise from not drinking enough.

IAN MCNAUGHT-DAVIS

The first time I really met Joe Brown was at his house in Manchester one rainy afternoon.

I had been looking for oil in Zanzibar and Tanganyika, as they were then called, and was being paid quite generously. Local expenses were enough to cover accommodation, food, and a fairly unlimited quantity of drink. The salary was banked in Kuwait, where it remained untaxed and untouched until the two-and-a-half-year term abroad was completed. Then the whole point of the exercise became apparent: between four and five months of holiday or leave, as it was called, in which to blow all the savings. I blew mine on an expedition to climb the Mustagh Tower.

It all started with a letter from John Hartog, a nuclear chemist and climber, inviting me to go and climb the peak I had only seen on a Sella picture that made it look impossible. The truly unclimbable mountain. It was clear to me that no one would invite me to join a large-scale, fully funded expedition, and the only way I was going to get to go to the Himalaya was to organize a trip myself. That was the problem. But as I had learned already from a good American friend, "There's no problem that you can't solve if you hose enough money at it." I agreed with that philosophy, but it simply removed the problem to another stage—where to find the money to hose. That was why I was looking for oil in East Africa, and by the time I got back to England early in 1956 I believed I had enough hosing money.

I had never met John Hartog and knew nothing about him, but he had invited Roger Chorley, with whom I had done several routes in the Alps. It came as a little surprise when I first met John that all the expedition consisted of was me, him, and a hundred empty cardboard boxes that covered the whole of his large flat in Earls Court, London.

"Where's the rest of the team?" I questioned. He looked at me with a kind of look a puppy dog does when it wants you to stroke it.

"There's just us two, but we do have permission and we have a grant from the Mount Everest Foundation. We're booked on a ship sailing from Liverpool on April 4 and on the 10:55 Khyber mail train from Karachi to Rawalpindi on the twenty-fifth. We'll take all our gear with us. I have a list of all the equipment we need and another list for the food."

This wasn't the last time John exposed his passion for lists. Make a list, that's strategic, then the job is for lackeys. On the way out he exceeded even his passion for organization by insisting on a list of all the lists we had to have when we arrived.

John walked with a peculiar stoop, and I never met anyone who looked less like a climber.

"Don't you think our party is a bit weak for the Tower? What other climbs have you done?"

He then reeled off a list of snow plods that were strangely popular at that time. Climbers climbed rock, mountaineers climbed snow and ice and got into the Alpine Club and were invited to join large expeditions to high Himalayan snow plods. The Tower didn't really look like a snow plod to me.

"What happened to all the people you invited?" I asked.

He put on the furtive, sheepish look again and muttered something about people getting married or new jobs or whatever. It seemed to me rather ominous that his friends would get married or change jobs simply to get out of going on this trip. Maybe they knew something I didn't.

"Do you think you could find someone to join us?" he asked.

I explained that all the people I knew before I went to Africa were more or less skint, and I couldn't see them having spare cash that they would like to hose at our expedition.

John then produced another list and proved that as long as we didn't have sleeping bags for the porters and took some weird secondhand RAF survival suits we could afford to take two people along free. That would make us just like the more respected expeditions to high places.

Well that's how I ended up outside Joe Brown's house in Longsite Road, Manchester, on a rainy day. I knocked on the door, and it was opened by a rather friendly-looking woman.

"Does Joe Brown live here?" I asked.

"Yes," was the reply.

"Er, could I speak to him?"

I was beginning to think it was like getting in to see royalty. In this long street of identical houses, perhaps he was a local hero. A gnomelike figure with arms that seemed to hang below his knees came to the door.

"My name is Ian McNaught-Davis."

"Ay, I've heard of you."

Well that was a good start. I wondered if my reputation was going to work for or against me.

"We're off on an expedition to climb the Mustagh Tower. We wondered if you'd like to come?"

The key question was, Would he go or not? He already had a fearsome reputation as a rock climber, as an Alpine climber, and he had just climbed Kanchenjunga, the third-highest peak in the world. There was no one in Britain more experienced and qualified to climb the "unclimbable mountain."

"When are you leaving?"

"The ship sails the week after next."

Was that good or bad? His kindly faced broke into a grin that was later to become famous.

"You'd better come in and have a cup of tea." I knew I'd cracked it.

We drank tea and discussed a third member, and Joe suggested Tom Patey, another powerhouse from Scotland whom I'd never met. And that was about it. As I was leaving, I asked him, "What about your business?"

"I sell from my handcart, and I haven't got a business."

As I retreated down the road the cackling laughter followed me, and I knew we were going to have a good time.

That's about it. Out of the four climbers only Joe and Tom, and John and I, knew each other before we left. On July 6, 1956, Joe and I were on the summit, where we spent the night. John and Tom climbed it the next day and also bivouacked, causing Hartog to lose some of his toes. Joe insisted that I kick the last few steps to the top.

"Well, you've paid for it. You might as well be the first on top."

Sentimental bugger.

AMY IRVINE

Amy Irvine

The niece of a veteran climbing ranger for Grand Teton National Park, Amy Irvine has been climbing since the mid-1980s. Her outdoor experiences have fueled her advocacy for wilderness; Irvine was formerly the director of development for the Southern Utah Wilderness Alliance, one of the nation's leading grassroots environmental groups. She has written frequently on both climbing and wilderness, with stories and essays appearing in *Climbing*, several outdoor adventure anthologies, and environmental publications. Recently "The Path of Destruction" appeared in the Patagonia catalog as part of a series of wilderness essays that included the work of Terry Tempest Williams, David Brower, and Gary Snyder. Irvine also wrote *Making a Difference*, a collection of environmental success stories, which was featured in the *Washington Post* on Earth Day, 2001. She lives off the grid, among the slickrock and sagebrush in southern Utah, her native state.

This article does not try to conquer the world, but it does speak to the important point that climbing does not happen in a void. Climbers should also be aware of the environment and participate in its protection.

The Path of Destruction

Climbers, myself most certainly included, can be outright narcissists. We, more than most, can narrow our lives to a single goal—a peak, a big wall, a boulder problem, even one isolated move. We will spend our last dime on another piece of gear, a tank of gas to get us to the crag. We will blow off time with our lovers, trips to the dentist, professional excellence . . . all for climbing.

In the past, while I took pride in having such focus, my myopic view of the world led to a sense of disconnect and numbness. I couldn't remember when I last voted. I had never donated time to a charity—except for rainy afternoons at the blood bank because I could make enough money off my platelets to get me to the City of Rocks and back.

I chose this piece because it is a symbol of my evolving view of climbing—indeed, of the entire world. In an era of plastic-plastered, temperature-controlled climbing gyms, I fear we are more disconnected than ever from the wild nature of climbing.

It is my hope that each of us can break our hearts and minds wide open—that we can expand our attention to include the places that give climbing its very soul.

AMY IRVINE

A ghost of a day. Damp. Silvery. Vaporous. We stand at the mouth of the gully, high above Provo Canyon, on the north flank of a mountain range managed by the U.S. Forest Service. Its narrow stairway of ice is the gateway to the high peaks above—the only part of the range protected by the Wilderness Act.

Outside the canyon, it is mostly private land. Nothing is sacred there. Bulldozers dig up the foothills to make way for more gated communities, displacing rattlesnakes and rabbits. Ribbons of pavement and a steel mill strangle Utah Lake and its great blue herons. But today I have escaped all that, climbed to a more pristine and serene place.

201

I uncoil the rope and gaze out. Surrounding us are monoliths of pale limestone, veils of ice, and a tapestry of snow. I am standing in a great white room. Spare. Lean with life. Beautiful.

I lead the first pitch. Water runs behind the column, marking my rhythm. First the delicate placement of a front point, then an explosion of power to bury my tool. A move of grace, then one of strength.

Finally, I top out in a small flat chamber and bring up my partner. I am more than happy to relinquish the lead—the next steep pillar of blue looks daunting. He pulls it off in fine form. I back away from the base to see him disappear over the lip toward a pine tree with a belay sling.

But there is more than that to see.

A thirty-foot wall of snow moving faster than a train is coming straight at me. A thunderous symphony. The snarling mass charges toward the lip of the waterfall. The last I see of my partner is his mad lunge to the downhill side of the belay tree. I run for the wall, hug it as the avalanche hits. The major portion of it falls away from the wall, but still I am buried.

I think one necessary thought: hang on to the rope.

This rarefied world, its gorgeous raw elements—at this moment I hate them more than anything. My black emotions catch fire; I burn through the ice coffin to the surface. Gasping, I look down to see the rope still in my hand.

My partner is waving from the tree, which somehow remains standing. He rappels down to me, and we humbly retreat. The slide's path has run to the canyon's bottom; we follow it to the road. We observe the violence: orange flakes of lichen. The crumpled carcass of a mountain goat. The debris covers the highway and the Provo River that flows alongside it, from this high mountain to Utah Lake below.

Two worlds connected.

Standing on the highway, the anger I felt for the avalanche slowly changes into rage at the road on which I stand. I see that its paved presence chokes the Provo River far more than the snow slide ever could. The avalanche brought down one goat, but the cars on this highway kill hundreds of moose, bobcat, and fox.

Protecting a high peak is easy: it's postcard pretty, and one can't build a Wal-Mart up there. But high mountains are habitat for relatively few species. It's the places humans *can* get to—private lands as well as public—whose rivers, lakes, forests, and valleys also need protection from the ravenous, ever-creeping crawl of human life.

Climbers are the gatekeepers between two worlds. From our vantage point, we witness the origins of water and soil, and we see where rivers begin their journeys to sustain vaster regions and the species that inhabit them. We know more than most what a place would look like if left undisturbed.

Climbing has turned me into an alchemist—to weld tenacity and courage from fear and discomfort. To move with grace and calm. To hang on no matter what hits. Today I realize that these same traits can close steel mills and stop strip malls when they threaten the ecological health of a place.

We climbers have a bright red fire in our bellies. For wild ascents. For wild places. What an indomitable force we could be, if we collectively bellowed a deafening, fearless No! to the vanishing of wilderness and other critical habitats.

It would be compensation for the privilege to climb in the world that tethers our sanity, a world outside urban madness. It would be an act of strength, an act of grace. An act of necessity.

DOUG ROBINSON

Doug Robinson on first ascent of Backside of Beyond, on Temple Crag in the Palisades, Sierra Nevada, 1998.

JIM HERRINGTON

William Broyles Jr., author of the screenplays for *Apollo 13* and *Castaway*, describes Doug Robinson as "John Muir meets Jack Kerouac." A pioneer of the "clean" climbing revolution in the late 1960s, Doug Robinson made the first clean ascent (without pitons) of Yosemite's Half Dome in 1973. He was the first president of the American Mountain Guides Association and produced a best-selling rock video, "Moving over Stone." Now he runs a guide service by the same name. His writings are characterized by wonderful titles, such as "Bringing Light out of Stone" and "The Climber as Visionary." His "Visionary" piece, discussing how climbing can trigger biochemical pathways in the brain leading to visionary experience, has appeared in countless anthologies, in many languages, and he greatly expands such ideas in his forthcoming book *The Alchemy of Action*. Doug Robinson guides Climber-as-Visionary seminars in California's High Sierra.

In a flier for those seminars he writes, "Why do we climb? The answer is simple, although startling: It gets you high. Literally. Have you ever noticed feeling inspired up there? Of course. Senses are sharpened, thoughts and feelings flow. We feel vital, more alive. We tend to think of inspiration as coming from the mountain scenery, or maybe a rare harmony with climbing partners. But we are producing it, right in our brains, by mixing the hormones of effort with a dash of fear and cooking them over the fires of stress into a hormonal cocktail that becomes . . . mind-bending. The act of climbing is strong medicine, no doubt about it, and the results can be—as I jokingly warn every novice—addictive. You become more open, receptive, and alert, which turns outward to landscape and partners, inward to yourself. At times a grateful sense of awe is kindled in the climber, a kind of clear-eyed ecstasy that the poet Rimbaud called *supernaturally sober*."

Mountaineering Just Means Glad to Be Here: Eight Alpine Poems

I chose these small, simple poems to include here because they come as close as anything I've been able to squeeze out of a pencil to hinting at that inexpressible high mountain feeling, the one that keeps drawing us back, beyond reason. These kinesthetic snapshots come boiling out anyway, like joy shouts, from the heat of the action. I pause to catch the lines as they come, like dictation.

Caution: These moods can seem too simple, obvious, and even a bit idiotic, until our minds once again approach the simplicity in which they were captured. To be receptive, stay active. Keep moving over stone. Chairs and couches just make it harder. Strive upward; only there can these lambent breezes loft you. Only then will it be, for a while, "as if gravity is become locally less important than rapture" (Thomas Pynchon).

DOUG ROBINSON

I
If you are more at home
In the mountains than anywhere
You are a mountaineer.
No climbing is required.
Being among the peaks it will arise spontaneously
With no other motive
Or justification
Than itself.
To be a mountaineer
Is first to love the mountains
Then to climb them.
Technique
Can never replace
Devotion.

I I
With all that evolving spread out behind us
We dance this frost fall morning away
On the sunward sides
Of granite boulders

I I I
Stone down
Boulder running
Falling light
Slab sailing
Wind building
Rock freckles dusking
Cloud pushed star dying
Dark

Light
Random rain
High dark south-wind sailors
Morning sleep
Rain wake
Heather clump back nestle
Cool fresh face rain
Short burst of sun warm
In a week you will be home

I V
Best of vantage points
Those high mountain days

V
No pencil comes out
Poets struck dumb by twilight:
Yosemite Point

VI
Waking these early morning hours
With mind abroad on the Sierra night,
Dreams of granite glory
Keep coming up.
Yet they drown each time
In return to present beauty.
My head is filled and scoured
Filled and scoured
By tumbling creek
Or trailing shooting stars to fluorescent death.
Against fresh feelings
Ego hasn't a chance.
A perfect pentagon of stars hangs in Contact Pass.
Ego dissolves in darkness
Soluble in starlight.

VII
On the best off days
A clean animal
Running down streams of white light
Through the clear wilderness

VIII
These high mountain days
Emerging from music into dance,
Re-merging to rhythm.
Not a thought.

ED WEBSTER

Ed Webster in 1988 on the Pang La pass, Tibet, en route to the East Face of Everest.

Well-known American rock climber and mountaineer Ed Webster has climbed, lectured, and pursued his art of photography for many years. A veteran of seven Himalayan expeditions—to Nepal, Tibet, Bhutan, and Pakistan—he also was the first American mountaineer to climb in Mongolia. He won an award for bravery from the American Alpine Club for his help in the rescue of a friend. His latest book, *Snow in the Kingdom: My Storm Years on Everest*, tells of the incredible fight to ascend the unclimbed and clearly difficult Kangshung Face of Everest and the tremendous act of survival in descending. Reinhold Messner calls the climb "the best ascent of Everest in terms and style of pure adventure." Chris Bonington describes the climb and descent by Webster and his friends as "among the most remarkable examples of survival in the history of Himalayan mountaineering."

The Fight

My choice was to live. At dawn on our team's summit day on Mount Everest on May 12, 1988, I removed my outer gloves for approximately two minutes to take pictures of the pink and gold alpenglow bathing the summit of nearby Lhotse. We were climbing without bottled oxygen; it was 5:00 A.M. and minus 30 degrees Fahrenheit. I took eight 35-millimeter slides. I put my gloves back on. My fingers were absolutely numb. I banged them together. I made windmills with my arms. My fingers remained senseless and wooden. They were too cold to feel any pain. I did not know it, but I had badly frostbitten my fingers by taking those pictures, and that single incident set the stage for the chapter that follows: of how, after Stephen Venables summited Everest without bottled oxygen (becoming the first British mountaineer to do so), we still had to descend the mountain, in our frostbitten, weakened, and incapacitated state.

My detailed diary entries provided the foundation for my Everest book, Snow in the Kingdom, *and it is these handwritten, scribbled paragraphs, recorded so dutifully in blank diary books over a decade ago, that I believe give such a vital life to my narrative of my Everest years. But after I returned home from this triumphant new route up Everest—a battered, thinner, seriously frostbitten waif of my former self—the fingers on both of my hands were gruesomely damaged by frostbite, and each finger was bandaged. I could not hold a pen or a pencil; I could not write.*

Over a period of about a week, as I convalesced at my godparents' home in Bedford, Massachusetts, my godmother, Judith Mc-Connell, patiently continued my diary for me, writing down my oral recounting of May 13 through May 17, 1988, and my reliving of the harrowing, near-death ordeal that follows: of how Stephen Venables, Robert Anderson, and I fought our way back down the Kangshung Face of Mount Everest without food for three perilous, joyful and agonizing, never-to-be-forgotten days.

ED WEBSTER

209

ED WEBSTER

Stephen Venables at 24,000 feet on Everest.

You've got to fight it. Sometimes you've just got to
fight it.

—Fritz Wiessner

It has often been said that descending a mountain is harder and more dangerous than climbing one. Perhaps nowhere is this truth more sharply evident, and statistically proven, than on Mount Everest. Now that the three of us were reunited, standing together outside the Japanese tent at 27,000 feet, it became imperative that we descend to the South Col. We needed to reach our own tents, sleeping bags, and stoves to rewarm and rehydrate our tired, parched bodies. As of yet, I hadn't begun to consider how difficult it would be to retrace our route down the Kangshung Face. Roping up somewhat symbolically on our 7-millimeter rope, we left the Japanese tent and headed back down to the col. Robert went first, guiding Stephen, who was very wobbly legged and weak, while I came last, wondering if I could belay the rope if someone slipped. Luckily the terrain quickly eased, and soon we were back on the flat, frozen, windswept desert of the South Col.

As we stumbled back to our two tents at camp 3, the full realization of how extended we were began to sink in. At this extreme altitude there was absolutely no chance of rescue, or help, really, of any kind. Helicopters don't fly much above the 20,000-foot level, and while several expeditions were currently climbing up the mountain's Nepalese side, none were close enough to lend assistance—nor did they even know we were here. We were three people very much alone, utterly exhausted, with virtually no possibility of any outside assistance. It was also now that we most felt the lack of the usual Sherpa companions to make hot tea and soup, care for us, carry our packs, and otherwise speed our safe return. Back down at Advanced Base Camp (a full 8,000 vertical feet lower than our present altitude), Mimi, Joe, Pasang, Kasang—and Paul, too, we hoped—would be searching for us through the binoculars.

When Stephen and Robert paused to rest, I hiked on ahead across the col toward our two tents. Then, still unaware of the extent of my frostbite injuries, I took off my gloves and pulled out my Nikon to photograph my partners walking toward me. I took two portraits of my half-frozen companions. In the first image, Stephen leans in fatigue against Robert, but in the second, Stephen stands alone, his ice ax raised in well-earned victory. It was a particularly proud moment.

I do not remember very much about the rest of that day. Oxygen deprivation, our overwhelming fatigue, and the lack of food, water, and sleep combined to make us incredibly lethargic. Our lives began to be acted out in super slow motion. I know that we lay down and rested in the tents, that we took our high-altitude climbing suits off and crawled willingly into the luscious warmth of our sleeping bags, and that we then made a brew of tea, only because somehow I took pictures of these things too.

I dimly recall taking off my overmitts and liner gloves to inspect my fingers. Gray in color, cold, numb, and woody feeling, the fingertips of my left hand, I noted, appeared considerably worse than those of the right. Fretting over what to do, I finally decided to rewarm them in our tiny pot of hot tea water. Stephen did the same with his frozen left toes. Then of course we drank the tea. While we knew that rewarming frozen tissue should only be done when all chance of refreezing the injured tissue had passed, we were positive we'd have little trouble descending the Kangshung Face. What could possibly be worse than the nightmare that we had just survived? Our previous hour-and-a-half-long descent from camp 2 to camp 1 made us assume that in two days time at the most, we'd be safely in Doctor Mimi's loving care at Advanced Base.

Finally we collapsed, dead tired and oblivious to the world, and slept. If we knew that we should have tried to descend to camp 2 that day, we never discussed it. Careful, rational observations were no longer terribly important, or even possible.

Subconsciously we knew that spending this third day above 26,000 feet was dangerous, perhaps even deadly, but our bodies craved only sleep and rest. The summit push had exhausted us almost beyond human limits. At last we were ready to go home; the question was, Could we still get there?

Time crept by. I blinked awake from the depths of sleep and peered at my watch's luminous dial. It was 2:30—but in the morning or the night? I no longer knew. My mind could not function. And what day was it? And where were we? Oh, right. We're on the South Col . . . on Mount Everest. After my long agonizing night huddled next to Robert in the Japanese tent, it felt so deliciously warm to be burrowed deeply inside my sleeping bag. Couldn't we just lie here a bit longer, I thought to myself. But wait. Who was I even asking permission of . . . ? I didn't know. I just didn't want to have to move a single inch, so I fell back asleep, never waking once, for the rest of that day and the entire night.

With no food left, the next morning we realized that our physical and mental condition had gone from bad to worse, as had our hopes for an easy, rapid descent. This was our fourth day above the 8,000-meter level without bottled oxygen. Our bodies would not respond to signals from the brain, movement was barely possible, and every effort, no matter how large or small, became a superhuman effort. Stephen's and my last gas canisters had run out the day before, but luckily Robert's stove was still going. Unable to make a single effort to prepare to descend, Stephen and I lay inert inside our bags and waited hours for Robert to deliver us a single, half-filled pot of hot water: our breakfast. We were a pathetic sight—unmotivated, listless, and uninterested in doing anything to save ourselves from the certainty of what would happen should we not act. I began to realize the terrible truth, that slowly and inexorably, we were dying.

Standing up required an effort we could only marginally begin to grasp; to carry the weight of our two tents, or any of our additional heavier equipment back down the mountain was virtually impossible. We decided to leave the tents here on the col, and we would risk bivouacking out in the open in our sleeping bags at camp 2, where we had left behind a few extra gas canisters—but no food. At camp 1, we had two tents and a large food cache. Trying to cut even more weight, I also left behind my wonderfully warm down-insulated bibs. Last, reasoning that my wool mittens (though by now fairly worn out) would be easier to rappel down our fixed ropes with, I discarded my thick overmitts, which saved only ounces, and in retrospect was yet another costly error.

I crawled outside the tent, alternately lying and sitting in the snow until the final, most awkward task of fastening crampons to boots was accomplished. But could I stand? I glanced over at Robert, flat on his back in his tent, boots protruding out the entrance like a dead man's. Yet every so often he would come to life, sit up, fiddle with his crampons, and collapse again. Stephen was also preparing to go, and lay on the ground, corpse-like, in front of our tent. I pulled out my autocamera to take a picture of him, and he waved at me halfheartedly to prove that he was still alive.

Yes, I could stand up, with difficulty. Shuffling to the east side of the col, I carefully stepped down the initial steep slope and plunged into waist-deep fresh powder snow—which was good for skiing, but not very easy to walk through! Afternoon snowstorms over the past two days were the culprits. Snow had also been blown over the col onto the leeward side by the powerful winds. The avalanche danger in the upper part of the bowl was extremely high.

Earlier in the expedition we had discussed the possibility of our descending into Nepal, into the Western Cwm, if conditions or circumstances high on the mountain warranted such an extreme change of plan in our descent. And while that escape down Everest's normal South Col route was probably now fully justified given that the snow conditions on the Kangshung

Face were so atrociously dangerous, in my debilitated condition I realized that several steps down Everest's East Face were several steps too many to reverse. As soon as we stepped off the South Col, we were irrevocably committed to fully descending our route. So, with no going back, I continued stumble-stepping down the slope, plunging each boot deep into the powder, my ears straining for the slightest sound of the snow cracking or settling. To make matters worse, thick moisture-laden monsoon clouds smothered my view.

I could only listen and wait for disaster.

"What's it like down there?" a voice yelled from above. It was Robert. I could see him standing in silhouette on the rim of the South Col, 500 feet above.

"Dangerous! Whatever you do, don't glissade," I shouted back. "Don't slide down the slope. Follow in my tracks!"

Minutes later, I shook my head in disbelief. Far to my left, Robert was now almost level with me! A small and lonely figure, he stood in the very center of the vast snowfield. How did he get there so fast?

"What are you doing!?" I yelled, with not a little consternation.

"I glissaded. It looked fine," Robert replied. "I guess I got going kind of fast . . . and, uh, I dropped both of my ice axes, too. Could I borrow your extra ski pole?" His voice revealed increasing alarm as he discovered the dire consequences of his slide. His two ice axes were nowhere to be seen; they were lost.

"I wanted to get down as fast as possible. So I jumped off the edge of the South Col," Robert later explained to me, using some high-altitude-riddled logic. "And everything was fine for the first few seconds. 'This is great,' I thought until I hit some rocks, tumbled forward, and the slope avalanched. Which sent me cartwheeling down the hill, but then fortunately, I stopped."

Stephen left camp 3 ten minutes after Robert, so he did not see Robert fall. When Stephen reached the col's edge, he saw only Robert's initial toboggan-slide dent in the snow. Now far below the col, Robert and I had already been swallowed by the clouds. Stephen also decided—just as unwisely—to glissade off the edge of the South Col and slide down the slope. And he also lost control and took a dangerous fall.

"It was the only time on the entire expedition that I heard Stephen's British reserve crack," Robert related. "I think he was truly frightened. He stopped above me, then he yelled down that his ice ax had been ripped off his wrist, nearly taking his Rolex with it. At least he kept his priorities straight."

Within twenty minutes of leaving our camp on the South Col, both Robert and Stephen had lost their ice axes. As a result, during the remainder of our descent of the Kangshung Face, I held in my hands our only ice ax—our one ice ax. I left my spare ski pole for Robert, and after his fall, Stephen now had nothing to use for safety or support, neither ice ax nor ski pole.

I continued down the snow slope. Peering through the enshrouding mists, I searched for a landmark to tell me that I was on route, hoping and praying that somehow I could still find the way to camp 2—which, after my teammates' falls, felt increasingly distant and perhaps unreachable. I made each plunging, plowing, downhill step through the fluffy powder with the greatest of effort, lifting legs and boots and crampons, moving always forward, but finding no food to eat except for my singular desire to live, my strength flowing from a hitherto-untapped reservoir, from a life stream flowing deep within me, and of course I was thankful this new supply of energy existed, but how long would it last?

Suddenly, I heard a dull muffled roar break loose from the mountainside high above me. I turned uphill; every muscle in my body tensed to iron. Hidden by the gray curtain of cloud, sounds of chaos and destruction multiplied wave upon wave as tons of unseen snow began to race downhill. An avalanche! Quickly I ascertained that it was not heading directly for me but had originated above and to my left. Then, to my horror, I realized that the avalanche had started from the direction of the huge, unstable snow slope where I'd last seen Robert standing alone and helplessly vulnerable. My stomach tightened into a fierce sick knot.

The clouds were so dense that I could not actually see the avalanche. I could only hear the crashing sound of the falling debris, emanating now well to my left, now below me, as multiple thousands of tons of snow and ice—carrying one human body—erupted over the edge of the immense Lhotse ice cliffs. A sharp, crippling wave of anguish overcame me as I imagined Robert being swept along with the debris. I could picture the terrible sequence of events in detail: Robert standing in the center of the snowfield one moment, hopeful of survival, then his sudden panic as the billowing white tidal wave overwhelmed him, sweeping him down, down, down, before tumbling him over that horrifying edge to his final, excruciating plunge into the abyss. Robert had just died—after everything that we had been through. The finality of such a death shocked me profoundly, even through my exhaustion, even as I grappled with disbelief.

Turning back downhill, breathing hoarsely, I resumed my descent. There was nothing else to do. I imagined the two of us, Stephen and myself, walking into Advanced Base Camp without Robert. What would we tell the others? How could we explain something so inherently unfair, that after all we had survived together, Robert had died in an avalanche on the descent? I didn't know. Robert's death was an impossibility; I wanted to cry out in anguish, to rage against Everest, to blaspheme God, to curse fate itself, but I fought back my tears and bit my lower lip to hold back my vile and desperate words. My body quivered with emotion; each breath came in a creaking, throat-tightened spasm.

My determination to reach the mountain's base became furious and indignant. Stephen and I had to survive; we could not give in and let ourselves die.

After a few minutes, I glanced back uphill. Only a single dot, a small black figure standing in the white snow, was following in my footsteps. Even as I tried to cling to the chance that Robert was not dead, I saw my worst fears confirmed. There was just one dot, not two. I was certain now that Robert had been killed. I crumpled into the snow, struggling once again to keep from breaking down. In the ultimate conviction of the truly desperate, I found myself proclaiming: "We are as alone as any humans can be. This is a fight to the end." There seemed nothing melodramatic in such a thought—in fact, I found that it clarified things wonderfully. "I am going to live," I insisted to myself. *"I am going to live!"*

Adrenaline carried me downhill once again. Stopping momentarily to rest, I turned around to check on Stephen. I saw two small dots in the distance! I counted them twice, and then even a third time, just to make sure that my eyes weren't deceiving me. I had been so sure it had been otherwise! I shook my head in disbelief, then felt a surge of gratefulness and joy as I watched the dots continue down the snowfield. As quickly as disaster had seemed to descend upon our group, it had passed away again, leaving me in stunned amazement.

I still thought that we could reach the Flying Wing and the snow platform at camp 2 before nightfall. Carefully, I stepped across a partially hidden bergschrund, trying to remember at what level we had diagonaled across the lower portion of the treacherous snow basin below the South Col. After descending vertically several hundred more feet, I slowly began angling to my left, facing downhill. We'd made a long traverse upward to the left from the right-hand end of the Flying Wing; I now had to reverse this section. Unfortunately, the snow conditions had completely changed since our ascent. Far from the easy hard-packed snow we'd savored on our climb up, I now waded forward through thigh-deep, unconsolidated powder ripe for an avalanche of massive proportion.

As I began to traverse across the snowfield, I was cognizant that it was heavily laden with freshly fallen and windblown snow. The surface could fracture at any second, and without warning. Traversing almost horizontally to get across it, I also knew that I was breaking a cardinal rule of mountaineering—traversing straight across an avalanche slope and creating, in effect, a man-made fracture line—but here there was absolutely no alternative. Somehow, somehow, we had to cross to the opposite side.

We were trapped; this was sheer and utter madness! And if the snow did avalanche, as I had every belief that it would, the tumultuous deafening roar of untold tons of falling snow would send me hurtling into one of many deep and waiting crevasses, or tumbling into eternity, into the Witches' Cauldron at the base of Lhotse, 7,000 vertical feet below. There would be no escaping death if the snowfield gave way, but maybe the others would survive. Maybe the snow would fracture below them, and only I would be swept away. Perhaps they would be spared. I continued forward, making each footstep as softly and gently as possible, my heavy boots sinking nonetheless into the snow's downy cushion. We were rolling the dice to win our own lives. If I heard or felt a crack or a settling of the snow, I was prepared to run for my life—in a last futile effort.

I endured these soft sinking velvet footsteps one by one, knee-deep, waiting for death, expecting to die, experiencing the embrace of eternity known only by the condemned and the dying. Thirty minutes later, when I at last reached the slope's far side above the Flying Wing's right-hand end, I hunched over with relief. The snow should have avalanched, but miraculously, unbelievably, it had not. Slowly I recovered from this torment and prepared myself for the next one.

Days earlier, on our ascent, we had crossed the deep crevasse formed by the detached uphill side of the Flying Wing snow block. This lethal gap was somewhere just below me. We'd crossed it via a fragile snow bridge, but where?

As I stumbled downhill toward this crevasse, an alarming thought found its way into my brain. Why weren't we now roped together for safety? In fact, where was our climbing rope? I didn't have it. And neither, I thought, did Robert or Stephen. Before we left the South Col, we hadn't discussed if we should rope up—tie into the rope—or not, presumably because during the summit climb we'd each become accustomed to climbing solo and unroped. No doubt we just assumed that we wouldn't need to bother roping up below the col either. Only months later, while looking at a picture I'd taken, did I discover the missing rope lying coiled in the snow in front of Stephen's and my tent on the South Col—right where we had left it.

Confused by the thick clouds and the almost total whiteout, I could see only about fifty feet, far enough to discern the Flying Wing's jagged and icy upper lip extending far to the right. I squinted my eyes and scanned the slope. An apparition materialized out of the clouds. Were my eyes tricking me? No: it was a tiny orange flag, the highest of our bamboo wands, which I had placed four days earlier to mark our route over the impasse. I hurried forward through the snow and grabbed the wand. It was real! Carefully I tiptoed downhill toward the snow-bridged crevasse. I couldn't tell if the snow was solid enough to support my weight, so I jumped across the span's midsection instead.

All I heard was a "Whoompf!" behind me when I landed on the far side—the sound of snow collapsing and falling into the mountain's unknown depths. Five feet from where I now stood, a round black hole clearly identified the part of the snow bridge that had given way. There the crevasse was much wider. I decided that the others would see the black hole and know to be careful.

Camp 2 was almost in sight. I descended the next easy-angled slope, circled around the overhanging ice cliff at the right end of the Flying Wing, and waded over to our old tent platforms. At dusk, I cleared away the loose snow from where we'd tented on the way up. Then I found four or five extra fuel canisters hanging in a stuff sack suspended from ice screws pounded into the Wing.

Robert straggled in. We got into our sleeping bags and lit the stove for a brew. Stephen appeared just as darkness fell. Robert produced some tubes of Japanese instant coffee and milk he'd found two days earlier, which we drank. Unfortunately, we hadn't cached any sugar, extra tea bags, or soup here. Later the weather cleared, and Makalu and Chomolönzo thrust into view above the dissipating valley clouds, and the cold black sky, in its turn, froze around us. At Stephen's suggestion that we should try to signal Mimi, Joe, and Paul at Advanced Base Camp—to let them know that we were alive and descending—I stood up and shone my headlamp for some minutes in the direction of our friends at the mountain's base. Several more cups each of hot water quelled our thirst before we each passed out, snug inside our warm feathery wombs.

On the morning of May 15, we could not move from our sleeping bags for several hours. Merely sitting up, let alone the astoundingly difficult feat of standing completely upright, demanded impossible physical endurance. Instead, we talked sluggishly between naps, or passed out collectively. Twice Stephen tried to melt snow for drinking water, but each time the hot stove melted into the snow—and when we fell asleep, it tipped over, spilling the hard-won liquid. Well, it didn't much matter, did it? Did anything really matter? As the daytime temperature grew hotter, in our collective, numbed stupor we were lulled into a passive denial of the truth—the stark, undeniable reality that if we did not leave the Flying Wing, it would soon become our grave.

Although nearly incapacitated by lethargy and inertia, I was becoming increasingly angry at the apparent hopelessness of our situation and the nearness of my own death. Stephen and Robert lay asleep in their sleeping bags, but for some reason I was slightly more alert. I didn't know why. As I fiddled awkwardly with the stove canister with my frostbitten fingers, turning the on-off key and fumbling with the lighter to ignite the burner, surges of anger and rage welled up inside me. I turned and shouted at Robert and Stephen. We had to keep going, we had to move, we had to act. We couldn't just lie here and die.

I suppose at this point I recognized that maybe I'd assumed the temporary role of leader, but it was leadership by default. I did not want this duty. I was much more comfortable with a shared democratic leadership, but I also knew that personally I couldn't hold out much longer. Another day without food, two at the most, and I thought I might be finished. If it was my turn to lead us through the fray, then so be it. If through my anger and outrage at my own impending death I could rouse Stephen and Robert, then so much the better.

All three of us had been frostbitten on summit day and during our forced bivouacs during that night of May 12, but Stephen and Robert's injuries didn't appear as severe as mine. Amazingly, Stephen's hands and fingers hadn't been injured at all during his 28,600-foot bivouac. (Back on the South Col, Stephen had related to Robert and me that the miraculous preservation of his digits during his summit bivy was thanks to the warmth of a yak herder's fire, and because of some solicitous care of his health given by the spirit—or presence—of Eric Shipton, the British Everest pioneer of the 1930s.) Stephen's nose, however, had been exposed to the wind that night, and the end had now turned a mottled ashen gray. The condition of our toes we could only guess at. Because of the extra insulating layer of the supergaiters that Stephen and I each wore over our plastic mountaineering boots, neither of us had as yet inspected our toes. And the toes of his left foot, Stephen mentioned, were numb. Nine of Robert's fingertips, like mine, were covered with the sickening bulges of black frostbite blisters, and Robert added that the toes of his left foot also felt cold.

It was with a growing mutual concern that we discussed our dwindling chances of survival. Our ascent of Everest's Kangshung Face had been the best climb of our lives. It had been so enjoyable, so thrilling, so tremendous. And Stephen had summited. As a team, with Paul, by our collective efforts, we had triumphed. Furthermore, we'd become the best of friends. We'd laughed, cried, and shared a great adventure. To be killed now did not seem at all fair.

As the morning waned, the weather turned cloudy and held off the midday heat as we tried to prepare ourselves to descend. Let's leave by eleven o'clock, we agreed—before our departure time slipped to twelve noon, one, two, and then three o'clock. Try as we might, we could not pack our belongings, or clip on our crampons, or stand up, that most demanding challenge of all. Every exertion had to be willed by a tremendous effort commanded from our oxygen- and energy-deprived brains. As Robert later phrased it, "we possessed the collective energy of a mouse." We talked very little. Had Joe and Mimi and Paul seen us descending? Or had they seen our headlamps last night? If not, then surely they would be looking through the binoculars from Advanced Base for signs of us.

Hours slipped away, fading seamlessly into mere seconds of consciousness. A third attempt at brewing hot water succeeded. Then Stephen discovered a packet of potato flakes, plus some freeze-dried shrimp and clam chowder. He suggested that we eat it, but the mention of food nauseated me. I declined, but he and Robert ate some mashed potato.

As the afternoon ticked away, a single thought kept circling through my mind. "I must get to Advanced Base so Mimi can take care of me." My fingertips looked increasingly ghastly; my frostbite blisters were growing bigger. After first propping myself up on one elbow, I succeeded in sitting up with a great effort. Two hours later, after repeatedly collapsing onto my platform, I had stuffed my sleeping bag. I continued to urge Robert and Stephen to descend. When I left camp at 3:45 P.M., they were still fastening their crampons. It would be dark at six. The fight for our lives was on.

Almost as soon as I departed, the sky congealed into a bleak gray sheet. Snow-laden monsoon clouds thickened around and above me, blending evenly with Everest's undulating snow slopes and ice cliffs. At least the clouds masked the sun's heat, but soon it was snowing again. Visibility diminished to forty feet. But the waist-deep snow was enveloping, somehow comforting.

To sit down for a long rest would be the easiest thing in the world.

Unconscious of any danger, I slid unexpectedly down a thirty-foot-tall ice slab that had been concealed by a two-foot layer of snow. Landing on a powdery bed, I brushed myself off and began angling to my right down a snow ramp leading into a maze of crevasses that we'd threaded through on our ascent. Nervously, I surveyed my surroundings. Near the ramp's base, I knew that I needed to turn sharply left above one of the largest crevasses. The turn was unmarked; we'd been conserving our remaining bamboo marker wands.

My fatigue was growing. Continuing downhill, I tripped over a short icy step and fell forward. My next thought was the unpleasant realization that I was sliding down the mountain head first, on my back. Instinctively, I clutched at my ice ax, jabbed the metal pick into the snow, swung my legs around, pivoted my body uphill, jabbed my boots and crampon points into the snow—and stopped myself—all in several seconds. Trembling with fear and surges of adrenaline, I kicked my crampon points viciously into the hard ice buried beneath the top snow layer and managed to reestablish myself on the mountain. Then I looked down.

One hundred feet lower, a gaping crevasse leered its icy grin upward, its fathomless blue void wanting to swallow me whole. By the narrowest of margins, I had escaped death again. I looked uphill. Stephen and Robert were descending slowly toward me; I could see their ghostly figures shuffling through the mist and lightly falling snow. Insanity! It would be dark in an hour; what did we think we were doing, descending so late in the day? I realized then that it would be better to return to camp 2, use our remaining fuel to brew hot water, get some sleep, and descend early the next morning. We had wasted the entire day.

"This is crazy!" I shouted up to Robert. "I just missed falling into a huge crevasse!" Robert soon arrived beside me and promptly slumped in an exhausted heap. A minute later, Stephen joined us. I pointed to the crevasse just below us, recounted my near-death experience all over again for Stephen's benefit, then launched into a high-strung exhortation on the foolishness of continuing our descent. "If we don't climb back up to camp 2, we'll be sleeping out in a snowdrift!" I knew that I was sounding unduly melodramatic, but I was adamant. To continue descending in such poor visibility, unroped, surrounded by hidden crevasses, risking a forced bivouac in the open, could easily have fatal consequences. In fact, to do so I thought would be suicidal.

Stephen eventually agreed with me that we had no option but to retrace our steps back up to the Flying Wing; Robert was too tired to care. Accepting our fate, we willed ourselves uphill toward camp 2. What had taken one hour for us to descend required three killing hours to reverse.

Just below camp, we were stopped by the thirty-foot, sixty-degree ice slab we'd slid over on the way down. With only one ice ax between the three of us, I was wondering how we would negotiate this section. Somewhat comically, Stephen and I balanced up on our front points, climbing side by side, while each holding on to the ice ax. Then, while Stephen clung on tightly to my jacket, I swung the ax until the pick lodged. After repeating this procedure several times, we reached easier angled snow.

Robert watched questioningly from below. "Don't forget to leave that ax!"

"Okay, I'll leave it here, partway up," I replied, then climbed down a move and slammed the pick firmly into the ice. The only problem was that the ax was still two full body lengths above him.

"How am I supposed to climb up to it?" he demanded. I wasn't quite sure, but Robert was inventive. He'd figure something out. He would have to!

Stephen and I continued to camp. It was pitch dark by the time all three of us were resettled under the Flying Wing's ice canopy. We collapsed, having eaten virtually nothing in two days. I made a brew of hot water, and we shared several meager grit-filled mouthfuls. We absolutely had to get an early start in the morning. My strength was dwindling, and I knew that our chances for escape had almost run out.

Everest, from Ama Dablam.

The sun rose gold over Tibet. Feeling the sun's warmth penetrate into my sleeping bag, I peeked outside to see towering Makalu resplendent in the dawn light. Inside my sleeping bag, I was deliciously warm. I could have stayed there forever. That was the problem. I struggled to prepare to leave, made two brews of hot water, and invariably knocked over the stove once or twice. Every action was made with a fragile economy of effort and in the slowest possible motion. Stephen and Robert were awake too, but they had hardly stirred.

I hounded them. "Stephen," I half-joked, "you're not going to be famous unless you get down alive."

We also talked about the mountaineers who'd perished on K2, the world's second-highest mountain, two years earlier. Trapped in a storm at 25,900 feet on the Abruzzi Spur, they ran out of food and fuel and died in their sleeping bags, or soon thereafter, making a last-ditch effort to descend the mountain.

Among those killed were two of Britain's best mountaineers, Alan Rouse and Julie Tullis. It was a tragedy we did not want to repeat.

I remembered what an ordeal it had been to stuff my sleeping bag, so I decided to abandon both my sleeping bag and my parka. By carrying an absolute minimum of weight, I hoped to increase my chances for living. But by abandoning my survival gear, I was irrevocably committing myself to descending to Advanced Base Camp in a single day—or I'd be stranded this evening without a sleeping bag or any warm clothing. I dressed in my Capilene expedition-weight underwear, my one-piece pile suit, a pile jacket, hat, and wool mittens. In my pack I carried half a quart of water, my two cameras, and the rolls of film that I had taken at the South Col and above, on summit day.

Again, I left first, departing from the Flying Wing at about 10:00 A.M. Robert and Stephen said they were coming, but glancing over my shoulder occasionally, I didn't see them for a couple of hours. Our Everest climb had become a battle. We could encourage each other, we could lend moral support, but physically, we could not carry each other back down Chomolungma. Ultimately, the determination to survive was an individual commodity. Robert later told me that when he'd left camp 2 that morning, he did try to get Stephen moving, but Stephen hadn't budged from his sleeping bag. Would he lie there and die? Robert couldn't tell, but finally Stephen did muster himself to stand up and follow us.

I waded through the softly enveloping snow like an automaton. More snow was falling from the heavens. My leaden limbs moved as if by magic, by rote muscle memory, driven by the primal instinct to live. I wasn't going to give in without a fight. My almost seething anger at our shared frostbite and our possibly impending deaths remained, but I sternly reminded myself not to do anything rash. I had to think my way out of this nightmare. I had to create my own destiny if later I wanted to live it. There had to be a way to escape from this crevasse-riddled, snow-walled prison. I realized, too, that my will to live had also spawned a deep hatred for Everest. Chomolungma, mountain of my dreams, how could you kill me? Our brief views of heaven had come at an enormous cost.

Soon I reached the ice step where I'd stumbled and self-arrested the previous afternoon. Sitting down in the soft snow, resting, I decided I'd gone too far right before. I gambled instead on traversing left around a steep snow rib to look for a big crevasse I remembered vividly from our ascent six days ago. But how much the mountain had changed! It was nearly impossible to recognize landmarks because of the tremendous amount of new snow and the smothering clouds. There remained only the slender hope that I could somehow choose a safe path and not be swallowed alive by a lurking crevasse.

But if I did fall into a crevasse, well, what then? I held our only remaining ice ax in my left hand. We no longer had a climbing rope. Even if I fell into a relatively shallow crevasse, I still might not be able to escape. Death would come quickly,

I rationalized, and Stephen and Robert would see which trail not to take. It was better to make the effort, to reach out for life no matter what the consequences, than to sit down in the snow and passively die.

Using every route-finding skill that I'd learned in twenty years of climbing, I began breaking trail through the crevasses in an increasing blizzard. I excavated a trench to my left through a deep snowbank, climbed down a steep fifteen-foot incline, and saw several crevasses directly in front of me. None of them looked familiar. Cautiously, I waded toward them, holding my ice ax at the ready in case I fell in. A snow bridge spanned the first crevasse; gingerly I trod out onto it and pooled enough energy to jump over the weak-looking midsection. Breathing easier once I reached the far side, I then jumped a second crevasse and plowed straight ahead, thinking now that maybe I knew the correct direction of our route to camp 1. Not altogether positive of the way, though, I moved ahead slowly and cautiously and prayed that some higher power would guide me.

Then, through the cloud, I caught another glimpse of orange. I'd found the next bamboo wand! We were on our route! The marker wand also gave me a tangibly solid connection with my not-so-distant past. I stopped in my tracks. Paul, Mimi, Joe, Pasang, and Kasang; they were all waiting for us below. We were not completely alone. Finding that slender stem of a once-growing plant shook me from my dream world and gave me new incentive to return to earth.

There was still no sign of either Stephen or Robert, but I was convinced that my partners were alive and would soon be coming. Though they'd been far from energetic looking when I left camp, I never once imagined that they were dead or in trouble. We had survived so much already through our collective will and by sticking together that I began to assume that probably we would all live. Death was a possibility, yet it no longer seemed as certain as it had the day before. But we still had over 5,000 vertical feet to descend.

I repositioned myself in my mind's eye at where I thought I was along our route, then set off downhill toward the next landmarks, Stephen's Ice Pitch and the next big crevasse. Halfway down the slope, I located another wand, fallen over and half buried by the new snow. "Keep going," I chanted under my breath, my optimism growing. "Keep going, keep going, keep going, keep going."

I felt as if the clouds surrounding me, thick as ocean fog, could have been sliced like a loaf of bread. Downhill through this misty uncertainty was the only direction that my legs would carry me. As I plunge-stepped down the smooth snow slope, my sixth sense prickled with awareness. An avalanche trap! The gently curving slope was smothered in three feet of new-fallen snow. Had the powder had time to bond with the old layers beneath it? I kicked at the snow with my boots. The adhesion seemed vaguely secure. I continued. What choice did I have? The lambs were being fed to the wolves for breakfast. I vowed with every stumbling forward and downhill step toward safety that if I did live through this climb I would never, ever, do another route that was this dangerous.

What I would have given to be transported virtually anywhere else from the hell of this frozen, frostbitten world! I fantasized warm, white sandy beaches, or sunny Colorado, or the normal everyday things in life—going for a walk, eating dinner with friends. Or events that perhaps too often I'd taken for granted. As soon as I escaped from this hated mountain, I would revel in the mundane.

My strength faltered. My arms began to feel light and buoyant. My legs were lead bars. I breathed from the hollow pit of my empty stomach. My breath gave me back energy to move, but my motions became jerky and slow, one foot placed marginally in front of the other as I pushed through the snow like a human plow, moving closer to salvation and a release from this wretched cage. I couldn't recognize any landmarks, but I knew I must be getting near the steep incline of Stephen's Ice Pitch.

My mind began to falter. Just keep moving, I told myself. Don't dare stop or you'll never start up again. Pace yourself, don't hurry. You don't have the strength to hurry! Don't even bother to think, just let your legs move. Walk. Walk slowly. Breathe. Breathe slowly. Slowly, breathe, slowly.

I heard a shout. Robert was a hundred yards above me.

My companions were alive! In my heart, I'd known all along that they were okay. Once more, I began my halting, awkward movements downhill. The next crevasse was 150 feet lower. It was wide—and unfathomably deep. One slip and I'd disappear without a trace.

Tilted straight into the crevasse, the snow slope I was standing on was church-roof steep. I began to traverse left across it, toward the snow bridge we'd used to cross this impasse on our ascent. The snow was bottomless. Each footstep collapsed into the one below it. I realized that I'd descended too far. I would have to climb back up and make a higher diagonal traverse. I began retracing my steps, and yelled up to Robert to head left earlier than I had.

"Left?" he responded weakly. I nodded, too exhausted to speak. I'd eaten nothing in over two days and had consumed only a few cups of tea and a bowl of noodle soup in over four days. I thought the climb back up those hundred feet would finish me off. Moving against gravity at that altitude, in our condition, was an incomprehensible trial.

"I'm not feeling very good, you know that?" my brain said.

"Neither am I," answered my body.

"Well, don't let me down now," said my brain.

"What do you mean?" my body replied. "You always told me you liked a challenge. You're getting one now, aren't you?"

My eyelids grew heavy; my head began to swim.

"Well, you always said you wanted to experience the ultimate challenge, to feel what life was like on the edge," yelled my body to my brain. "And guess what, you idiot—I have news for you. *This is what you wanted, and this is what it's like!* How much longer do you think you can hold on?"

I managed to take another uphill step. Through the mist and the clouds I saw a second stumbling figure appear. It was Stephen! "So you're alive, too," I thought. Good for you.

We had reached Stephen's Ice Pitch, now buried beneath several feet of powder snow. Angling left, we carefully plowed a trench down the slope. After passing Robert, Stephen and I tiptoed along a ledge underneath a vertical ice wall, across the snow bridge spanning the crevasse, and began the final slog toward the top of our fixed ropes, still a thousand feet below.

Again, I went in front, breaking trail. The snow bridge and ice wall were solid landmarks I remembered from our ascent. We were definitely on route, and I felt a new burst of energy. However, we'd placed far too few wands to mark this section, and I followed my instincts down the short ridges and small snowfields that characterized this portion of the route, relieved that the worst of the avalanche and crevasse danger was at last behind us.

Eyes shifted nervously from side to side, searching for the correct route. Here? There? Maybe that way. Legs faltered, stopped, then started. Energy, what was energy? Air was food. My muscles had degenerated into near uselessness, but with each downhill step I began to gain nourishment from an invisible ally: the increasing percentage of oxygen in the atmosphere.

Move legs, move! You've got to keep moving! I remembered Fritz Wiessner's words, and began to chant them over and over again in a solemn incantation:

"Sometimes you've got to fight it."

"You've just got to fight it." Rest. Breathe.

"Sometimes you've got to fight it."

"You've got to fight it." A few more staggering steps.

"You've got to fight it."

"You've just got to fight it."

My breath became labored. Stay in control! Left foot, right foot, another few steps. Good!

"You've got to fight it."

"Fight it!"

I found another bamboo wand at the start of a snowy prow. I walked to the end of the plank; the ridge was corniced and overhung on both sides. We must have climbed up one side. I returned to the wand. Stephen and I walked to the drop-off for a second look.

"I think we went this way," he said with surprising conviction, and began to descend a steep snow trough. Suddenly there was a loud crack, then a whoosh, and Stephen was caught in a small avalanche. Riding atop the wave of falling snow, he flew down a fifty-foot drop and landed in a huge mound of soft snow on the flat terrace below. Springing up out of the drift like a hippo jumping out of a mud hole, Stephen shouted cheerfully: "Yes, that's definitely the right way!"

Shaking my head in disbelief, I returned to the wand. A shorter trough led down to the left. Several steps later, I was also avalanched and fell twenty feet. I brushed myself off. We continued. Stephen broke trail. We could no longer see Robert, but Stephen assured me he had seen him coming.

Then I noticed Stephen had stopped. I joined him.

"Don't you think we should try over there?" I suggested, motioning to our right down the next snow slope.

"What?" Stephen said, seemingly perplexed.

"Well, it looks better that way to me," I replied.

"Ed! We're at the fixed ropes!" he blurted out, pointing to a short piece of orange 8-millimeter rope emerging from the snow.

My gaze settled fondly on the colored length of rope. I couldn't believe it. We were going to live! I reached over, embraced Stephen in a bear hug, and shook him in celebration. All we had to do was rappel three thousand feet to the glacier. Maybe we could still get to Advanced Base Camp tonight. Before starting down the ropes, we glimpsed Robert some distance above us.

"You okay?" I shouted up to him.

"See you at camp 1!" he yelled, adding that he was fine, just slow.

"No—not at camp 1. We're going to Advanced Base no matter what!" I shouted in reply. Robert waved back, and Stephen and I once again began to descend. We dug our harnesses and descenders out from under three feet of new snow (we'd cached them here to save carrying their extra weight any higher), and I strapped on my harness and immediately began racing down the ropes, hurrying from one anchor to the next across the Jumble. I'd been so concerned with staying alive that, until I started rappelling, I hadn't given my stiff, wooden fingers much attention. It took a while to get used to holding the rope, and for the first time I began to realize that my fingers, especially those of my left hand, were very, very cold. I now began to worry. My fingers were not mending as I had hoped. In fact, they felt much worse.

Laboriously, I ripped the fixed ropes out from under their snow mantle. I felt a surge of relief seeing that the Jaws of Doom crevasse had not widened or collapsed. But the seracs had definitely moved downhill, because the ropes spanning the Tyrolean Traverse were stretched tighter than ever! I crossed Jaws and continued down to the Webster Wall. There the rope disappeared into the snow, so I unclipped from my rappel and walked without a belay to the edge of the 75-foot overhanging ice cliff. The pink 11-millimeter rope down the Webster Wall was buried deeply, but by stamping out a platform and carefully peering over the edge, I just caught a glimpse of it hanging free.

I dug the rope out of the snow and rappelled to camp 1. It was 5:30 P.M. when Stephen joined me. We had a short discussion about whether we should continue down or remain here for the night. What little body warmth I still possessed I was rapidly losing through my frostbitten fingers. Since I no longer had a sleeping bag or a parka, I told him that at all costs I must keep moving, to generate heat and to stay warm.

When we'd left camp 1 almost nine days before, we'd collapsed our two tents to protect them from damage. They were now buried under several feet of snow. I hardly recognized the campsite. Stephen pointed out a large trough created by an icefall of recent vintage, directly over where our tents had been pitched. It would have taken us an hour of hard work to excavate them, and since the descent from camp 1 to Advanced Base took two hours in good conditions, I lobbied strongly to continue. Reluctantly, Stephen agreed.

I started down the snow slope below camp. The fixed rope here was also completely buried. All of our 9- and 11-millimeter static fixed ropes were white in color (we'd gotten a good discount on the price), which made them virtually impossible to detect (hence the cheap cost!) against a white snow slope. Now where was that darned rope? Unroped, I gingerly climbed as far down as I dared and began digging with my ice ax. Below me was a two-thousand-foot drop straight into Big Al. As I continued to chop at the snow, suddenly I heard a pronounced crack—and the slope avalanched just above me. Two feet of silky snow cascaded through my legs and into the fearsome abyss. I gripped my ice ax with a burst of adrenaline—and didn't fall.

"Oh, there's the rope," I said matter-of-factly, spotting it at the base of the avalanche fracture. Stephen volunteered to go first, and we rappelled to the bottom of Paul's Ice Pitch, with Stephen digging out each rope length from under the snow. It was a peaceful evening, the bad weather was clearing, and I remember even being nostalgic rappelling past the Greyhound Bus—the first Cauliflower Tower—thinking fondly that I'd never see it so close up again.

Once more, we were about to be caught out in the dark on the mountain. I became increasingly worried and told myself to stay calm and in control. We'd soon be down. Paul, Mimi, and

Joe would take care of us. It was getting dark, no stopping it, and we had no choice but to deal with the situation like we'd dealt with the rest of this hellish descent. Which was as best as we could.

As darkness closed upon Everest, we discovered that neither of our headlamps worked. Then Stephen fumbled and dropped his spare headlamp bulb.

When Stephen couldn't pull up the next section of fixed rope, I rappelled down and joined him at the bottom of Paul's Ice Pitch. Taking my ice ax with him, Stephen headed down and chopped the rope free, inch by inch, from beneath a two-inch-thick layer of ice that had frozen over it during the previous week. It was painstaking work—and one poorly aimed blow could cut through the rope. I hadn't thought our situation could worsen. It just had. I was shivering so hard my limbs trembled. For the next several hours, all I could hear was Stephen's chopping, then his much anticipated signal of "Right!" or "Off!" which meant that he'd reached the next anchor and it was my turn to descend.

But something wasn't right. I looked down. The toe bail of my right crampon had come unclipped. Held by its ankle strap, the crampon dangled uselessly below my boot. With frostbitten fingers, I couldn't fix it. Rappelling down the ropes at night with no headlamp, frozen fingers, and only one crampon became an endless nightmare. Multiple sections of rope were so well frozen into the mountain's icy coating that it was impossible to pull up enough slack to clip our figure-of-eight descenders in for a proper rappel. The painful alternative was a wrist rappel. This meant clipping the rope into a short safety sling and a locking carabiner attached to our harness, then wrapping the ice-encrusted rope around our wrists and forearms for friction. Gripping the rope as tightly as I could with my useless fingers, I would begin to slide down the rope. Several times I lost my grip, and proceeded to fall, slide, and bounce down the slope until my safety sling stopped me at the next anchor attaching the rope to the mountain. I prayed that a stupid mistake wouldn't kill me when I was now so close to safety.

Stephen led the entire descent down the buttress. We were more dead than alive when we reached the Kangshung Glacier at about 1:00 A.M. Using our short length of 11-millimeter rope stashed at the resting rock, we roped up. The recent warm

Stephen Venables

weather and monsoon clouds hadn't allowed the glacier surface to freeze at night, and the crust was now in about the worst
possible condition. Instead of well-frozen snow which would
have supported our weight, a thin, breakable snow skin masked
over a mush of unstable depth hoar—loosely packed snow resembling large Styrofoam pellets. When the crust broke, as it
did about every thirty feet, it was like plunging feet first into a
jar of marbles. Extricating oneself was extremely difficult, especially in our weakened state.

We attempted to keep our sense of humor about the situation. This too became impossible. Hopefulness and grim determination gave way to anger and sudden outbursts. I slipped
back into my old habit, getting pissed off at Venables for moving too quickly, for pulling the rope tight and yanking me off
my feet, while Stephen became increasingly angry with me for
not moving faster to get back to camp.

About halfway to Advanced Base, Stephen began a ceaseless
tirade for a hot cup of tea. "Paul! Mimi! Joe! *Tea!*" he shouted at
the top of his lungs about every five minutes. I was craving a
hot orange drink, and Stephen wanted his bloody cup of tea.
That wasn't too much to ask for, was it? We stumbled across the
glacier, got lost, finally found our way through the crevasses,
and inched progressively closer to camp—to safety, to warmth,
to our friends.

"Paul! Mimi! Joe! *Tea!*"

Suddenly I fell into another pit of unstable snow. We were
roped together about fifty or sixty feet apart to safeguard each
other from hidden crevasses. Stephen's patience grew thinner
and thinner as I struggled to escape from this new bear trap.
But my right leg—and the loose crampon dangling uselessly
beneath my boot—remained firmly rooted in the oatmeal-
thick concrete.

"Ed, can't you do something?" Stephen protested after
watching me struggle in vain for fifteen minutes. I could tell his
patience was at an end.

"You look like a bloody floundering bird!" he bellowed.

We were in the middle of a now-starry Everest night, barely alive, and it seemed we were never going to reach camp, even though safety was probably only minutes away. Stephen was angry, my leg was firmly stuck, and all he wanted was a hot cup of tea. I didn't know what to do. I couldn't budge my leg or my boot, and I was completely exhausted. I leaned back against the snow to catch my breath. We were so close to camp, but I couldn't escape from this damn hole! Then I glanced back up toward Stephen—but Stephen had gone.

After untying from his end of the climbing rope without a word, Stephen headed toward camp. I watched his ghostlike figure disappear into the darkness. Moments later, from the crest of the moraine ridge off to my left came a sudden and animated commotion. Other voices rang out, friends' voices, Paul's and Mimi's voices, shouting and exclaiming, and I knew we were safe. I struggled again to free my boot from its slushy prison, but I couldn't. Slumping backward, I simply waited and looked up at the stars.

Then, momentarily, a wavy beam of light ran along the moraine beside me and a familiar soothing voice shouted out my name. It was Paul Teare. I had never been so happy to hear a friend's voice, a voice which a day or two earlier I was not sure I would ever hear again. I shouted his name back, and Paul bounded across the snow toward me, falling in and leaping back out like a gazelle, springing forward until he reached me and threw his arms around my neck.

"Why didn't you let us know you were alive?" Paul demanded. My attempt to signal from camp 2 with my headlamp had obviously been unsuccessful. Paul asked if I was all right, and I had to admit that . . . well, actually, I wasn't. I told him that my hands were frostbitten, but that my feet, I thought, were all right. In his exuberance over our survival—that we were, amazingly enough, still alive—our frostbite was fairly inconsequential.

"I'm so glad you guys are okay!" he exclaimed. Then Paul asked after Robert, about his condition, and where he was. I replied that Robert was fine, just a bit slower, and that he would be following us down soon.

With Paul shouldering me, I pried my right boot out of the snow, and we retraced his tracks back to the moraine where the walking was easier. Minutes later, back in camp, I was greeted with a joyous welcome home hug from Mimi. Joe was in Base Camp, sending word to the Chinese for a helicopter to come look for us, and Paul and Mimi had been so distressed, thinking we had all died, that they could only sleep by taking sleeping pills.

It was 4:00 A.M. on May 17.

I collapsed beside Stephen inside my dome tent, grateful, so very grateful, for sleep and rest and warmth, just to lie down flat and rest and be warm, and to drink a hot drink, even if it was grapefruit juice, to feel it trickle past my parched lips and down my scratchy sandpaper throat before consciousness failed me. I do not really remember what happened during the next two days. I can recall only a string of hazy dreams: Paul putting me on warm, hissing oxygen, the clear plastic mask slipping over my face, while Mimi tenderly soaked Stephen's and my fingers and toes in sterile warm water baths and fed us soup and crackers, and later, Kasang stared blankly at us, not understanding and very worried, and Ang Chu's brother, Sonam, was crouched beside Kasang, and Sonam's body was trembling, he was so frightened and concerned for us, but then Pasang's fatherly face looked down at me, gave me his comforting smile, and his calm hand reached out to gently hold my shoulder and reassure me that everything would be all right, before Robert, after spending the night sitting alone in the mountain snows one last time, finally returned safely to camp with Joe, who'd hiked out to help him, and Robert stood in the sunshine outside our tent before he bent over, peered quizzically at

Stephen and me lying inside, looking like death—and Robert said to us, grinning that Robert grin: "So, boys, how are we feeling today?"

What I remember most is the sweet delicious sensation of being alive, of lying in my warm sleeping bag on the soft foam pad inside the yellow tent, and of savoring that simple radiant joy, that great gift, of having survived.

And drinking the hot grapefruit juice.

ALISON OSIUS

Alison Osius

Alison Osius has served as the president of the American Alpine Club. She is senior editor at *Climbing* magazine and has contributed to many newspapers, magazines, and anthologies, as well as writing *Second Ascent: The Story of Hugh Herr.* She studied English at Middlebury College and received a master's degree in journalism at Columbia University.

Climbing competitions, a relatively new aberration of the climbing culture, have become popular among the young and eager and allow audiences to watch people attempt steep, man-made walls indoors (sometimes outside), with plastic (and other kinds of artificial) holds. In the past, Osius was winner of three such national women's climbing championships as well as invitational and regional events. She placed in the top ten in a handful of international events. She lives with her husband and two young sons in Carbondale, Colorado.

The Squalor and the Glory

I chose this story simply because it makes me laugh. I liked competitions—having to prepare, focus, and try hard. Comps brought me a lot, mainly lifelong friends. Since this article was written, the efforts of a national youth program have helped more Americans to attend international events as organized groups. But participation is still a big expense.

ALISON OSIUS

There they were at the Nuremberg airport, just the way they were supposed to be, Kurt Smith and Tim Fairfield, waiting on a bench with their elbows on their knees. The two were my travel partners for the next three and a half weeks, three competitions, and some good cragging. We were a trio in a rental car, two rad boys in their twenties and, somehow, this elderly lady in her thirties.

They stood up and offered hugs. Both were wearing tall black new storm-trooper boots, Tim's steel-toed. He explained, "They'd be better in a mosh."

I got into the back seat of the rental car, my official position for the rest of the trip. Back seat, right side. When my friend Susan Price joined us a week later, she would sit in the back left. Neither she nor I would drive unless we were alone in the car; apparently we could not be trusted to maintain requisite velocity. The boys drove alertly, both hands on the wheel.

From this first moment, I looked at the backs of their heads. Their hair was amusingly opposite, Kurt's straight and black, bristling short on top and long down the back; Tim's blond, long on the top and shaved underneath, and sprouting a hair wrap with a feather and beads. They often wore backward baseball caps, so then I'd face Chicago Bulls and J-Rat logos.

We three, plus one other friend collected from a train station, stayed in a local climber's studio apartment. Wolfgang

Stegherr's place contained a kitchenette, loft, and desk, where he sat smoking cigarettes and answering constant phone calls. On the wall were climbing photos, rock-concert ticket souvenirs, and music posters including three of the Red Hot Chile Peppers wearing just socks. The loft sported a campus board, but no ladder; each night Wolfgang got in bed by facing outward, grabbing the big edge, and kipping his legs overhead. Each night we other four arranged ourselves below in a phalanx of sleeping bags.

I normally have no problem sleeping, except when there's a full moon and, unfortunately, before competitions. Especially in a room packed with people, which is how it generally is on the World Cup.

The World Cup is exciting, and it's fun, and there are transcendent experiences—like watching Lynn Hill rise higher and higher to flash the women's superfinal (the same route on which all but two men had fallen) at Lyons, France; or watching François Legrand, just about any time; or maybe even the times you did well yourself. But especially for the Americans, the World Cup doesn't come easy. No American climbers, whether U.S. Team members or not, get any general funding to go, and it's hideously expensive to fly to Europe and live and rent vehicles and drive around.

You don't really climb as much as expected, either. On this three-and-a-half-week trip, I went cragging seven days. We seemed to spend more time driving, changing money, reading city maps, finding stadiums and registries and rooms.

The last time I had been to a comp when traveling with a noncompetitor, Mike (my husband) and I arrived in Switzerland for a competition, hoping to be able to climb locally. But we had to drive south till it stopped raining, and two days later come twelve hours back again.

I drew number 51, and by the time it was my turn, after nine hours in isolation, building workers were sweeping and hosing down the floors.

Then I missed a foothold and fell low. Between the flight, the hotel, the gas, the entry fee, and those few days in the rental car, I figured I paid $360 each for the three bolts I clipped.

"Or, if you consider I climbed 25 feet . . ."

"Max," Mike put in cruelly.

". . . that's $27 a foot."

Fortunately, we were staying longer to climb (driving back south), but Mike never came to another European comp with me.

It's best to go to comps with others doing the same thing, whether you know them or not. Then you sleep three or four to a motel room, cooking on camp stoves. You try to sleep. You listen to Kurt sniff or thump or say "N-n-n-n-n-en" in his sleep, and Timmy chuckle and clack his teeth. Kurt swears he heard me say in my sleep, "Maybe our children will climb hard."

After the World Cup in Nuremberg, we drove south, stopping at the French border. Laughing, Tim tossed francs into the toll basket one by one. Within seconds, two border patrolmen shone flashlights into the windows, looked at each other from beneath the rims of their crisp caps, and ushered us to the side of the road.

The guards asked for passports, and we produced them. In his photo, Tim had amused himself with sucked-in cheeks and demented Popeyes. The guards immediately motioned us out of the car. Neither took any interest in me, and I stood foolishly off to the side.

One man pointed at Kurt's pockets. Kurt turned them out, coinage bouncing all over the bricks. The other cop pointed at the car hood. Tim smartly splayed both palms on it, spread his legs, and bent over. ("That's what I had to do last time I was arrested," he later explained.) The cop tapped his shoulder—he had only wanted Tim to set out the contents of his waist pack.

The patrolman knelt to search with his flashlight under the driver's side floor mat, his shoulder accidentally honking the horn. Tim watched to make sure he didn't plant anything.

"If he did he'da had my boot up his a——," he said as we
drove away.

"I'da grabbed his gun!" said Kurt.

Their chipper bluster was already normal to my ears, like
their gleeful insults of each other.

Kurt added, to Tim, "Thought you were all cool when you
had that photo taken, didn'tcha."

In America we have some good scenes, but in Europe
climbers are more used to being competitive and, partly because of their closer geography, have an advanced level of sharing, working, and training together. In the south of France,
scads of climbers live within two hours of each other; they all
have walls, they go to the crags together. They also have backing. A competitor good enough to have made the finals in
Laval, France, mentioned that he would not have come if he'd
had to pay his own train fare. The Italian B team (let alone the
A team) rides around in a van and climbs full time.

We arrived in southern France for what would be a great part
of the trip. Climbing in Europe, you have more opportunity for
on sighting, come upon stern grades, learn new techniques.
And we stayed put for a bit, ending up with a group of other
people in a threadbare house in a village.

Ah, what a pleasant life. Climbing or resting during the days,
cooking light simple meals, group Scrabble games, reading (we
passed around dinosaur and vampire books, Anne Tyler, Wallace Stegner, guidebooks).

You talk about routes, tell stories, imitate yourselves.
There's usually recreational bashing of our sport's journals
(even if a given basher had just the other day requested a cover
photo).

Seven of us had chipped in to rent a chilly, moldy little
house, humid as Vietnam, with no hot water. Our feet slid on
moisture beads on the floors, Tim bought incense to mask the
rot, and everyone coughed on each other and passed colds
around, and several threw up out the windows and passed flu.

Last year the two-bedroom house had held ten Brits. Hard to believe they fit, but we admired their organization: apparently each cooked dinner every ten days. (This year, at one houseful of Brits nearby, someone had decorated the walls with cutouts from an American climbing magazine and deftly hybridized onto them photos and themes from a porn mag.)

One night as Kurt, Tim, Will Gadd, and I drove back from Buoux, Will picked up a quick three-pack of chocolate bars. We pulled off the wrappers in the dark and ate pieces with gusto, starved after being out in the cold air. It was only later, inside the house, that someone saw on the last bar a misty fungus and the long white dots of maggots. General chaos ensued.

Someone: "I'm not worried about the worms, I'm worried about the mold."

Kurt (hands over face): "I'm worried about the eggs."

Soon after, Will shook habanero powder onto the dinner he was cooking. A mustard-gas-like haze arose, visible even from outside the windows, where violent coughing drove us. I threw up a small amount on the ground. "Are there any worms in it?" Kurt asked.

Kurt, Tim, Susan, and I left early one morning for the St. Polten, Austria, contest, the organized Kurt having scientifically packed the car the night before. In the dark, a peacock squalled. A nearly full moon shone over the fields and through the bamboo trees.

We drove, often through snow, to St. Polten, stopping at one hotel on the way. In the crowded registration area, one of the boys reflected, "We drive here fifteen hours, sit here five hours, we wait in iso five hours, and climb five minutes."

"I hope," said Susan. In Laval, we stayed in a seedy dorm-like motel, where the toilet rooms were supposed to self-clean when you turned out the light. But the system didn't work, and the lights rarely came on in the first place. One sleepless night I went in, closed the door, and heard a loud "whoosh!" in the blackness. Waters exploded on me from all sides. One morning as Susan and I drove to the comp, she asked in concern if I'd been watching the belayers, noting some casual miens.

"You know," I said, "one of these days someone is going to get dropped in one of these things. But don't worry, it won't be us." That very day Susan was dropped 40 feet to land half on a mat, half on a cement floor. She was essentially unhurt but badly bruised, as I could attest the next two nights watching her struggle to get into her bunk.

After Laval, I flew back home and to work, a little burned, though knowing I'd do it again. (I did, but only once to Europe again. Today I still climb, but no longer compete.) Despite the effort it takes, I've mostly enjoyed my short infiltrations into traveling bands, and on this trip was touched when, for example, Kurt asked, "So are you having fun, traveling with us?" and by Tim's lasting amiability.

I'd hoped that Kurt and Tim would go on and compete at the season's final event, in Birmingham, England. But they were tired and wanted to climb—and it would be seven tanks of gas, at $40 to $50 each, with a $200 ferry cost, hotel and entry fees . . . In fact, Kurt never competed again, though his climbing continued at the same raging pace. Tim has. He even moved to France for a time and won a world bouldering contest.

That month, Susan drove with the boys back down to southern France. The first day back, Tim looked into her face and said, "We are going out today and you are going to fall." And she did, with unwillingness and relief, trusting him to catch her. Years later, she still says, "If Tim hadn't done that, I don't think I would have ever climbed again." She and I live in distant places now, but try to climb together annually. In fact, we'd like to go to Kurt's place in El Potrero Chico, Mexico, next.

Leaving Laval, we all gained perspective from two climbers from Romania. It had taken Stefan and Marius six months to save up for their climbing shoes, which they resoled themselves (the edges didn't quite match). One of the two had made his own harness out of seat belts. At home, they had to take three trains to get to their rock gym, which had twelve members. At competitions, they slept in their cars.

"It is no problem," they said. "We are happy just to be here and see François Legrand climb."

KURT DIEMBERGER

Kurt Diemberger

One of the world's great mountaineers, Kurt Diemberger has climbed five of the world's highest mountains. He made two first ascents of 8,000-meter peaks: Broad Peak in 1957 with Hermann Buhl (and two other climbers) and Dhaulagiri with a Swiss-international team in 1960, both ascents done without supplemental oxygen or high-level porters.

Diemberger was with Buhl when, tragically, Buhl walked off the edge of a cornice in a storm on Chogolisa. Diemberger cut his teeth on famous climbs such as the North Wall of the Eiger and the Walker Spur. In 1978 he climbed Makalu and Everest and, the following year, reached the top of Gasherbrum II. In 1984, twenty-seven years later, he climbed Broad Peak again. He reached the summit of K2 with Julie Tullis in 1986, an ascent famous for its tragic culmination.

In a career spanning nearly forty years, Diemberger has been on about twenty-five expeditions. He has filmed three Everest expeditions and has made twenty or so beautiful mountaineering films, winning an Emmy in 1982 for his film work with the Americans on the east face of Everest. He has written three books; his *Summits and Secrets* is widely viewed as a mountaineering classic. He lives in Italy and Austria, though he spends most of his time traveling, climbing, and filming, visiting jungles, deserts, mountains, and seas.

The piece Diemberger has selected is poignant. Descending Broad Peak, "carefully probing the steep new snow above the blue serac walls," Kurt Diemberger and Julie Tullis were caught in an avalanche. Kurt uses this experience to frame that memory of the tragic loss of his friend Hermann Buhl years earlier. The account also seems to portend the loss of Julie, the love of his life, who would die later on K2.

Excerpt from *The Endless Knot*

I like the idea of this book and would contribute something from
The Endless Knot.

KURT DIEMBERGER

Everything is spinning: down is up, up is down; terrible forces
against which all resistance is vain; they toss you, carry you,
twist you, crush out your breath . . . your mouth is stuffed
with snow . . . you grab another gulp of air, and then you're
sucked in again . . . moving down Broad Peak . . . remorselessly.
That's it . . . the end . . . I think, but . . . no! Not yet . . . air.
Don't give up! A pause. Then the tug of the rope again, pulling,
pulling . . . more of this terrible tumbling . . . Oh, Julie! You,
too . . . caught somewhere in this never-ending whirl. Don't
give up! We must not give up—never—even if this is the end
. . . air . . . horrible twists . . . somersaults . . . bumps . . . air . . .
there's no stopping this whirling . . . until it stops by itself . . .
I don't want to do it . . . I have to try and stop . . . need air . . .
a kick! Another impact . . . the rope pulls onward . . . No! I
won't give in. Hold on! . . . Stop! . . . It's stopped!

Stopped. I'm jammed between blocks of ice. The avalanche
has moved on.

Sky up there. Blue. I can move, try and get up. Blocks of ice
near me, the rope goes straight down . . . Where is Julie?

. . . There's a figure, immobile on her back, arms widespread,
head downhill, sprawled on the slope below me. I cannot see
her face.

Julie!

Great God, let her be alive.

I yell: "Are you hurt?"

Seconds of eternity. Answer, please answer.

"I'm all right, but I can't move. Please help me get up."

Her voice. Alive.

Soon I have her freed from her awkward position. The
avalanche, when I came to a halt, had carried Julie on, catapult-

251

ing her head over heels into the slope, where she stuck on her back. We can hardly believe we are still here . . . and unhurt. When we look up, we see a vertical wall of ice, as high as a house, over which the avalanche has carried us before depositing us onto this steep slope of ice blocks. We've come down more than 150 meters over the seracs, and we're incredibly lucky to be still alive. The snowfall has stopped. There's blue sky looking down on us through a hole in the clouds . . .

In the shelter of a huge ice tower we crouch in the snow, the events of the past minutes still etched in our faces. We are badly shaken, even if we appear to have got away unscathed. As we brew some tea, we slowly calm down. Julie is in some pain from a bruised thigh, and I have a hematoma above my left eye— small matters. I lost my snow goggles, and the avalanche pulled the gloves from Julie's hands (luckily she has spares in her rucksack), but such things do not bother us at present, when we think of what might have happened. We keep looking at each other in disbelief: here we are, both of us! If we hadn't been using the rope, we would each of us be, if not dead, on his own somewhere, without any possibility of help, and unaware whether the other was alive or not. We might never have found each other.

That was how I lost Hermann on Chogolisa in 1957. We had no rope. "When I was lying on the slope," I hear Julie say, "there was only silence all around me. I couldn't see anything— my goggles were choked with snow. Then suddenly your voice asked if I was hurt, and I knew you were alive . . ."

Reflectively, I sip my tea from the lid of the aluminum pot and my eyes slide up from Julie, who is now also engrossed in drinking, to the ridge of the mountain.

What made me want to climb Broad Peak again—after half a lifetime?

Did I want to recapture the memories of my first summit experience in the Himalaya? Or was it simply that I wanted to see the places again, stand there, where I had been with my companion—the ridge, the face with its seracs, the high gap and the view down into China, the summit with its cornice—to see if they were still the same, or whether Broad Peak had changed over the years? Did I perhaps want to know whether I could tackle an eight-thousander at the age of fifty-two as well as I had at twenty-five . . . ?

Or was it a totally new challenge: for Julie and me as a team of two to make a "lightning raid" on it—to climb it again in quite a different manner?

Probably it was a combination of all these things.

While we slowly sip our tea below the huge ice tower and gradually recover our composure after our devastating adventure, in my mind images of the first ascent in 1957 dissolve into those of the present. When Julie and I, a fortnight ago, during a first push, got to 7,000 meters I suddenly found something . . .

A twisted, rusty piton—a piton that I recognized. A heavy piton with a ring, both of solid iron, one of those pegs which long ago in the fifties were equally good for rock and ice but which nobody uses these days. I clearly remember Hermann hammering it into the rocks here—twenty-seven years ago—for anchoring our tent at camp 3. He was swearing, as the piton did not want to grip in the friable limestone of the rocky island which we called the Eagle's Nest. Several pitons had to be used in the end. Finally, in the evening of that day, 28 May 1957, we had two tents up and our assault camp was ready for the first summit bid. Ready for the final stage of what others had so often called "madness," the "first eight-thousander in west Alpine style"—without high-altitude porters or oxygen respirators. A hard adventure: a true Buhl enterprise. One giant mountain and just four climbers: Hermann, Marcus Schmuck, Fritz Wintersteller, and me, the "Benjamin" of the expedition. God, what a lot we carried! But it was one of the last unclimbed 8,000-meter peaks. A dream—my first Himalayan trip. With the great

Hermann Buhl . . . so thin and frail he looked. But he was the idol of a whole climbing generation—not only in Germany and Austria: the whole world had been electrified when he got to the summit of Nanga Parbat on his own. At the time, that icy giant, the "Naked Mountain," had already claimed nearly forty lives. Coming back down, he'd had to stand the whole night on a narrow ledge leaning against the rocks at 8,000 meters, a "bivouac" few others could have withstood. Yet he made it. I still remember the famous picture: his face ravaged by sun and wind under the slouch hat, goggles pushed up onto his forehead, that staring gaze. In the forty-one hours of his summit ordeal Buhl's face had aged into that of an old, old man—it was an image that moved the world. And me with it: I worshiped him from that moment. And when, after going to one of his lectures, he wrote "Bergheil" on my Austrian Alpine Club membership card, I guarded it like a treasure. I was twenty-one and could never have imagined that in just four years I would be standing with him on the summit of Broad Peak watching the sun go down behind a savage sea of peaks.

When we climbed down the West Spur, I saw that face again—haggard from the struggle of the long, steep nighttime descent and his own iron determination to return to life, just as he had been on Nanga Parbat. The unforgettable face of Hermann Buhl.

Our acquaintance was far too short. We only reached this one summit together. But we had great plans for the future . . .

Neither of us could imagine that barely three weeks after that sunset on our eight-thousander, Hermann was to die on Chogolisa when he simply stepped out of this world, over a cornice in a storm . . .

"We plan to stay on here for a while: make some excursions, perhaps do one or the other six- or seven-thousanders . . . " Buhl wrote home. To me, it's as fresh as yesterday: after Broad Peak, the expedition divided. Marcus and Fritz dashed off to grab a lightweight Alpine style ascent of Skilbrum, a seventhousander in the nearby Savoia group; Hermann and I—moving with just one tent, which we planned to carry with us and set up day after day—had as our target the beautiful "roof in the sky," 7,654-meter Chogolisa.

It all seemed to work well. Our "mobile high-altitude camp" was fine. At 6,700 meters we left the tent on the ridge and set off toward the summit. It was 27 June 1957. Hermann was in fine form and really pleased with life: climbing such a high mountain in only three days, rather than three weeks, was like a dream, even for him.

But it was to turn out very differently . . .

A little cloud came rolling up the slope below us. It grew larger, enveloping us, enveloping the peak. Without any warning, all hell broke loose. Gray veils of mist scurried across the ridge. We fought our way forward through clouds of blown snow, bending double to meet the fury of the gale. Yet such a deterioration in the weather seemed impossible after the glorious morning we had had.

"We must turn back at once. The storm is wiping out our tracks," Hermann said suddenly. "We'll end up over the cornices if we're not careful." And he was right. Those were his last words at 7,300 meters. It was soon after that it happened.

"Whummm!" The noise ran through me like a shock. Everything shook and for a moment the surface of the snow seemed to sink. Terrified, I jumped out to the right.

It was the cornice breaking under Hermann Buhl. But I did not suspect that until later when he failed to join me, when I waited for him and he didn't come. I hurried back and discovered footprints, his last steps, leading to a fresh fracture line: at a bend in the ridge, he'd left the track and gone out toward the edge of the cornice . . .

And supposing we had been roped? Could I have held him, or would he have pulled me with him into the void?

I still do not know, and so often have thought about it. Hermann fell down the north face of Chogolisa, probably 500 meters—there was nothing to see on account of further avalanches. A later search revealed nothing. That I got down from there at all in that storm, I put down to a lucky star. And to myself—never giving up.

Hermann Buhl's face dissolves and the white roof of Chogolisa blurs into the distance: above me soars the huge ice tower, the sheer, vertical serac wall over which we have fallen. There is still a patch of blue sky above the rocky ridge of Broad Peak, but already the clouds are moving together to block it out.

Yes, I am infinitely grateful to the fate that has allowed Julie and me still to be here, sitting in the snow. It is nothing short of a miracle that we have both survived. It was the rope that prevented us from being separated by the torrent of snow.

I clasp the pot of tea in my hands, knowing that Julie and I need another lucky star to get us down to the place where I found that old piton; we have to descend at least another 400 meters across these avalanche slopes.

WALTER BONATTI

Walter Bonatti,
England, 1984.

Perhaps the most famous of all alpinists, the great Italian climber Walter Bonatti has also been regarded by many as the finest alpinist of all time. Reinhold Messner has credited Bonatti with "ushering in a new dimension to classical Alpine climbing." Bonatti's ascents in the Alps, Himalaya, and Patagonia set a standard for courage and boldness. A first ascent of the east face of the Grand Capucin in 1951 marked the introduction of artificial aid climbing in the western Alps. His first ascent of the Southwest Pillar of the Dru, in 1955, was at the time viewed as the "last great problem" of the Alps. That ascent was done in a five-day solo, a bold stroke and one of the greatest feats ever. It certainly lifted the concept of adventure to a new high. In Patagonia he made a visionary attempt on Cerro Torre from the west, and in the Himalaya in 1958 he made the first ascent of Gasherbrum IV with Carlo Mauri. His career culminated with a solo ascent of a new route on the north face of the Matterhorn in winter in 1965.

Bonatti for many years has continued to travel, create, lecture, and live a life of adventure. He is an accomplished photojournalist. He has written eleven books in Italian, three of which have been translated into English: *On the Ice, The Great Days,* and *The Magic of Mont Blanc.*

The following excerpt from a talk he gave is almost like stepping into the middle of a conversation. In fact, the subjects of spirit and adventure and style have dominated Bonatti's writings. What he has to say is important to hear, as it seems fewer and fewer of today's climbers have much interest in what makes an achievement a worthy one. It becomes easier and easier, for example, to reduce climbs and overcome their difficulty by technology, modern gear, or bolts. Bonatti speaks of the limitations he has always placed on himself to keep true adventure intact.

Concepts of Adventure

I wrote the following reflections for a talk I gave at a conference in 1999.

WALTER BONATTI

To solo the north face of the Matterhorn in winter wasn't anything new for me. In fact twelve years earlier, when I was still a boy (in March 1953), I climbed the Matterhorn, finding a way through the overhangs of the Fürggen Ridge via a new route. With the completion of the winter ascent of the Matterhorn, in 1965, I brought to a fulfillment the type of mountaineering I had lived for sixteen years at extreme levels of difficulty.

Assuming that we are all free to think as we like and are able to embrace and live by our own personal, most desirable rules for existence and therefore also to practice the kind of mountaineering that is best for us, I too, for the same reasons, have chosen an approach to climbing that conforms best to my personal philosophy. From the beginning, I have taken my inspiration from traditional and classic ways of climbing, in which one measures oneself against a great mountain, and where everything about oneself—physical and emotional conditions and principles—is put to the test, and one must give all and spare nothing. Furthermore, a mountain that I define as "great" becomes particularly severe and exacting because of the limits imposed by the technical means that we have, and accept, to climb it.

An ascent is even more fascinating if we see its historical and ethical value as well as its aesthetic value.

I conformed myself to the mountaineering of the thirties, adopting, of course, the essential but still elementary and very limited technical means used in those times. But why should I have chosen, and continue to embrace, these anachronistic limitations? Certainly not out of some perverse masochism, but rather to be able to preserve an unalterable method of comparison, a kind of Greenwich meridian that remains unchangeable

260 • Walter Bonatti

throughout time and its conditions: the sole reliable constant by which one can achieve an impartial judgment of things, and a judgment also of oneself.

I therefore imposed this on myself from the beginning, and I would do it again, in order to have a firm link with the past—which has always been my reference point. So, engaging in my endeavors on my own mountains, I say again, I have been able to measure myself deeply, and in relation to those who have preceded me, and I have been able to stay in touch with the physical and psychological conditions those predecessors faced in their exploits. Not least, I have been able to objectively evaluate the entirety of what I have been able to do, with respect to what had been done until then.

In assessing alpinism, if we ignore the past and refer only to the present to judge our climbing—a present ever more saturated with technology and concerned only with the difficulties, the unknowns, and even aimed at pulling down a climb and its peculiar difficulties and uncertainties, and often also the impossible—then I believe we never will be able to form a clear and unbiased criterion for understanding what alpinism really is. We fail if we do not truly consider what the limits and motivations of alpinism have been in the past.

Thus, after my 1965 success on the Matterhorn, I extended my adventures to the entire globe, moving through natural settings that were different but no less rich in emotion, wonder, and authenticity, in the farthest, strangest, and most demanding places of the world. I therefore transferred my extreme alpinism, with all its psychological components, from its vertical context into an equally intense and much more varied adventure. And on my life's journey, there are still great mountains that will never cease to fascinate me.

SUSAN FOX ROGERS

Susan Fox Rogers

Susan Rogers started climbing at age fifteen (1976) in central Pennsylvania and soon made her way to the Shawangunks. Loose Woman was one of those early climbs, and writing about the subtle but pivotal moments in climbing has been the focus of most of her personal essays, which have appeared in *Climbing* and various literary journals. She has edited nine book anthologies, including *Solo: On Her Own Adventure*, *Another Wilderness*, and *Two in the Wild*. She received an MFA from the University of Arizona in creative nonfiction and now teaches writing at Bard College, across the Hudson River from the Gunks.

Loose Woman

My choice, "Loose Woman," is a personal essay about an early climb, a time when the possibility and mystery of climbing were just emerging. This climb, short, not very hard, unknown except to locals, sparked my love of climbing and oriented me in my life.
SUSAN FOX ROGERS

Munch and I coasted down the far side of Pine Grove Mountain, the red VW Bug picking up speed. The Doors, blasting through three speakers, seemed to push the car faster. I wanted Munch to slow down, or at least focus on the road, on the sharp turns ahead. Instead he smiled at me, his round freckled face spread so wide into a grin that his eyes became creases.

"You have to do it," he said.

I shook my head, uncommitted, and stared through the bug-splattered windshield at the light green blur of the spring forest.

It was a climb named Loose Woman. Several times I had tried and failed at the crux, which involved a traverse that led into some fancy laybacking. But it wasn't only the technical challenges that fascinated me. It was the name of the climb and what or who I might become if I did it.

"It's your nemesis," Munch said. "Every climber has their nemesis."

I didn't know what a nemesis was, but I smiled.

Loose Woman. Age fifteen, while all of my girlfriends were experimenting with various degrees of sex, I was walking around the house singing "Fifty dollars says you can't make me come." The only curiosity I had about sex was why others were so obsessed with it and why it made my girlfriends so dumb. And yet, I wanted to be Loose Woman.

Loose Woman was not my mother or my sister. She was not the woman who made boys giggle and girls blush. I'd never met her, never seen her, even in the movies or the adventure books I read. She traveled in the shadows, spoke slowly, and smiled only

when she was happy. She was strong and knew it, walked tall
and said no. She did as she wanted, felt desire and acted on it.

I still want to be Loose Woman.

Loose Woman was one of a several dozen climbs in a small area
called Donation, smack in the center of Pennsylvania. None
of the short cliffs in that narrow valley ran to more than sixty
feet high, and the rock looked like rough elephant skin, lined
and ridged and pockmarked in no rational way. Soft and ab-
sorbent, the rock was often moist and green with moss. After a
spring rain, we had to wait for days for everything to dry. If you
didn't know where Donation was, hidden deep in the woods
and split by a dirt road, you would never find it.

Dunk's white Chevrolet van, dinged and scratched from
many climbing trips, nested in a pullout in the valley. Voices
on the left side of the road told us a top-rope was set up on
Royal Delight, a climb named for Royal Robbins, a legendary
Yosemite climber. Years earlier he had passed through this valley and put up the climb, a series of overhangs on an overhung wall.

Working on the climb were Dunk, Mac, and Vicki. Mac was
living in State College while Vicki finished her degree at Penn
State. Vicki was tall and slender, with short reddish blond hair
and round wire-rimmed glasses. Talkative and enthusiastic was
the polite way to say it. Dumb blond is what others said. In our
area she was the only other woman who climbed, so I expected
a lot of her, wanted to be her friend. I wished the rumor that
Loose Woman was named for her wasn't true. She laughed too
much and played along with the boys. She was given that
name; she didn't take it.

But the rumor extended: she had never done the climb. I
could be the first.

Munch called "Rope!" The yellow coil dropped through the
air, nicking the branches of a nearby tree. With a sure thud it

landed on a smooth patch of dirt. I grabbed both ends of the goldline, which felt stiff in my palms, then pulled to see if the rope ran smoothly through the anchors Munch had secured on top. From one anchor, we could do three climbs: Loose Woman, Damnation, and Salvation. Moving left to right, each climb was harder than the last, with sections where the wall overhung, bulged out past ninety degrees.

I sat on a fallen tree, the bark gone and the wood soft, flaking like Styrofoam. Shoes off, I wriggled my toes in the cool spring air to dry them. I climbed barefoot, my feet solid, sinewy, and callous. My exposed feet sweated, smeared and edged on holds that cut. The pain was a sign of my devotion, my love.

My harness was a single black nylon band wrapped neatly around my waist. I tied a square water knot and stared up at Loose Woman, imagining how I would feel: graceful, controlled, powerful. But the details of this waltz—left right, right left—were not clear, even though Munch had told me a dozen times: you have to grab the arete with your left hand, move your feet, then match with your right hand.

Or was it right, then left?

When someone asks, Did you jam the crack or did you reach through to the jug? I can't answer. My memory doesn't work that way. When I climb I rely on knowledge lodged in my muscles. The memory there emerges through smells or the rhythm of movement and is fully reliable—I count on my feet to step high when needed, for my triceps to mantel me through onto a ledge. But these memories are not specific or logical, cannot account for how I got from here to there, how at the bottom of the climb I was one girl and at the top another. How twenty-two years ago I was her, and now I am me.

And yet I do remember everything from that day so clearly: the tone of Munch's voice, raspy and full of enthusiasm, the humid tick of the woods, the slur and dip of that Pennsylvania rock. Maybe in the memory I'll find her, that girl who was fully loose woman. And I'll transform her into words, let her reenter my body.

On the first 10 feet of the climb the holds were cool and faintly moist against the tips of my fingers. Small ledges served for footholds, a narrow vertical stairway. At the traverse, I stopped and inhaled as if drinking ice water through a straw. I looked between my legs to where Munch stood on the ground, holding the rope loosely around his waist.

"Do it." He no longer grinned.

For a moment I wanted to back off without trying, downclimb to the solid ground. But I looked up the rock, toward the top, then reached for the ridge with my right hand. I pawed the rock, hoping for a more solid purchase. A slight tug from the rope around my waist reminded me Munch was there.

"Give me some slack." I didn't want tension from the rope to help me through the move, I wanted to know I'd done it alone.

My feet stuck to the rock, and I shifted my weight to the right, leaned in toward the ridge. The hold cupped in my right hand like an oversized baseball started to slip. If I hesitated or retreated, I sensed the holds would draw back. So I pushed forward, and with more weight the hold became secure. My left hand snapped over to join my right. With hands stacked one on top of the other, my fingers wrapped around that bulky ridge, I inched upward. My toes splayed against sloping dishes in the rock as I positioned to layback the next few moves. Laybacking was awkward, hands and feet in alignment, like climbing a flagpole, while my body flapped out like a barn door that at any moment could unhinge. Shifting from left to right, my body adjusted to the form of the rock. Something else shifted as well in how my body gave over, leaned into the rock with a hope that rested only in my forearms. My body trusted what seemed doubtful.

At a horizontal band, I leaned out hard against my arms, my breath short gulps. Though past the crux, I didn't linger—

because the rock continued steep. With strength quickly drain-ing, I pulled on rounded holds large enough for my palms. When I rolled onto the top ledge, I lay for a brief moment lis-tening to my gasps, short, high, as if I might start crying. Next to my face rested a small mound of deep green moss that smelled of dark, rich Pennsylvania soil. The ledge disappeared into darkness, a sealed cave.

"Nice work, loose woman," Munch called up from the ground thirty-five feet below. Congratulations felt all wrong. I wanted silence, to hold onto this fleeting sensation, the way my heart beat in a strange and insistent way, thrilled and guilty at once.

Later, after Munch had waltzed up Loose Woman and we'd both thrown ourselves at Damnation and Salvation, we crossed the road and found Mac, Dunk, and Vicki. Munch bragged for me. "She did it. She's a loose woman."

"How'd it go?" Mac asked.

"It's hard to explain," I should have said. Instead, I looked down at my feet, shyness swooping down to rest on my ex-hausted shoulders.

I remember my mother announcing to my father when my period began. I see his face still, the shift from surprise to em-barrassment. The change was so subtle yet absolute that he didn't need to be told. And neither did Mac, Dunk, and Vicki. My transformation was evident in my feet and my swollen fore-arms, in the way I kept my smile to myself.

APPENDIX

Glossary

abseil—A rapid method of descending on steep rock, snow, or ice by sliding down a rope or double rope. Same as *rappelling*.

acclimatization—Letting your body adapt to the "thin air" at high altitude. Usually this entails gaining height slowly, exercising gradually at progressively higher altitudes, and not staying very high for very long. An actual physical transformation takes place in the blood cells.

aid climbing—Climbing where gear placements and other equipment (pitons, nuts, slings, etc.) are used for *handholds* or any other type of direct support in making progress up or across the rock.

aiders—Two slings that can be attached to gear placements to stand in during *aid climbing*. Same as *aid slings*.

Alpine style—A means of climbing high mountains or peaks without a massive buildup of staff and equipment and, in the purest sense, without *fixed ropes* or siege tactics.

anchor—Any tree, rock horn, climbing nut, bolt, or *piton* that climbers anchor, or tie themselves, to for a *belay* or *rappel*, to secure a *bivouac*, and so on.

approach—The hike, scramble, or rock route required to get to the bottom of more serious roped climbing.

arete—A somewhat sharp ridge.

arm lock—A technique in which the climber bends an arm sharply at the elbow and wedges it into a crack 9 to 15 inches wide for support. Usually the elbow is head high against one inner wall of the crack and the palm is at chest level against the other inner wall (fingers pointing toward the chest or downward).

ascenders—Handles that can be attached to a rope. Because they slide up but not down, a climber can use them to ascend a rope.

base jump—To parachute from the top of a large rock to its base.

belay—Anchoring to the rock, then pulling in and feeding out the rope to protect and, in the event of a fall, catch a fellow climber.

belay anchor—Any device such as a climbing *nut*, *piton*, or *sling* around a *horn* or tree, used to keep a belayer from being pulled off if a person belayed falls.

belay plate (or belay device)—A metal device that attaches to a rope and to a belayer, or to a double rope, to provide friction for belaying, lowering, and sometimes *rappelling*.

bergschrund—A *crevasse* between a glacier and the main slopes or rocks of a mountain.

biners—See *carabiners.*

bivouac—To pass a night or wait out a storm in the open, such as on a rock ledge or in a hammock suspended from *pitons.*

bivy bag (or bivy sack)—A body-sized covering that serves as a small tent in a *bivouac.*

bolt—A small piece of metal hammered into a drilled hole in the rock, used only where there are no natural cracks or other forms of *protection.* Also, to drill a hole, or several holes, in the rock and drive in an expansion bolt or a line of bolts.

bolt hanger—The metal ring on a bolt to which a *carabiner* is clipped.

bong—A large aluminum *piton* used for wide cracks (usually 2 to 4 inches wide).

bouldering—The art and pleasure, and also training, of climbing on small but very difficult rocks. Usually bouldering is done without a rope, although some "boulder problems" are high enough to be viewed as serious climbs or warrant a *top-rope* belay.

bridge (or bridging)—Stretching your legs across a space between two points of rock. Standing with your feet on two separate rock points to support yourself by opposing force with your legs as you climb. See also *chimney technique.*

bucket—A large *handhold* or foothold.

buttress—A large mass of rock protruding from a mountain or rock formation.

cagoule—A waterproof jacket, usually with a hood.

cam—A metal *protection* device that locks into a *crack* by rotating and wedging. There are several different types and sizes for various sizes of cracks.

carabiner—A circular (or oval) ring or snap link, typically aluminum, through which a rope is clipped to a climbing *sling, piton,* or other points. The carabiner holds the rope and lets the rope run. Carabiners are also used to anchor the rope, such as at *belays.*

ceiling—A large, flat overhang. A protruding rock that blocks the way.

chalk—The gymnastic powder magnesium carbonate, spread on hands and fingers to neutralize skin moisture and keep sweat from making handholds slippery.

chalk bag—A small bag filled with *chalk* and clipped or tied somewhere on the body where the climber can reach it with either hand.

cheval—A method for crossing a narrow ridge with one leg on each side.

chimney—A *crack* large enough for your body to fit inside. Also, to ascend a chimney by wedging your body inside and worming upward or *bridging*.

chimney technique—Most often, using opposing force (back against feet, for example) in a *chimney* or wide *crack*.

chockstone—Any rock wedged in a *crack*, *gully*, or *chimney* (or between two walls) that might serve as a *stance*, a hold, or something to tie a *sling* around for an *anchor* or for *protection*.

cirque—A circular area of mountain or rock, forming a kind of amphitheater, a contour roughly forming a half-circle or quarter circle.

clean climbing—Doing a route without placing pitons or bolts. Making an ascent that does not damage or scar the rock (or litter the rock with unnecessary *slings*, cigarettes, and trash).

cleaning a pitch—Removing the *nuts* and other gear placed by the leader. This is done by the person going second on the rope, who has the advantage of a *belay* from above.

cling hold—A regular flat, ledgelike handhold.

clipping in (or clipping)—Attaching your climbing rope to an *anchor* or a point of *protection* by placing a *carabiner* on the anchor and then clipping the rope into the carabiner through the carabiner gate.

col—A type of dip in a ridge, for example between two peaks, or between a higher summit and a lower summit of the same mountain. A saddle.

committed—Having reached a point on a climb where retreat is very difficult or nearly impossible.

cord—Slang for a rope or *sling*.

cornice—A lip of snow projecting over the edge of a ridge or the top of a rock or *gully*.

couloir—A large gap between two areas of terrain.

counterforce—Simultaneous exertion of force in opposing directions, such as an *arm lock*.

crack—Any small or large fissure in the rock.

crampons—Steel spikes that are strapped onto boot soles. Used in climbing ice and snow.

crevasse—A crack in the surface of a snowfield, glacier, or rock, sometimes hidden and usually deep.

cross-pressure—Two limbs (or hands or feet) pressing in opposite directions against each other to hold a climber on the rock or allow upward progress.

crux—The most difficult section of a climb or *pitch*.

cwm—A word from the Welsh, meaning a *cirque*.

descent—The hike, climb, scramble, or *rappel* required to get off a rock, mountain, or climb.

dihedral—A place where two planes of rock come together like a corner, formed by the intersection of two walls.

direct aid—The use of gear for support in climbing. Gear is placed to support a climber's weight in making upward progress. In *free climbing*, no direct aid is allowed.

draw—See *quickdraw*.

dynamic move—A quick, controlled swing move or a lunge from one hold to another.

dzong—A Tibetan fort.

edge—A sharp corner of rock, or a small foothold or *handhold*. To edge means to use the sides of your shoes on small holds.

8,000-meter peak—A mountain 24,000 feet above sea level or higher. Everest, the supreme 8,000-meter peak, is 29,028 feet.

etriers—French word meaning *stirrups*, used for the slings climbers stand in that are attached to *pitons*, climbing *nuts*, or *prusik* devices such as knots or *ascenders*.

exposure—Being exposed to very open air or a long way down. An airy place and rock, with a long drop, or where a slip would have frightening, if not serious, consequences. Exposure can also mean a loss of body heat, leading to hypothermia or *frostbite*.

face climbing—Moving over a face of rock using holds. People sometimes face climb a *crack*, finding holds to pull up on and avoiding the usual crack-climbing techniques.

feeding rope—Paying out the rope as a climber *belayed* needs *slack*.

finger jam—Using fingers wedged in a *crack* to support body weight or hold a climber into the rock as the feet support body weight.

finger lock—Positioning fingers in a *crack* so they lock downward and can be used as a *handhold*.

finger pocket—A hole in the rock that fits a finger or several fingers.

fist jam—Wedging your fist into a *crack* for support.

fixed piton—A *piton* left by a previous ascent or established for successive ascents.

fixed rope—A rope left in place on the rock or a snow or ice slope for a return to the climb. Fixed ropes are sometimes established in mountaineering to aid porters and other members of a climbing team.

flake—A piece of the rock that is very thin, juts up sharply, or is not fully attached to the rock.

free climbing—A technique in which equipment and rope are used only for protection in a fall but are not used to support weight or grabbed with the hands to make upward progress. Not to be confused with *solo climbing*.

free solo—Climbing with no rope or *protection*.

friction—A type of *face climbing* where you smear (press) the bottoms of your shoes to a relatively holdless slab of rock. See also *smear*.

Friend—A spring-loaded *camming* device set under *flakes* or in *cracks* to provide *protection*. A *carabiner* is attached to the *sling* on the Friend, and the rope then is run through the carabiner.

front point—To climb ice or hard snow, with *crampons*, jabbing the sharp front spikes of the crampons into the ice, in order to support the weight of the climber. Walking up ice, with each successive jab of a cramponed foot.

frostbite—A condition in which ice crystals form between the cells, constricting blood vessels. The oxygen supply to the cells is reduced, resulting in deterioration and infection of the tissue.

gear sling—A loop of sling placed around a shoulder and hanging down toward the opposite hip, for attaching and carrying various items of gear, such as *carabiners*, *nuts*, and *Friends*.

gendarme—A pinnacle on a ridge.

glissade—Sliding down a snow slope, dipping the ice ax into the snow (or ice) as a brake.

goldline—A nylon rope, one of the earlier prototypes, the color of gold.

gully—A somewhat deep, wide groove in (or across) the rock, usually not difficult to climb but often having loose rock.

handhold—Anything that serves as a hold for a hand, in climbing, such as a *flake*, or a small ledge, or a crystal.

hand line—Any fixed rope that allows a climber to pull up, usually in mountaineering, but occasionally where a fixed rope is used in rock climbing.

hand jam—Placing a hand in a *crack* and cupping it into a wedge to pull the climber up.

hand traverse—Climbing horizontally or diagonally along a series of *handholds* or a *crack* or *flake*; usually the hands and arms take the brunt of the climber's weight.

hangdog—Hanging or resting on gear and lowering from fixed *protection* while piecing together a series of climbing moves.

harness—A sling or webbing contraption fitted around the legs and waist, attached to the rope, and used to support a climber comfortably during a *rappel* or in case of a fall.

haul bag—A sturdy duffel bag or other large, well-made equipment sack for hauling heavy loads up a big wall.

hauling—A technique for big-wall climbing where *bivouac* equipment, water, and such are pulled up, *pitch* by pitch, in a large bag by a rope independent of the climbing rope. On a shorter climb, you can haul a small pack.

headwall—Usually a vertical section of rock that is noticeably steeper than the general angle of a rock. An especially steep and vertical section of rock that impedes the way or must be climbed.

hook—A small curved piece of steel designed to hook onto a small ledge; used for support or *protection*.

horn—A projection of rock suitable as a *handhold* or as support for a *sling*.

hung up—Getting the rope stuck while climbing or *rappelling*.

icefall—An unstable series of huge *crevasses* and enormous fractured blocks of ice and pinnacles formed where a glacier falls over a steep area.

ice screw—A *piton* to be driven or screwed into ice.

inside corner—A place where two faces of rock come together like an open book. Same as a *dihedral*.

jam (or jamming)—Wedging any part of your body into a *crack*.

jam crack—A *crack* in the rock that is ascended by *jamming* the body, or the hands, or any combination of other body parts, including the climbing shoes.

jug—A large *handhold*.

jumar—A mechanical *prusik* device with a handle, like an *ascender*, attached to a rope for ascending it.

knife-blade piton—A thin *piton*, about as thin as a knife, that is driven with a hammer into a thin *crack*.

knob—A small natural knob of rock protruding from the surface and used for a hold or to drape a *protection* sling.

layback—See *lieback*.

leading—Going first on the rope.

lieback—Ascending a *crack*, *edge*, or *flake* by pulling with the hands in opposition to the feet. The climber leans back against the arms while holding on to a flake, with the feet pressing on the wall not far below the hands.

lowering—Coming down with the support of a rope passed through a piece or pieces of *protection*. Being *belayed* down from above.

lunge—A committing, somewhat uncontrolled leap for a hold, sometimes becoming detached from the rock.

mani stone—Rock that a prayer has been carved on; common in Nepal and Tibet.

mantel—A climbing move where a climber places hands on a flat or slanting ledge above, pulls up, and then pushes down with the hands on the ledge (usually until a foot can be placed on the ledge). A mantel can also be done with one hand and arm, while the other hand uses a normal handhold. To mantel is to perform a mantel up onto something. Not to be confused with *mantle*.

mantle—A rope's braided covering or sheath. Not to be confused with *mantel*.

moraine—Banks of stone and earth pushed aside by the movements of a glacier.

move—Whatever action is physically required at any given point of the climb. Any particular step of climbing.

nail—To hammer *pitons* into *cracks*, for direct aid, in ascending steep rock. See *direct aid*.

neve—Snow slopes of a mountain above a *bergschrund*.

nut—A small metal wedge (with a wire or sling) set in a crack and used for *protection*.

objective dangers—Dangers that cannot be overcome by skill, such as unpredictable weather or avalanches.

off-width—Term referring to a *crack* where nothing seems to fit: too wide for fists or hands, too narrow for an *arm lock*, too narrow to *jam* with heel against toe. Such cracks are usually 5 to 10 inches wide.

on-sight—Leading a climb on your first encounter with that climb.

opposition—Connecting *slings* and *nuts* in opposition so they hold each other together or in place in the rock and cannot be lifted out by the movements of the rope.

overgrip—Holding to the rock too hard and tiring your hands.

overhang—A protrusion of rock that creates an obstacle. See also *ceiling*.

palming—*Smearing* (pressing) your open hands onto the rock or on a slab to force it to stick and to support yourself or push yourself up.

pendulum—Swinging back and forth across a wall on a rope to reach a *crack* or ledge to the side or more climbable rock or to create a *traverse*. Also, a fall where the position of the rope allows the climber to swing across the rock.

perlon—Nylon rope.

pin—A *piton*.

pitch—A section of a climb measured by the length of rope required to reach a *belay* spot. For example, "The first *pitch* was only 60 feet to a ledge, then the second pitch was a full 100 feet to a *stance*."

piton—A tapered metal wedge hammered into a *crack* for *protection* or support, now almost obsolete since pitons scar the rock and are not as aesthetic or expedient as *nuts*.

placement—The setting of a climbing *nut* or *piton* or other piece used as *protection* or as an *anchor*.

pocket—A cuplike hole in the rock, deep or shallow, that serves as a *handhold* or a hold for fingers.

protection—Gear such as *slings, nuts, pitons,* or *ice screws* placed in the rock or snow. Natural points such as small trees or *flakes*. All these are used by a climber to fix a *carabiner* or sling with a carabiner and run the rope held by the *belayer*, to minimize the distance of a fall.

prusiking—Ascending a rope by sling knots or metal *jumar* handles (or *ascenders*) that attach to the rope. The knots or jumar handles slide up the rope but not down. Usually the climber is attached to the knots or ascenders by slings and also stands in slings attached to the ascenders.

pump (or pumped)—A condition where the forearms are puffed up, tired, and tightened from strenuous climbing.

quickdraw (or draw)—A short length (or loop) of *webbing* (usually no more than 6 inches long, sometimes with a loop sewn into each end) with a *carabiner* attached at each end for quick clipping of *protection*.

rack—A selection of different-sized climbing *nuts* or other gear and different-length *slings*, carried by a leader.

rakshi—Liquor made from rice.

rap—See *rappel*.

rappel—To descend rock or snow by sliding down a single or double rope, usually with the rope running through a friction (braking) device such as a figure-eight ring that is attached to the climber. Sometimes a rappel is done by wrapping the rope around the body (for example, held by the left hand first, then run between the legs, around the backside near the right buttock, around to the front and up the chest, over the left shoulder, down the back, then held by the right hand).

rappel anchor—Whatever gear is necessary to anchor a rope at the top of a *rappel* and to support the rappeller's weight.

roof—A sharply cut overhang. A smaller "ceiling." See also *ceiling* and *overhang*.

rope drag—Difficulty in pulling or feeding the rope because too few *runners* were placed or because the rope runs around a corner of rock or through a tight *crack*.

runner—A loop of sling designed to add length to *nut* slings or any other *protection* point. A loop of *webbing* clipped to a point of protection so that the rope runs more freely. Runners also are draped over *horns* and *flakes* for *protection* or may be left to reinforce *rappel anchors*.

runout—A section of climbing that has no *protection*, where a leader must risk a longer fall than is normally considered feasible.

rurp—Acronym for *realized ultimate reality piton*, a tiny *piton* about the size of a guitar pick.

safety—A protective knot to back up another knot.

scree—The slopes of loose stones along the bottoms and sides of cliffs (and sometimes the tops).

serac—An ice tower or ice cliff.

Sherpani—A *Sherpa* woman, originally Tibetan but now also Nepalese and others, who helps carry loads on Himalayan expeditions.

Sherpa—A person, originally Tibetan but now also Nepalese and others, who helps carry loads on Himalayan expeditions and also sometimes serves as a member of the actual climbing team.

siege tactics—Repeated attempts, *fixed ropes*, and any other method, such as alternating climbing teams, to force victory in climbing.

sirdar—Head *Sherpa* of an expedition.

slab—A surface of rock that slants away at less than vertical.

slack—Extra rope. To keep the rope loose for a climber or pay out rope so that a climber can move freely or clip an *anchor* without resistance.

sling—A relatively short loop of *webbing*, or *perlon* rope, used for various purposes in climbing. A length of rope tied in a loop, such as a *gear sling*.

smear—To push the sole of your climbing shoe into the rock, creating friction so that the shoe sticks to the rock. Smear is related to feet, or shoes, as opposed to *palming*—which is related to the hands. Hands, however, can smear.

snow bridge—Hard snow creating a bridge over a *crevasse*. It is often difficult to judge the strength and safety of a bridge.

snow hole (or snow cave)—A shelter found or dug in the snow for a *bivouac*.

solo—To climb alone, without rope and *protection*. Or to climb alone while self-*belayed* with the rope.

spindrift—Light powdery snow blown about by wind that tends to penetrate clothing and tents.

sport climbing—Competitive climbing, usually on artificial (man-made) climbing walls, or on natural rock, or climbing up small but difficult rocks, usually with preplaced *bolts* for *protection*.

spot—To stand underneath a climber and keep hands upward to catch the climber in the event of a fall.

stance—A small foothold or place on the rock where you can stand and rest or, if *anchored*, can *belay*.

stemming—Basically the same as *bridging*, using opposing force between widely spaced footholds or between two planes of rock (such as a *chimney* or *dihedral*).

stopper—A type of climbing *nut* large at the top and small at the bottom.

stupa—A Buddhist shrine.

style—Individual expression and merit, regarding one's approach to climbing.

talus—Boulders that have piled up along the bottom of a cliff.

tension—Keeping the rope tight.

thin—Term for a section of rock with a scarcity of holds.

tie in—To attach the rope to the climber or to an *anchor*.

top-rope—A *belay* rope arranged through *anchors* above, or a belay given by a climber who has reached a point above (or the top of a rock).

traverse—To climb horizontally to the side (or diagonally).

tsampa—Barley flour used for traditional Tibetan and Nepalese dishes.

undercling—A *lieback* performed with palms upward (pulling on the underside of a *flake*).

verglas—A thin coating of ice, usually on rock.

webbing—Strong, closely woven nylon or *perlon* used as sling material or for climbing *protection* or for seat harnesses and such.

wire stopper—A tiny wire climbing *nut*, set in thin *cracks* to hold *protection* or other *anchors*.

Grading Systems

Climbers use various grading systems to indicate the difficulty of climbs, or the individual pitches of climbs, or the length of climbs, or danger factors, and so on. Gradings will always be debated. They are at best estimates. Often a grade varies greatly depending on a person's size or reach or factors so small as finger size and shoe type. A small person may be able to fit fingers all the way into a crack, whereas a larger person with thick fingers finds the climb significantly more difficult. Someone with a long reach is able to use holds out of reach of others. A difficult face climb on the steep granite of Tuolumne certainly must have been much more difficult wearing a pair of Cortinas in the early 1960s than in today's modern sticky rubber shoes. A climb done in the 1940s without chalk might be found to be substantially easier now with the use of chalk. All these variables, and others, including time of day, temperature, and humidity, make accurate grading troublesome.

Writers in *Climber's Choice* occasionally mention a grade. Below are a few samples of different grading systems now in use.

California Decimal System (developed in the late 1950s and early 1960s by Royal Robbins and Don Wilson, for free climbing)

1 —walking
2 —moderate scrambling
3rd class—actual rock climbing, but not technically difficult
4th class—slightly more difficult rock climbing
5th class—rock climbing where a rope and belay are recommended
5.1
5.2
5.3
5.4
5.5
5.6
5.7
5.8
5.9

5.10—the top of the free climbing standard in 1960
   a.
   b.
   c.
   d.
5.11—extremely difficult, the top of the standard in 1965
   a.
   b.
   c.
   d.
5.12
   a.
   b.
   c.
   d.
5.13
5.14—the current highest standard of free climbing

The a-b-c-d system was added during the 1970s by Jim Bridwell, who began to develop it in Yosemite. Before the a-b-c-d system, a plus or minus was sometimes used to suggest the upper or lower end of a grade. The plus-minus system continues to be used in some cases today.

Danger Factors

Danger factors exist on certain climbs and are sometimes indicated by an R or X, indicating a long runout or some similar type of danger. The terms "runout" and "serious" simply mean a leader must move above the protection and risk a long or dangerous fall. Acute skill, concentration, and control are required, since the only real protection in such situations is the climber's mind, technique, and ability to master the rock and the fear.

Climbing Length

Climbing length is indicated by the occasional use of a roman numeral, a system developed in Yosemite in the 1960s.

I, II, III, IV, V, VI . . . indicate various degrees of magnitude. Most short, one- to three-pitch free climbs are grade I. A grade IV climb must be more serious and quite long but can usually be done in one day by relatively skilled, experienced, and well-equipped climbers. The Salathé Wall of El Capitan, 3,000 feet of steep granite, is a grade VI. The Diamond on Longs Peak, a 1,000-foot sheer wall, is a grade V. Yet the Diamond is higher than El Capitan and is on a 14,255-foot mountain. Weather easily can turn this grade V into a grade VI. Indeed, climbs at altitude and with notorious weather possibilities can be strenuous and serious.

Aid Climbing

Aid is where equipment is used to make upward progress. A climber hangs from a piton or a nut placed in a crack, standing in sling material, a loop (called an aid sling) attached to the piece of gear. If the placements are difficult to make or hard to find, the aid climbing becomes progressively more difficult. This is indicated by an aid-grading system of A1 through A5. The numbers mean easy aid to gradually much more difficult.

Bouldering

John Gill's B system, for grading difficult boulder problems, was never really intended for use by the masses. It was Gill's own private system, although climbers soon began to attempt to adopt it. Most climbers even today still do not understand how Gill originally used the system. It was simple in its conception.

B1, approximately equivalent to 5.11 or 5.12

B1+, approximately equivalent to 5.12 or 5.13

B2, extreme bouldering difficulty

B2+, the upper extreme of bouldering

B3, a route of B2 difficulty that is unrepeated. As soon as it is repeated, it automatically is downrated to B2 or B2+

John Sherman's V System for Bouldering

V1	V7
V2	V8
V3	V9
V4	V10
V5	etc., through V15
V6	

About the Editor

Pat Ament has ridden freight trains, mastered chess, walked high wires, and done one-arm handstands on the tops of impressive rocks. He has a black belt in karate yet composes music, sings, plays the piano, and is a poet and writer. He has won awards for film and for his line drawings and for many years, through word, photography, and lecturing, has related the beauty and adventure of rock climbing. A pioneer rock climber in the 1960s, he established several of the first 5.11 routes and, with John Gill, developed extreme bouldering. He is married, with three children.

Pat Ament climbing in Eldorado Canyon, 1976.